IN AND AROUND
SWINDON
WORKS

P1·465
Sept 1948

" DOWN YOUR WAY" - Richard Dimbleby interviewing Swindon railway
workers in the "Down your way " feature to be broadcast on
Sunday week. Left to right - Richard Dimbleby, Miss D. Guy,
clerical worker G.W.R. fire station, Mr. John Shuter, son of
Brig.-Gen Shuter, of Cirencester, B.B.C. producer, Mr. George
Morse, chargehand at No. 4 Shop, and conductor of the Male Voice
Choir, and Mr. Tom Wheel, chargehand in R. Shop.

IN AND AROUND
SWINDON
WORKS

PETER TIMMS

AMBERLEY

In memory of John 'Jack' Fleetwood:
'I would do it all over again if I could'

FRONTISPIECE
A picture taken during the BBC outside broadcast unit's visit to Swindon Railway Works on or around Thursday 19 August 1948. They were making a radio programme for the *Down Your Way* series with the well-known broadcaster Richard Dimbleby and producer John Shuter. The format of the show was that each week the team would go to a location and talk to people, asking them about their working life and to name a favourite piece of music. Their choice was then presumably played between interviews. I think there was some effort made in advance to choose people who were likely to come across well in front of the microphone.

The programme was due to be broadcast on 29 August at 4.30 on the Home Service. No doubt many 'factory' workers gathered round the wireless that Sunday teatime and listened in. It is thought that Raymond Baxter also did a radio broadcast from the Works sometime in the days before television was widely available.

Another photograph and mention of Doreen Guy appear in chapter ten. Tom Wheel of Wootton Bassett Road was 'chargeman pistons' in R Shop and prominent in the Amalgamated Engineering Union. He had two brothers inside: Benjamin was chargeman on the valve setting plant, and Bill was a fitter somewhere on the loco side. Tom had about 44 years service in the Works when this picture was taken. 'He chose 'Look for the silver lining' from the musical *Sally* as his record choice,' said his nephew Reg Bullock. Reg was a coppersmith 'inside' and not long out of his apprenticeship in 1948.

This photo is credited to the Swindon Press Ltd, with copies supplied for the Swindon Works Drawing Office files. Another photo of this occasion appeared in the *Evening Advertiser* on 20 August. It shows Mr Dimbleby interviewing Bill Dando, chargeman fitter in AE Shop, in front of the newly built Castle Class engine 7017, named *G. J. Churchward*.

First published June 2009

Amberley Publishing
The Hill, Stroud
Gloucestershire, GL5 4EP

www.amberley-books.com

British Library Cataloguing in Publication Data.
A catalogue record for this book is available from the British Library.

ISBN 978 1 4456 0656 9
ISBN (ebook) 978 1 4456 1120 4

Typeset in 10pt on 12pt Sabon.
Typesetting and Origination by Amberley Publishing.
Printed in the UK.

Contents

	Acknowledgements	6
	Introduction	7
1	Raw Materials	13
2	General Stores	22
3	Working in CME Accounts	27
4	GWR Locomotive Development	34
5	Steam Locomotive Repair and Overhaul in the 1950s	47
6	FT&E Apprenticeships and other Recognised Training	64
7	'Loco Side' Work	78
8	The Drawing Office and D800	97
9	Accidents	112
10	The GWR Estate and Hospital	117
11	The Works Fire Brigade and On-call Arrangements	132
12	Wartime Work	140
13	The Carriage and Wagon Works	156
14	C&W Tradesmen and Women	169
	Tailpiece	190
	Bibliography	191

Acknowledgements

It was my privilege to hear at first hand stories of the 1930s, 1940s and 1950s from the following ex-employees: Colin Bown, Des Griffiths, Jack Fleetwood, Ken Farncombe, Bert Harber, Jim Lowe, Stan Leach, George Butt, Terry Couling, Dorothy Cook (née Grimes), Daphne and Colin Kibblewhite, Ian Sawyer, Gordon Nash, Ernie Ruggles, George Connell, Roy Taylor, Reg Willcocks, Dave Viveash, John Walter, Ray Eggleton, Manfred Spindler, Bob Grainger, Alan Lambourn, Beryl Stanley (née Hunt), Brenda Hedges (née Berry), Mary Parkhouse (née Almond), Reg Bullock, Terry 'Curly' French, Ray Townsend, Maurice Parsons and Margaret Painter (née Eveness). Thank you all.

Also, thank you: Beryl Wynn (née Odey), Myrtle Harber, Dianne Timms, Sarah Roe and her Mum – Jane Hill, Michelle Couling, Hugh Freebury, Bev Usher, John Partridge, Richard Woodley, Derek Wiggins and Elaine Arthurs, who was very helpful when searching for specific documents in the Steam Museum archive.

Thank you Dave King, editor of the *Swindon Advertiser*, for allowing me to use information contained in reports from the *Evening Advertiser* in the 1930s and 1940s. I made full use of the extensive research material of the Swindon Central Library local studies section over the last five years. Darryl Moody and the staff there are all enthusiastic and helpful: thank you all.

Thank you to Louis Archard and Campbell McCutcheon and everyone else at Amberley who was involved in helping put this together.

Finally, I am especially indebted to Mr J. Birch BSc MD FRCS for giving me back the will to start this project.

Introduction

Anyone living in this country up until the 1960s associated Swindon, or to be precise new Swindon, with just one thing: the Railway Works. The railways of this country were once so much a part of everyday life; they represented reliability and stability in almost every community, no matter how rural. From London to the north-west and down to the south-west, it seemed that everyone knew where those fine-looking locomotives that sped them to favourite seaside resorts were built. Swindon men on war service often said that mention of their home town abroad got a favourable reaction from foreign engineers.

Some observers noted that the railway town was ordered and self sufficient with low unemployment, its inhabitants educated, law-abiding and hard working. On the other hand, writers including J. B. Priestley and John Betjeman had an aversion to industrial towns, especially Swindon with its proximity to rich countryside and ancient villages. A writer in *Wiltshire Life* in 1946 said:

> To most Wiltshiremen Swindon is, I am afraid a name which merely brings to mind a blurred and rather depressing memory of drab streets and industrial gloom – a town not to be visited unless necessity demands it. They think of it as a region where men and women, mainly employees of the Great Western Railway reside only because their livelihood demands it.

In some weather conditions a low-lying smog hung over the town; John Partridge remembers that this was particularly noticeable from the top of Liddington Hill.

For a long time after the coming of the railways, Swindon was almost unique as an industrial town in southern England, away from the coalfields and iron-making of the Midlands and the north. Something of the size and scale of its Works can be imagined by the fact that around 12,000 men and women worked or were based there at any one time, but much of the site was very thinly populated: the 86 miles of sidings made up the largest single part of it. Building carriages, wagons and particularly locomotives is what Swindon Railway Works is best remembered for, but 90 per cent of work in the shops was repairs. They also repaired and maintained the company's cranes, boilers, pumping gear and all other mechanical equipment or sent men from the Works out to work on site. Here too was the accounts and administration centre of the Stores and the Chief Mechanical Engineer's Departments. A part of the Works not connected to manufacturing was the offices of the Locomotive Running Superintendent, later the Motive Power Department.

Designers at Swindon had incorporated many features of North American practice in their rolling stock and locomotives. There, the cost of manufacturing the latest aluminium alloy railroad cars was around £15,000 in the early 1930s. The cost of the finest GW carriages was a little over £2,000 at the time. In return for such an outlay, the American vehicles ran at high speeds over long distances and initial costs were recovered quicker than the GWR could hope for. Although designed for different requirements, the GW carriages had only one distinct advantage apart from the cost: they allowed the carrying capacity of the trains to be altered by adding or taking away carriages individually. The American trains could not be split, which in itself offered some advantages and indeed nowadays our own high speed trains are built this way. The stainless steel Zephyr trains of the Chicago, Burlington & Quincy Railway had cost £70,000, including the diesel-electric locomotive. This was more than twice the cost of the Cheltenham Flyer in 1934, with its 'Castle' locomotive and lightweight train of six coaches. The 'Flyer' cost more to run and was slightly slower (no longer the fastest train in the world) but possessed twice the seating accommodation of The Zephyr. Obviously, because of the different operating conditions the comparison is of limited value but it does show that the GWR's approach to initial costs was more about long term stability than progressive development.

The GWR was among the most respected companies in this country and prospered, despite enormous restrictions placed on them and on other British railway companies. By an Act of Parliament, the money they raised from revenue was to be used to keep user charges down once the shareholders had been paid, so as to check the accumulation of assets. In retrospect, we know that the success of the GWR company belonged to the pre-war era, when everyone and everything was carried by train. The government imposed a 'common carrier' status on British railways, requiring that they carry everything offered at a rate set by a parliamentary tribunal. No such obligation was imposed on the road haulage industry; they were free to undercut the railways, a situation that was to last until the mid-1950s. It wasn't until well after nationalisation that the 'Western', along with the others, started to run at a loss. Goods traffic was always slightly more profitable than passengers, but it began to decline from the end of the Great War, with a temporary recovery during the Second World War. The government-controlled railway companies worked well during the war of 1939–45 and the backlog of maintenance and shortages of materials and coal was certainly not due to inefficiency.

From 1940 onwards there were restrictions in capital investment for transport. The post-war redevelopment plans for the CME Department worked out in 1944 had to be scaled back at a time when expenditure was badly needed for 'renewals and additions'. The situation got worse after the war with the shortages of materials and, in 1949, the devaluation of the pound. Even modified capital investment programmes could not be met by the start of the 1950s because now there was a shortage of steel as well. The railway workshops could not replace 'old for new' plant and machinery on anything like the scale they required. Replacing locomotives was down by 50 per cent in 1952, new wagon building down by 65 per cent and no new coaches were to be built at all that year. As prices and wages continued to rise, it became more expensive for the railways to achieve the same amount of work. Despite all adversity, the products 'built at Swindon' continued to inspire a loyalty and pride not seen elsewhere.

The A Erecting Shop seen across the rooftops from Okus. Ted Baden worked there; his house on Kingshill Road had an attic room, seen here in the middle right.

Colin Bown was in charge of his school allotments, somewhere in the foreground: 'I was standing there alone on that day in 1944 when all the planes went over to France. Everyone remembers where they were when all those aircraft flew over the town.'

Jack Fleetwood can't remember what his father made of the spectacle now but: 'It was the only time I ever heard him swear.' Presumably they are referring to planes and gliders taking part in Operation Market Garden in September 1944, or was it the prelude to the D-Day landings in June that year? (*Author's collection*)

147. Cheney Manor Road Swindon.
(6724)

GREAT WESTERN RAILWAY.

No. 4301

CHIEF MECHANICAL ENGINEER'S DEPT.,

SWINDON.

24/7/47.

The bearer, Mr. W. Gough formerly employed in the Loco./Carr. & Wagon Works, Swindon, is authorised to obtain free and privilege tickets at the Works Booking Office from 10.30 to 11.0 each week-day morning and tickets for coal and wood at the Mess Room on alternate Tuesday afternoons. This card must be produced on each occasion.

F. W. HAWKSWORTH,

Issued by

Chief Mechanical Engineer.

3,000—Est. 525. 7/46.

Retired staff enjoyed some privileges in the 1930s and 1940s, when the 'shop floor' workers did not receive a Works pension. Whether this was negotiated by the unions or shop committees or whether they were incorporated in Employment Acts I do not know.

William Gough had been a chargeman vertical retort stoker in the Great Western Gas Works and presumably retired just before the date shown. Despite years of heavy and dirty work, Mr Gough was able to use this card for many years to come. The company records would have Mr Gough listed by name, former occupation and check number and these are written on the reverse of the card.

Railway families in Swindon were provided with medical, recreational and spiritual facilities by their employer. Perhaps this was why they were less militant than some groups of industrial workers. Low wages resulted from these concessions but smaller families in the 1930s were at least as well off as their parents and grandparents – the yardstick by which they compared their lot. The threat of being without work preoccupied the 'factory' man during the years from 1928 to 1938. On the one hand, the men wanted to work fast and earn their piecework bonus but on the other hand there was a real fear that once finished there would be little or no work tomorrow. Under these conditions the men knew their place, but that is not to say there wasn't an underlying resentment towards a system that kept them down while others appeared to have plenty. It was said at the time with some reverence: 'The English working man feared God, honoured his wife and obeyed his conscience.' The collective conscience had been controlled by the Church but by the 1930s things were not what they used to be. Fred Uzzell of Kingshill Road wrote his life story when he retired from the Loco Stores in 1936. He was a strong critic of the bad language used by a minority of Works men: 'The swearing done there is awful, though I don't suppose it is worse than other large factories for wickedness, but at Swindon there are many who never use a bad word and yet never go to a place of worship.'

The various trades had labelled each other with unflattering terms. The loco side fitters called their carriage colleagues 'five-eighths fitters' because the work they undertook was comparatively light and therefore, according to them, easier. Carpenters were known by some as 'wood butchers', moulders were 'sand rats' and a 'wagon basher' riveted up wagon underframes. The boilermaker, whose work was particularly heavy and noisy, was a 'fitter with his brains knocked out'. With such a close-knit community, there was bound to develop certain phrases not immediately recognisable to outsiders (anyone beyond walking distance of the Works). A typical opening gambit when two Swindon men met was, 'What ja know then snow', which meant: 'I don't mind stopping and having a chat with you'; upon hearing some interesting gossip, he might then exclaim: 'Oh bugger I are.' Even now elderly Swindon people say old so and so has 'gone on', meaning they had died, and all the houses had 'backsies' – back alleys to us 'outsiders'. R. J. Blackmore worked in 'the factory' and regularly wrote an eloquent piece for the staff magazine, *Swindon Railway News*. Of the London overspill years in the 1950s, he said: 'Terms like 'trip' and 'inside' fall on new ears with arresting effect.' A lady recently told me about the time a new vicar in the district came to their school – Ferndale Road Girls: 'This was during the war and he asked some of us whether our fathers were away fighting for the country. It wasn't till later that I realised why he looked so disappointed, he thought half of them were in prison.' This type of misunderstanding was not unusual around the town.

If you ask old Swindon people if they thought life was tough for them and their parents before the war, they are likely to say: 'Only in retrospect because we knew no different.' Was working life tough for the wages grades? The consensus seems to be that conditions were tough but there was a family atmosphere about the place. 'If you needed assistance there was always someone willing to help you,' something noticeably lacking when workers moved to higher-paying factories after the war. Men that had left were not always complimentary about the railway factory. Lewis Carroll's line about 'cabbages and kings' was sometimes used by ex-railwaymen to describe the

A 1932 handbill for one of the many excursions run to see the place where the King Class engines were recently built. Interest in Swindon's famous Railway Works was never greater than in the period after the company's most powerful steam locomotives were introduced and the publicity department made the most of it. (*Author's collection*)

two types making up the workforce 'inside'. There was no denying that there were those who were content and those with ambition, but both were equally important. Ambitious workers became frustrated because they would not be promoted on ability alone. Out of necessity, the exception to this was men being promoted out of the Drawing Office and taking up management positions. Many capable people, especially men, left after the war when the Works had to compete with other local industry; they were not prepared to wait in a seniority queue, as was the way of things 'inside'. 'Waiting for dead men's shoes' generally persisted long after nationalisation.

It is said that the men returning to the Works after demobilisation had a different attitude to authority. This, together with the introduction of procedures to ensure an individual's grievance would be independently investigated, meant the foreman could no longer do what he liked without question. Nationalisation in 1948 was never going to suit the 'Western', who did everything their own way and appeared to be influenced by very little of what was going on elsewhere. Building standard rolling stock and answering to a Railway Executive with little Great Western influence was bound to affect the attitude of the fiercely loyal Swindon workers and management, many of whom retired earlier than they would have done otherwise. By the mid-1950s, the new British Railways were starting to lose money. The reasons given for this were: 1) the growth of private transport; 2) rising costs, together with controls on fares and charges; 3) political and public pressure to maintain services making losses; 4) a sharp fall in the amount of coal needing transportation; 5) a long delay in getting resources required for modernisation.

The Railway Executive had been brought in to try to make the railways more competitive. The resulting 'rationalisation' inevitably destroyed the goodwill and loyalty of the workforce, something the old company had been blessed with, although this was more to do with the attitudes of the times generally. Under the old regime conditions and, later, certain payments were dealt with by the Works and Shop Committees. Representatives of both sides had far more scope to settle matters locally and it rarely led to industrial action. The RE's only choice now, given the totally different circumstances, was to prune the network and cut jobs; any pay increases were to be linked to higher productivity.

In the Works, this led to difficulty in attracting and retaining skilled staff while trying to undertake an ambitious schedule. Not for the first time, Swindon was having to fight on too many fronts. While maintaining the fleet of ex-GWR locomotives, they designed and built BR standard steam locos. From the mid-1950s, workshop space had to be transformed for diesel production, repair and testing. They were about to build diesel mechanical shunters and repair diesel electric shunters, repair engines and transmissions for diesel rail cars and, on the 'carriage side', build the multiple unit sets complete.

THE RAILWAY EXECUTIVE
Western Region.

SWINDON WORKS & OFFICES

All persons, with the exception of the Executive's Officials furnished with Periodical Passes and others holding Special Permits, must enter and leave the Works or Offices by the authorised entrances and exits for their particular place of employment.

They are not allowed to walk along or across the Lines or to enter or leave the Executive's premises by other entrances or exits.

Watchmen are instructed to see that this Order is carried out.

BY ORDER.

H. RANDLE,
Carriage & Wagon Engineer,
SWINDON. *May*, 1950.

K. J. COOK,
Mech. & Electrical Engineer.

The Works' printing requirements for circulars and notices were usually contracted out to various local printers even though they had their own facilities. This one was done by Twitcher & Co. Ltd of Swindon.

CHAPTER 1

Raw Materials

A 15-inch pipeline brought water of a suitable chemical composition to Swindon Works from Kemble, 13 miles distant. As the Works and the adjacent running sheds expanded, so the wells were deepened to increase the supply. A 24-inch diameter bore was sunk to a depth of 72 feet in 1935. In the same year, the Lancashire steam boilers and pumps were replaced by electric turbine pumps capable of pumping 75,000 gallons an hour. During the period covered by this book the Kemble supply never fell below 40,000 gallons. Men from Swindon kept the earlier pumps in working order by running them once a month in case of emergency. At the surface, the water was pumped into the pipeline and ran down to the tanks at Swindon, assisted by gravity. During the 1930s and 1940s, the Works used 160,000 gallons of water per hour at peak times. The deficit was made up from storm water and some reuse of waste water.

After use in 'the factory', waste water was pumped away via the branch pump house to the 'back cutting'. This ran parallel to the railway line beyond the northern perimeter. Ken Farncombe said: 'The cutting always stunk of the oil gas' (Oil gas was made in the company's Gas Works: it was compressed into liquid and used in restaurant cars and carriages before electricity). Stan Leach remembers that the lake always seemed to be giving off steam, possibly hydrogen sulphide or perhaps because of warm water from the Central Laundry. Once it had stood and the sediment and oils separated, some of this 'return' water was pumped back and reused for such things as flushing toilets, washing hands and hydraulic use. Kemble water was used at the fire points to guarantee a constant supply and gauges in the Works Fire Station registered any reduction in pressure. When it arrived at the Works, the pipelines were divided to provide industrial and drinking supplies.

The Works had access to water from the local authority if the Kemble supply was temporarily stopped. A 5-inch main had been laid under the railway estate and came into the Works near the tunnel entrance. Stopping the Kemble source might be done if: 1) the periodic chemical analysis was not right; 2) maintenance or repair of the pipeline joints was to be carried out; 3) while the royal train, on its way to Cheltenham Races, ran over the route, in case a leak washed away the ballast and track. If the pipeline did spring a leak, signalmen along the route were warned by a pressure gauge installed in their signal box. The reason for the loss of pressure had to be ascertained first, so the alarm in the Fire Station was reset after 30 minutes. If it was then still active the pumps would be stopped and the line closed. The CME

G Shop Maintenance Fitter Norman Sanders is lubricating the moving parts of one of two steam engines kept in reserve at Kemble. Their boilers were no longer used, so when the electric pumps were switched off for maintenance the standby pumps were driven by steam from a tank locomotive. The photo was taken by apprentice 'Bob' Grainger, who accompanied Norman 'outstation' on this occasion.

Department were responsible for the pipeline so a shunting engine and platelayer staff would be sent out from Swindon to find the damaged part. The 'PL' Shop kept a large covered rail van, stocked and ready to be taken out.

The largest elevated water tank was above the Pattern Stores and was known as 'the pattern loft'. It was divided into four separate tanks and held a total of 230,000 gallons. The elevated tanks provided sufficient head to reach distant points and the top of the CME building. A booster pump in a nearby cabin increased the water pressure at the fire hydrants if necessary. It was tested every Monday morning at 9.00 a.m. With the pressure increased to 60 lbs per square inch, a jet of water would reach the top of the A Shop roof in the event of fire. There were also balancing tanks at the running shed coal stage, and just north of 15 Shop. The Fire Station tank was 20 feet higher than the others and held 41,000 gallons. All the tanks were divided up to allow cleaning and maintenance work without shutting off the supply. The largest water tanks in the Works were at the same level as the regulating tank at Kemble. Therefore, when the ball valve in the Kemble tank shut off, the Swindon tanks also stopped filling and the two electric pumps cut out. However, Bert Harber remembers that occasionally the Pattern Store tank would overflow into Rodbourne Road.

A service tunnel ran under the GWR estate between the carriage body shops and the Medical Fund building in Milton Road, allowing water for the baths to be emptied and refilled by sluice gates somewhere under 3 or 4 Shops. The company, and not the MFS, bore the cost of supplying the swimming, slipper and Turkish baths with water, heated by the boiler house in No. 2 Shop or the Sawmill. Water used for filling boilers and for drinking was regularly checked by the Works' assistant chemists. They would carry out chemical and bacterial analysis of the supply at the Works and throughout the company. If they encountered a problem they would, with the help of the chief chemist, find ways of improving the quality of the water. They might, for instance, increase chlorination to destroy harmful bacteria. Men from the Works G Shop maintained the chlorination plant at Kemble.

Water mains maintenance was the responsibility of the 'PL' Shop, over near the running shed. Steam and hydraulic power was produced from the water supply and distributed around the factory. Hydraulic water at 1,500 lb psi was used for larger lifting appliances and presses; it was also available at 800 lb psi for smaller plant and hydraulic hoists. Again, it was the men from G Shop who maintained these services. The steam supply was obtained from eight Stirling Boilers, two of which were converted to be oil-fired during the 1940s. Steam at 160 lb psi was available, but most passed into a Ruths storage accumulator near X Shop which had a capacity of 34,000 lb and from which steam was drawn off at 80 lb psi. A second accumulator was built in 1944–5 on the other side of the Gloucester line, next to 18 Shop, for powering the drop stamps and steam hammers there.

The metals section of the Stores Department, later the Supplies and Contracts Department, was responsible for ordering and receiving all metals required at the Works. It came in a million and one different grades, sections and sizes. In my first book, I said that the Works could melt down and recast iron and some other ferrous metals and alloys. Steel in particular had to be 'bought in' as there was no foundry facilities 'inside' for producing it, although the Rolling Mills had furnaces capable of melting down and casting steel, mainly from old wagon axles. Statistics released from Paddington state that in 1936 the Stores Dept issued: 3,793 tons of pig iron, just over 5,000 steel locomotive tyres and a combined total of 4,500 tyres for rolling stock. These figures represent three times the stock held on site at any one time. From the 1930s, welding was starting to be used to fabricate steel rather than rivet it or buy in expensive castings. In some applications cast iron could be used but it was generally inferior and difficult to weld at that time. The *Swindon Railway News* said in 1960:

> Tons and tons come in every day for the construction and repair of rolling stock. Steel for carriage underframes, panels and roofs; tyres, wheels and axles; frame plates; steel boiler tubes; gas and water pipes; conduit for cables; angles, channels, joists, flats, rounds and hexagons; steel for platers; for machinists; for spring and toolmakers.

Open Hearth Basic or Acid steel was preferred for locomotive working parts. The plain carbon steel used for connecting and coupling rods had a strength of between 32 and 38 tensile tons per square inch. A-grade cast iron was used for pistons, chimneys, tender axleboxes and other engine fittings. Cast steel parts such as wheels were bought in from the Railway Works at Crewe.

After the war, the output of British Steel could not meet the demand and priority was given to projects of national security and to exports. Consequently, the Western Region allocation, as elsewhere, was limited and new building programmes increasingly affected. Later in the 1950s, when conditions improved, the Works received around 35,000 tons per year from outside steel mills. Mr Basham, the Locomotive

The central supply of steam for industrial use in the Locomotive Works came from this Boiler Station. By the 1930s there were eight Stirling water-tube boilers here and after the war some were converted to burn oil supplied from a service tank nearby. Each boiler was capable of producing 14,000 lb of steam and evaporating 1,400 gallons of water per hour. In 1938, 23,775 tons of coal was used; it was discharged from wagons and fed by conveyor into overhead hoppers. From there, the coal gravitated to the moving grates from the coal boilers, the ash being discharged into a pit. An ash-handling conveyor took it away to a plant and discharged it into wagons. The high chimneys, made of old boiler barrels, were a well-known landmark on the skyline until 1960, when the last boiler was converted to burn oil and they were all halved in height. (*GWR and R. Grainer*)

Storekeeper, claimed that his department had 16,000 tons of steel and £1 million of scrap on the premises at any one time. These figures excluded the considerable amount of manganese steel used around the site for track renewal, of which most but not all was carried out by the Engineering Department. More steel was now needed than before the war and it continued to replace timber in certain forms of construction. Some grades of iron, copper, brass, tin, antimony, zinc and aluminium sheet were also received; the latter, non-ferrous, metals were being increasingly used in rolling stock construction.

Mr Humphries said of purchasing and selling scrap:

> Each day brings its quota of demands, enquiries, phone calls, correspondence and visits from firms representatives. Prices of the valuable metals can fluctuate considerably, and a watchful eye must be kept on the market so that, where possible, advantage may be taken of any fall in basic prices.

As with timber, inspections were carried out at firms' premises, in this case by staff of the Works' metallurgy section. Frank Webber from G Shop took samples from forgings such as connecting and coupling rods and had them tensile tested in the Test House.

The way steel and all raw materials reached the shop floor was by the 'slip system'. When work orders were issued by the foreman, slips or requisitions were made out by the chargeman of the gang doing the work. They were sent to the Stores Department, who issued the material and recorded details on the slip. The purchase price and handling costs were also recorded and invoiced to the CME's Department. Unused or scrap material could be sold back to the stores. Defective material and any work done to it was charged to the Stores Department, who then had to make a claim against the firm who supplied it. The departmental accounts were settled every four weeks.

Even though less timber was being used for carriage building from the 1920s onwards, the majority of the work in the carriage shops continued to be done in

Mr Humphries was in charge of the eight staff of the Supplies and Contracts metals section in the 1950s. His title would still be known as Assistant to the Stores Superintendent (Iron and steel purchases and sales), joint third in line to the person in overall charge: the Supplies and Contracts Manager for the Western Region. (*Swindon Railway News*)

wood. It was sometimes referred to as 'The Carriage, Wagon and Timber Department' before the war. Despite this, the company's (Civil) Engineers used more timber than the CME's Department, for their buildings and sleepers. For wagon and non-passenger vehicle bodies and carriage interiors, there was no substitute for timber at that time. In 12 Shop the carpenters produced furniture for waiting rooms; platform seats; ticket stocking and issuing cases; label racks; platform trolleys; and barrows as well as work for other departments. In the Pattern Shop on the loco side they used mahogany or New Zealand pine for smaller patterns and White and Yellow pine from North America for making large patterns. Yellow pine was ideal because it was straight-grained, free from knots, easy to work and not liable to twist or warp (patterns in frequent use were made of metal).

The timber storekeeper from 1933 was Mr Bezzant; he placed the orders from his office in 4 Shop. Before they became area inspectors in the mid-1950s, the company's timber inspectors were based at Swindon. They would go out to inspect the orders before they left the merchants. Gabriel Wade & English Ltd, who had a depot (Baynes) in County Road, was one timber merchant that supplied 'the factory' from its earliest days. Imported shipments were checked before they were brought ashore. The inspectors were looking for water and other damage, fungus or disease. Gordon Nash, a former Works inspector, said:

> The exporters could not afford to have timber shipments returned so their inspectors checked it over before it left. It was the home grown consignments that were likely to cause problems if any. Sometimes different wood or different grades were mixed in to make up a load. There were several similar types of Douglas fir for instance; I would view it close up using a small lens (which we had to provide ourselves). Sometimes I would refer to the grading manual or to illustrations of wood structures known as the 'lens key'. I also had to check the dimensions and calculate the quantity in square feet against the order. When I was satisfied I would stamp it with my mark which was originally GWR 1, later they swopped it for BRW 1.

The timber-stacking ground, looking east towards A Shop in the 1920s. As can be seen, the timber was stacked with spaces between each piece. (*GWR Magazine*)

At the far west of the Works site was a timber stacking ground and '1' Shop – the Sawmill, built in 1908. Walter Timbrell was timber yard foreman until he retired in 1944. He received the incoming wagons of wood, many of which were specially constructed to carry large logs or trees. It was cheaper to buy it this way than as ready-cut boards and it could arrive in lengths of up to 40 feet. The largest cut lengths were called 'flitches'. If it still had its bark, the wood could be seasoned in the open air (I use the term wood for the pre-seasoned, and timber for the workable states). Seasoning reduced the moisture content over a period of time if air could freely circulate through the pile. The intention was that any distortion happened before the timber was cut to size. In later years, an instrument was passed over all surfaces to detect nails, pellets or pieces of barbed wire embedded in the wood. Damage to the cutting teeth of the machinery, which had in the past proved costly, could now be minimised. Softwood logs usually went to the sawmill for 'breaking down' after 12 months but hardwoods took a lot longer to season.

No. 1 Shop or Sawmill had a 10-ton overhead crane and two log bandmills capable of handling logs of 4 feet 2 inches and 3 feet 6 inches square. There was an art in cutting very large sections and it was usually done by the chief sawyer. Other machinery here included a bandsaw; high speed planer; cross cut; and circular saws, all capable of handling large wood sections. One such job required 25-foot or longer lengths of 1 foot by 6 inches and 1 foot square elm to be cut for use as fenders and piles at the company's docks. In 1935, 3,170 full-size logs were cut up here, about twice the number being done in 1959. An artificial drying kiln was adjacent to No. 1 Sawmill: this was an external fan type with four compartments into which logs could be winched; the heat was controlled by steam jets and fans. The total surface capacity was about 8,000 square feet when full. Ash was a hardwood used in construction and was particularly suitable for kiln drying.

On the south side of the main line were the original carriage buildings, including what had become known as 'the old sawmill' – this was 2 Shop Sawmill. A little further west behind Dean Street was the Timber Stores. Beyond them were the timber sheds, which were stacked with softwood battens such as European white deal or Scots pine. A lot of softwood was used for wagon panels, sheeting and floors after it was seasoned naturally. Some smaller batches of seasoned timber were sent to the Stores Department, who held it in there warehouses. These were divided up as wagon; carpenters; coachwork; body repairs; or loco side. Larger consignments did not physically go to the stores but were issued out by them all the same. Douglas fir from British Columbia and pitched pine from the USA usually arrived as logs or trees. Yellow pine was one of the best softwoods but was very expensive and the company encouraged the use of red or white deal as a substitute. Hardwoods were used for constructional purposes such as coach frames. Teak, elm and oak all had particular qualities and drawbacks. Elm could be worked with less fear of splitting and had more resistance to decay from moisture. Canadian rock elm was kept in water until cut up. Teak from Burma had restrictions on felling, so it was expensive. Polish oak was not as strong as British oak but was less prone to distortion. Walnut and mahogany were decorative in section and used mainly for coach interiors.

Gordon said: 'Tenders were sent out every three or four months to the timber trade, and the Stores staff had to find the best prices. We used home grown timber

No. 1 Sawmill was built in 1908 and thereafter called the new sawmill. (*GWR*)

when possible.' There were occasional difficulties importing timber from outside the Empire, particularly in wartime. Then, the Ministry of Supply had to find substitutes for imported woods and their controller of timber decided how the depleted supply was distributed to each railway company. English elm and beech were being used for construction instead of various pines from the Americas and hardwoods from the Far East. White pine for pattern making was now being cultivated at home and was known as Weymouth pine.

Some of the information on the types of wood purchased and its use comes from a paper given by Mr S. N. Matthews to the GWR Lecture and Debating Society in 1932. At that time, he was timber storekeeper for Swindon. Mr Richards was about to retire as foreman for the old saw mill and timber mill and Mr Waterhouse took over. Hundreds of thousands of planks and battens were machined in No. 2 Sawmill. One of the large horizontal bandsaws was acquired during the 1914–18 war by contraband control. Gordon Nash thought it might have been from a Danish ship heading for Germany. The last of the machinery still to be altered was converted to electric power in the 1930s. Bandsawing, planing, boring, tenoning and bending operations were carried out there, among other types of wood machining.

Timber sections were formed to shape in the 'bending house', an area of the shop next to the Fire Station yard. Oak was used in particular for bending into carriage body parts, and ash or hickory used where wagon timber was shaped or formed. Oak for carriage roof sticks (supports) had to be 100 per cent free of defects. They were put into a pressure steamer for 4 hours then formed on a Fay & Egan bending machine. They were then removed and clamped into a jig for 24 hours, then left to dry for 3 days. Battery box separators that were fitted underneath carriages were made of cedar from the US; later, British Douglas fir was used. They were made of end-grained 'flitches' and had to be cut down from large sections, making them very expensive to produce. Buying them in ready-made was no cheaper, said Gordon Nash. 2 Shop Sawmill stopped making battery (Leclanche cell) boxes by the end of the war; they were presumably made of other materials by then.

Previously called sawyers, the men became known as wood machinists. The majority of their work was carried out using jigs and steel contour gauges. Some items were made in 2 Shop complete, such as brake sticks for pinning down wagon brakes. They were made of American White elm, which was expensive; later, they went out to tender. Shunters' poles were also bought in, from a firm in Cardiff, as they could produce them more cheaply. They were made of hickory, a very durable wood, so when they became unserviceable the Works hand-turned them into ladder rungs, handles for locomotive controls or hammer shafts. 'Trepanning holes in axlebox shields was a very dusty job until they fitted an extractor,' said Gordon. A section of the shop was laid out for the machining of rail keys by Len Mackie's gang. Oak and teak bars were planed, cross cut and tapered, and the keys had to have no imperfections; teak keys were to be used for main lines only. The inspector checked each one individually and stamped them to show the type of rail they were compatible with. Oak was also made into telegraph pole arms; later, they used jarrah for this. The resulting scrap timber and sawdust from both sawmills was burned in a boiler and the steam generated was used for heating, timber drying and bending.

CHAPTER 2

General Stores

The GWR described its stores department as its 'housekeeper and universal provider'; its importance was reflected in the fact that senior stores staff had all been senior mechanical engineers. The majority of work in this department was centralised at Swindon but it was necessary to site many small stores around the system. To attempt to minimise handling and damage, a statistical analysis of all materials moving between the workshops and the stores was completed in 1955. It was compiled using punch-card accounting and showed that 2,000 tons was moved every day. Although by this time the Works used hoists, fork lift trucks, power shovels and many types of crane, most still had to be moved by hand.

The large building with the ridge and furrow roof between the Station and the Running Shed was the General Stores. It came into use in 1896, just one part of the vast system of stores throughout the Works. The General Stores differed from the rest of the Stores Department in that it had no particular connection to the CME Department. It dealt with all the cleaning and consumable supplies required throughout the company. The vast majority of general stores were supplied by outside contractors. One section of the department perused the trade and economic journals as well as the daily press so that the best prices were not overlooked. Raw materials in particular were subject to fluctuations in prices, and these were recorded. If oil, steel or leather for instance came down in price, the superintendent was notified and he would decide whether to authorise purchases ahead of schedule. Once the quality of the product had been established, not only cost but reliability was a prime consideration. Breaking standing contracts could prove to be a false economy. Where applicable, the superintendent was under no obligation to buy from Swindon Works; if he could buy in cheaper from outside, he would do so.

The storage areas were arranged over three floors, with some items stored outside. Some deliveries were made each week to stations, offices, carriage depots and running sheds; other types of items were despatched quarterly. It was considered more economical to do this than to keep stocks of spares at each point. The weekly deliveries were taken out by Stores railway vans, each working to a strict itinerary. They were manned by an attendant known as a 'vanman', previously a 'tallyman'. From about 1930 there were five travelling vans, which were converted brake vans. They were loaded outside in the 'station despatch depot', then attached to the front or rear of normal service trains. Stores van No. 2 was rumoured to be a converted clerestory royal coach.

Such things as brooms, brushes, shunting poles, towels, dusters and lamps were issued on an exchange basis, new for old. This was strictly adhered to and items lost or stolen were investigated. Large amounts of laundry were exchanged too, clean for used.

A postcard sent to firms and departments that dealt with the General Stores, Christmas 1950. (*E. Ruggles*)

Among the items which took the most wear and tear were broom heads (five times more of these than handles were dispatched) and light bulbs and shades for carriage compartments (here they did have to allow for a percentage stolen). Other items sent out in large numbers are more difficult to understand: nearly 2,000 padlocks and many signal, train and hand lamp burners were supplied annually. The 'vanman' checked the worn items being exchanged to ensure a replacement was justified. Labels were attached to them for accounting purposes, so that the correct department was charged. Around seventy different types of articles were carried in the vans; the quantities depended on the anticipated demand on that route. Sacks were also dispatched for the collection of waste paper, which was sold for recycling. The Loco and Carriage Works too would use the vans for delivery of manufactured equipment on occasions.

A further fleet of sixteen vans was based at the General Stores for a quarterly delivery and collection of consumables, protective clothing and tools etc. A requisition book with the station or depot's requirements was received at the commencement of each quarter. Their entitlement depended on their category (status): the larger and busier places had a higher category. For instance, one van could hold enough stores for four small engine sheds in the Welsh valleys, whereas a large shed such as Old Oak Common might need three or four vans to itself. Cotton waste for cleaning and 'lighting up' locomotives was one of the main items delivered to running sheds: it arrived in hundredweight bales. Items were ordered by description, using the authorised name, group letter, number and quantity. The orders were made up in the packing room on each floor of the warehouse. Warehousemen collected the orders in large trolleys and did the loading up; when they were ready for dispatch, the four-wheeled Stores vans were marshalled into ordinary goods trains.

At the age of 15 and a half, Ernie Ruggles went to work in the General Stores. Ernie, from Stanier Street, said the date was easy to remember: it was 12/3/45. His father Arthur had come to Swindon from Stratford Railway Works in east London in 1911. He obtained work 'inside' on factory transport (later, when the maintenance

General Stores staff outside their building; the rest room is in the background. From left to right: 'Bamp' Shepperd, unknown, Davies, Alec Romans, Charlie Miles, Ernie Ruggles and Pete Aldridge. (*E. Ruggles*)

section was enlarged, this was known as Z Shop). Arthur Ruggles was for many years churchwarden at St Paul's church (behind Woolworth's) and caretaker at the church hall in Dowling Street. His first son naturally took up the 'free trade' arrangement, so Ernie would remain unskilled, something he feels bitter about.

This out of date policy of offering only the eldest boy an apprenticeship took no account of ability; it split up families and made no sense whatsoever. I started as 'stores lad', the only one on 'B' floor in the General Stores building. The three floors were known as A, B, and C, A being at the top. Within these three floors were three further warehouses: D, M and O, the clothing/uniform store (M) was in the corner of the top floor. Compton's, who had a factory next to the Works in Sheppard Street, supplied most of this stock.

The warehousemen went on strike over the right to get piecework payments. I was not yet in the union on account of my age so I worked on my own. Management gave in after a couple of days when they realised the disruption it was causing. The piecework price was the same for all entries on the requisitions whether they took a few seconds or 15 minutes to deal with, but it did make people work harder. As I was under 16 years I was to do only light work. I branded brushes and bass brooms with a branding iron heated on a gas grill: they were made at the Institute for the Blind in Bristol. I also stamped GWR on small brush handles using a rubber stamp and inkpad. Many of these were made in the Works and were used for clearing swarf from machine tools. The department could get items ready marked but it was cheaper for me to do it. I put away incoming stock, taking care to stack it correctly so: 1) the maximum could be stacked; 2) they would not fall out; and 3) they could be removed easily.

Each type of item was held in a unit with an identification tag on the front stating the reorder point and quantity held. We soon learnt the reorder points of many items in frequent use, how long they took to arrive from the manufacturers and the minimum and maximum they would send at a time. At the end of each bay there was a board which we updated whenever we removed stock: this the senior warehouseman referred to when he reordered. Material inspectors and 'green card men' (those with physical disabilities) checked and tested random articles. Some articles such as shunting poles were all tested, in this case with a man levering on one end. Fabric weave had to be counted per square inch, bass broom bristles were counted and padlocks were opened and locked. Lamps were lit and bellows used to see if draughts would extinguish the flame. Exterior paint was taken and applied to a wall at Challow station to see how it weathered.

Each consignment arrived with three copies of a receipt. One stayed with the goods, another went to the office and a third went to the inspector; after clearance from him the clerk would release payment to the supplier. B floor held: life belts for the company's ships, guards' watches, sheets of asbestos of varying thicknesses for steam pipe connections. Rolls of 'balata belting' were also kept here: after riveting into loops in the Works, they drove the older machine tools. The belt came in thicknesses from ½ inch up to 6 inches wide. In my early days I remember they kept wartime tin hats and stirrup pumps, horse shoes and stable equipment. Pipe fittings, guard's lamps, fire buckets and padlocks we stocked, we even had combs for stationmasters above a certain grade.

The laundry bay was also on B floor, where hampers of clean laundry for the hotels and refreshment rooms etc were held. They were dispatched to the outstation room at the junction station for delivery by ordinary train. Ernie remembers that there were three or four women in B packing room, including Florrie Browning; the men there were Dick Ellis, Reg Arthur and Alfie New in charge. Heavy items and large loads were moved by sack truck or trolley, which each gang guarded as their own. Outside, on the Station side of the building, glass was stored in the 'dingo huts', which had open sides and galvanised sheet roofing. There was also an 'empties yard' close by. Some items stored outside could be affected by the weather; laminated carriage and wagon springs, for instance, had to be stood so that rainwater ran off the leaves. On the far side of the yard, next to the canal path, was a large, open building holding platform trolleys awaiting either repairs in the shops or dispatch. Occasionally, notices were put up around the Works announcing the sale of surplus stock. Workers could come over and buy things like overcoats, overalls and brushes.

Ernie returned from his national service in July 1949 and went onto the 'platform gang' with chargehand Arthur Spreadbury. There were about a dozen men unloading the stores from outside firms and from 'the factory'. The vans were run in between wooden platforms in the adjacent Goods Receiving Depot; they could be moved along by levering the wheels round with a steel shoe attached to a long pole. Coming in were: screws from GKN; cork lino from Scotland; first aid equipment (some of which was purchased in 'Boots the Chemist' in the town); flare lamps and lump chalk from south Wilts for marking wagons; brickdust for cleaning restaurant car silverware; cadmium screws (not be used in food preparation areas); hand tools; and galvanised water containers. There were several young ex-servicemen in this gang at the time: 'They were a cheery bunch, men like 'Curly' Keele, Bill O'Connell and Eric Codling,' said Ernie.

'Bamp' Shepperd was a labourer in the Receiving Depot; he was paid an extra 6*d* to operate the hand crane on the platform. The story goes that 'Bamp' (from Bampton) took a load of timber to the home of Mr Tomes, the Assistant Storekeeper, as arranged. Mrs Tomes omitted to give him a tip, so he brought the load back. Reg Cripps, the chief warehouseman, kept his eye on the 'platform gang' from his office window: 'But he was a good boss.' His boss, Mr Bingham, was the Assistant to the

Stores Superintendent; he always wore a bow tie. Mr Eveleigh took over from him at around this time. It was this person who liaised with the departments using stores commodities; the General Stores dealt mainly with the Traffic Department.

In 1956 Ernie became a 2nd grade issuer in 'D' warehouse, back on the middle floor, with Ken Watts: 'Promotion indeed, I was entitled to my own pair of ex ambulance box scissors to cut string around parcels. We issued out stores according to Works requisitions which might have up to three items requested; outstation departments normally ordered on multiple reqs.' Products kept in 'D' warehouse included pumice powder; brick dust; cotton waste; chalk; paint; oils; and spirits. Detonators, which were used to alert enginemen of dangers on the line, were received here from Penistone. They were tested randomly by one of the inspectors, usually Bert Hillier. He placed them on the track and got the Works pilot engine to run over them while he counted the bangs. Atlacide weedkiller for clearing the sides of railway embankments was handled here too – until it was discovered to be a fire risk, that is. It dried the weeds as it killed them, so that sparks from locomotives could easily start lineside fires.

The Oil Store was at the rear of the building: paraffin; turpentine; sulphuric acid; rape; and gear oil were stored here. Ernie didn't like the Oil Store:

> It always seemed bitterly cold and stank of oil. It was sheltered from the sun but not the wind which would blow across the tracks and in the winter the rape oil would freeze. Occasionally the five gallon carboys of sulphuric acid broke and you could get splashed: two 40 gallon drums of water were kept for such an accident. Ken Watts once got acid all over his legs and had to jump into a drum. We had a box with an oil stove to keep warm during breaks. The G Shop cranemen were our only contact with the rest of the Works, they came across for oil regularly.
>
> In 1960 I applied for a job as warehouseman but presumably because I was the youngest applicant they offered me a position as a clerk instead. They asked me some general knowledge and maths questions as a sort of test. As was well known, if the questions were easy, and they were, they wanted you. So in September that year, at the age of 31 I went into the General Stores Office on the invoice section. There were about sixteen clerks here of which about six were females; Ralph Butt was the chief clerk. I was put to work matching up the cleared invoices with the order forms and filing them. As with most newcomers in any department, I was not supposed to answer the telephone. Now I could join a superannuation scheme: the GWR fund were not taking any more so I joined the LNER scheme.

The annual turnover of the General Stores in the late 1950s was around £171,000. This was the purchase price of the items dispensed and did not take account of repairs. For instance, the value given for the 23,800 guard's lamps that were exchanged each year was £37,500. However, most could be 'turned around' after perhaps replacing the lens and a repaint. As a result, the majority were old GW lamps that had been 'patched up'. The next most numerous item summarised in a Stores Department booklet for general circulation were shunters' sticks. They were used for coupling and uncoupling wagons as they were loose-shunted. Thousands were sent back broken; the steel hooks could invariably be reused and the hickory shafts could be made into smaller items, as described elsewhere.

CHAPTER 3

Working in CME Accounts

Daphne Kibblewhite lived in Cricklade Road and attended Euclid Street School until the age of 16. She had obtained a place at teacher training college in London but her father, a boilermaker in the GWR, did not want her to go. This was 1939 and with the possibility of another war, he thought Daphne should stay put. Therefore, she applied to become a clerk in the Railway Works and after a short while sat the entrance exam at her old school. When a vacancy came up she was accepted, subject to a medical. Waiting for a vacancy to come up would soon be a thing of the past. Daphne started her working life in No. 40 office on Monday 4 September 1939, the day after war with Germany was declared. Her friend from school Betty Crouch started about the same time – she went into the Printing Office. Percy Richards was 'clerk in charge' of 40 Office (Mechanical Accounting); his personal secretary was Nora Hunt.

The work of the clerk in the accounts' offices was to compile and record: 1) expenditure and receipts (financial accounts); and 2) work or assets exchanged (statistical returns). Mr Gardner, the Assistant Works Accountant in the 1930s, summed up the work as: 'To tabulate in the most convenient form, the results of past working.' Junior clerks were expected to attend evening classes at the College's Commercial Department to study subjects appropriate to their work such as shorthand, typewriting, commerce, book-keeping and office appliances.

Daphne said:

Mr (Frank) Dance was Mr Richards' assistant and Mr (Steve) Wheeler was next in line of seniority and not far off retirement. Mr Gregory and Mr Jones were there to start with as well but as the younger men got called up they were moved, possibly to No. 48 (Mileage) Office. Gladys Hamblin was the senior clerk in the machine section where all operators were, since the early days of accounting machines, females. Presumably because of a good report from school and because I was 16 I was not given errands to run and tea to make, the normal initiation duties of an office girl. I was put on an electric 'Muldivo' machine; I can't remember how much training I got but soon I was calculating fortnightly piecework payments on my own. I totalled up the amount of work done (expressed as £.s.d.) according to the chargeman's certificates, this I then divided by the number of men in the gang or gangs. The clever part was converting the figures to suit the metric machines then reverting back to a figure in sterling and doing it quickly. Later I was also calculating the cost to the company, of producing sawn timber: the machine made light work of compounding

Staff of No. 40 Office at Christmas 1942 or 1943. Those identified are left to right, standing: Maurice Chequer the office boy, Eunice (?), unknown, Joan Hazel, unknown, Betty Workman, unknown, unknown. In the front are: unknown, unknown, Norah Coole, Daphne Kibblewhite. Some of the men here may have worked in other offices. (*D. Kibblewhite*)

dozens of different sized batches. Sometimes I sorted coal tickets into street order by hand if another operator was using my machine. I was sent over to Milton Road post office on occasions, to buy stamps to stick on enginemen's insurance cards.

Girls in the office I remember were: Ethyl Brust; Bethyl Stiles; Morfydd Row; Joan Lane; Connie Simpkins; Peggy Reeves; Marion Ruddle; Nata Hayes; Nancy Verrinder; Gladys Ackrill; Nora Hunt; Barbara Dening; Olwen Nash; Lorna Scott; Betty Workman; Norah Coole; Joan Hazel; Hilda James; Lucy Fell; Mrs Pomeroy; Kathleen Maslen; Pat Nash; Joan Dafter; Doreen Pullen; Olive Ogden; Beryldene Hunt; 'Flossy' Banner; and Molly Adkins. There were three sisters in our office too, Doreen, Joan and Beryl, I can't be sure about their surname, possibly it was Hicks. Edith Cavill always wore black including woolly stockings and had her braided hair wound round in a bun. Muriel Whale joined the staff in 1926 and had been in charge of the Powers-Samas machine sections at one time; she resigned to be married in 1947. Sally Haskins was the senior person on the small section printing the actual paybills and cash slips. Some girls liked to sing whenever they were not having to concentrate too much, Ivy Davies was one of those.

I had an uncle who was courting Doris Wells, she worked where the administration of the workforce was centralised. (They dealt with staff records, retirements and pensions, accidents, military service, free and privilege ticket applications and vacancies. The initial applications to travel on the Works annual holiday trains were also dealt with here). Doris worked with a Renee Patten in this, the Staff Office, until she married my uncle.

Presumably this was before the rule was changed and women were required to leave their employment upon being married. Women were replacing men in the factories as they were 'called up', so this tradition was abolished. Widows, too, were encouraged to return to the Works, although this had always been the case.

After three years, Daphne was offered promotion if she moved onto punched card machines at the other end of the office, which she did. As with all mechanised work, the operators received a period of training at first. Engine, boiler and tender repair costs, piecework payments, stores orders and paybill figures were produced by the Powers-Samas 'punched card' system. So were records of the current value of machinery and plant throughout the department: all calculated over the four-week accounting period. Cards were fed into a key punch and perforations punched in (if there was a wedding coming up, someone would take a bag of punchings for confetti). Standard cards made up for paybill deductions were reusable and bypassed the punch. Each card had forty-five columns across, each with ten numbers printed downwards; the position of the holes determined the information held. Next they were put into a sorting machine, which placed them in sequence. Then the information on the cards was converted back and printed out onto sheets by a tabulator. The advantage of the punch-card system, once up and running, was that it was fast and accurate.

Daphne's next move was to a desk to be a 'coding clerk': when the multiple piecework certificates came off the Muldivos, she checked that the chargeman had entered the correct coded charge against the various types of work completed. 'Only rarely did I have to sent anything back to the shops; if there was a mistake I could usually correct it myself.' The expenditure could then be appropriated by the punched card system. After a period on this work, Daphne was asked to act as section head to a group of punch-card operators.

> Mr Richards was quite strict and we called him sir, like being at school. His wife was in the Women's Voluntary Service and they were knitting for the troops. So Mr Richards brought wool in and asked us girls if we would do some knitting at home too, which we all did. We were not allowed to leave the office apart from going to the ladies cloakroom, of which there were two, one on the ground floor and one on the top floor [when Brenda Berry was there the cloakroom on the top floor was for senior female staff or those working overtime]. If the siren [Works hooter] sounded, we all went down to the long tunnel under the office building which was our air raid shelter. In the early part of the war if it was after 5.30 in the evening when the 'all clear' went we could go home but lose the overtime. Later we worked 12 hour days like everyone else. After the war I got another chance to do my teacher training, and so I left the Works in 1946.

Shortly after the war it was possible to get into the Works offices, including CME accounts, by successfully completing a two-year Day Commercial Course at the Secondary Technical School (the College). The syllabus was made up of the old school subjects, including physical exercises, French, commerce, shorthand typing, craftwork and handwriting. However, parents were not always willing or able to support this. Otherwise, a prospective employee would be required to hold the Higher School Certificate or, in the 1950s, five GCE passes including Maths and English; they then did not have to take the 'difficult' entrance test. By this time other, less well-qualified girls were being taken on as office machine operators only, previously known as class 2 clerks.

Brenda Berry lived in Hughes Street and in 1953 she left school and went into 'the railways' (the Works) aged 16. Like many people in Swindon at that time, she came from a railway family. Brenda's brother Ron and sister Kathleen were 'inside' the Works, as was her father and his father before him. Ron went into the 'carriage side' offices in 1950: 'At least I assume that's where he was because he wasn't in

The Powers-Samas machine section of 40 Office in the mid-1930s. The photograph gives the impression that the office was smaller and more congested than it was. On the left are the printing tabulators, on the right the automatic sorters, and at the far end the key-punching machines. 'This mechanical machinery was electrically driven and was noisy,' said Daphne: not very nice for the staff trying to concentrate at the desks in the centre.

Limited photographic evidence seems to suggest that the glass partitions between some offices replaced earlier solid walls, something which no doubt improved the natural daylight when the electric lighting, high up in the air, had little effect. This was probably done when the CME offices were refurbished to accommodate staff who came in from the railway companies absorbed by the GWR in the 1920s. Some offices in the CME block also had glass partitions between them and the central corridor. Whether or not this was also a later addition, I have not been able to ascertain.

This mechanical accounts machine room was not the only one at the Works, nor was it the only one using Powers-Samas machinery. Mr Bartlett, the clerk in charge of the Statistical Office, had applied the punch-card system to locomotive and train mileage statistics. His office also had sections dealing with loco and rolling stock records, stationary, duplicating and addressograph work.

A snapshot taken by Miss Vera Prior, who later became second in charge of the CME Powers-Samas machine section. It shows her office decorated for the Coronation of 1937.

the CME offices,' said Brenda (not necessarily the case). Older sister Kathleen was a comptometer operator during the war; later, when her husband's job took him to London, she got a job on the Western Region at Paddington. Brenda's father Robert was a riveter in the Carriage and Wagon Works, making it likely that his son Ron was in the C&W side too.

Brenda was set to work in the Mileage Office:

Our working hours were 8.30 a.m. to 5.30 p.m. and we regularly worked overtime to 7.30 p.m. My wages started at £2 9s 6d a week before stoppages and I gave my mother a pound a week. 'The mileage' was a mixed office at the top of the CME building (within a four-storey extension completed in the late 1920s).We shared the floor with the Comptometer Office, which was on the other side of the central corridor from us. At one end of our office was a small lift used to haul up work from the floors below, at the other end was a long coil of rope which, in the event of evacuation, would be used to abseil to safety. I never heard of it being necessary for anyone to try.

The wooden desks we had were long and seated three people; along the inner wall of the office glass fronted cupboards were fitted. All the furniture and fittings looked very antiquated. There was an assortment of chairs of varying comfort and when a senior person left their chair was inherited by the next in line. The bosses: Mr Lewis and Mr Fluck, worked in a separate section known as the Glass House with half a dozen general clerks. My first section head was Mr (Reg) Pickering and his deputy was Mr (Ernie Mafeking) Smith, so named as he was born in 1900. Most of the unmarried females in the office were 'old maids'.

Office staff worked closely together and several have told me that they soon got to know each other's business, both professionally and socially. Perhaps this is why

The view from the top of the CME offices, possibly the Mileage Office, looking west across the Locomotive Works. The chimneys were those of the Central Boiler Station and the building in the right foreground was the G (Maintenance) Shop. The photograph was taken by clerk Jean Ockwell in 1948.

Brenda and two former colleagues can still recall the names and more of at least sixty mileage staff from the 1950s.

The Mileage Office, like No. 40 Office, was one of the larger ones, employing more than fifty staff, and again the work was largely that of compiling figures without aids or machinery, then passing it on to Powers-Samas machine operators. They were separate from the Works accounts but, like the CME machine office, both came within the Chief Accountant's Departmemt under statistics, possibly the largest single sub-section within the Works. There were, however, dozens of other offices doing different types of work for either the Chief Accountant; the Carriage and Wagon Works Manager; the Chief Mechanical and Electrical Engineer; the Locomotive Running Superintendent; or the Stores Superintendent. After 1948 some of the main departments were renamed and their responsibilities changed. The biggest change was that all carriage and wagon work now ultimately came under the C&W Engineer, a new position, and not the CM&EE. The 'Chief' was dropped from the latter title and the Loco Running Superintendent became the Motive Power Superintendent.

The work of the Mileage Office staff was to compile locomotive/train mileages run, over a four-weekly period. The figures were used, among other things, to assess the cost-effectiveness of modifications, overhauls and repairs; measure coal and oil consumption; and determine the 11,000 footplatemen's mileages worked, for paybill purposes. Enhanced payments and hours in excess of 'ordinary time' also had to be recorded at this stage. Guards came under the Traffic Department but Brenda thought their mileages may have been compiled somewhere at Swindon too.

Each section within the office covered an operating division of the GWR, later the Western Region. Each member of staff was responsible for a different depot or, if sufficiently small, depots. Brenda received the drivers' reports for engine diagrams worked from Worcester shed. Consignments of these 'returns' arrived daily, possibly in leather satchels according to Brenda. Another person on her section (there were five of them) dealt with Hereford running shed and so on. They used mileage charts but the main routes were soon learned by heart. The distance from Worcester to Paddington was 120 miles, remembers Brenda, with an extra three quarters of a mile out and back to Ranelagh Road for servicing the locomotive before the return trip. There were six London turns a day from Worcester.

As well as passenger and goods train services, engine drivers and firemen also worked light engine movements and engineering trains, the man-hours of which also had to be totalled up. Engineering trains in particular were often out at night, bank holidays and weekends and the mileage staff had to work out enhanced payments of up to time-and-three-quarters. Every other Tuesday the rates for permanent way 'ballasting work' were calculated. All the tabulated information was passed onto the machine section to be converted onto standard Swindon forty-five-column punch-cards. 'Finally we stacked each driver's records together and over a piece of wood we pierced the left hand corner with a screwdriver, then we tied them together with string and sent them back, care of the relevant Divisional Superintendent.'

When prompted, Mary 'Nutty' Almond, who worked in a different office in the CME building, also remembered a rope fire escape. She worked in the Stores Ledger Office on the clothing accounts section from 1955. This was on the second floor overlooking the main line.

The rope was elasticated and was anchored at one end to the radiator. If there had been a fire it could have been a disaster as there was so much wood and paper everywhere. The stairways at each end of the building, also partially made of wood, could barely cope at the best of times. When the gong (electric bell) went the stairways immediately became packed with staff and you got swept along with the flow. Some smaller offices still had open fires when I was there.

Another thing I remember about the CME offices was the dirt and dust coming in from outside: to compensate, we were all issued with a towel and a bar of soap. Keeping the windows closed all the time helped but of course in the hot weather it was tempting to open them. One girl did and a pile of invoices was swept out and she had to go and try to retrieve them all.

CHAPTER 4

GWR Locomotive Development

The steam engine was a simple idea and, as it turned out, not easy to replace with a viable alternative. However, there was always much potential for improving steam locomotion and reducing maintenance and production costs. Converting heat into steam into power (or work) ever more effectively within the limits of the loading gauge preoccupied the designers at Swindon Works.

On the subject of combustion, Mr W. H. Pearce, a senior draughtsman, said in a paper he read to the GWR Swindon Engineering Society in 1936 that less than six per cent of the heat units in coal can be converted into its equivalent work at the drawbar of the locomotive. Up until the 1930s, the GWR needed to produce locomotives to pull ever faster, heavier trains and use less fuel. The staff magazine said nearly two million tons of coal was used in 1942. In 1945 it was claimed that the company spent £4.7 million on locomotive coal, well over double the 1938 figure. Little wonder they tried oil as an alternative. The steaming qualities of British coal varied considerably. It was no good improving designs and educating the footplate men in economic use, only to then use inferior fuel. For heavy passenger and fast express trains in particular, the company purchased the best Welsh steam coal. Later, however, when forced to use coal of varying quality, the GW experienced more problems than other companies. Coal burned produces energy in the form of heat; the ability to raise heat and draw in air (combustion) was dependant on a good fire combined with a good firebox design. With the pursuit of ever-higher temperatures came the problems of containing the huge stresses on the joints and seams in the firebox and the boiler.

The problem of supplying only softened water for locomotive boilers was never fully overcome. Despite the water softening measures taken, locomotives still came in to the Works from some districts with badly chalked-up boiler tubes. Scale would gradually decrease boiler efficiency and increase maintenance. Locomotives where expectations were highest were fitted with 'blowdown' apparatus designed to discharge boiler water where there was a build-up of salts. Later, the 'Alfloc' water treatment developed with ICI gave good results as long as the locomotive was filled with hard water.

Lubricating the moving parts of locomotives sufficiently was always a problem, especially when travelling long distances. In the 1930s it was said by the GWR that: 'The loco consumes 3½ times the amount of oil that its train does.' The reasons for this were: 1) cylinder oil lost its viscosity as it got hot and was expelled through the exhaust; 2) the oil was thrown off the open motion and not contained by axleboxes. It was not thought practical to fit catch wells beneath locomotives to save oil. Another

A photo taken from the window of the Research and Development Office showing engines awaiting Works attention. In the foreground are two Dukedogs, 9004 and 9015, which by this date (August 1960) had been withdrawn. This class were involved in an amusing saga when they were chosen to be named after earls, all still living and connected with the company, most as directors. Although they were excellent examples of Collett's policy of modernising older engines where possible, the titled dignitaries objected because their names were not used on the new express engines being built at the time, the Castles. Some say that Mr Collett did this knowing the outcry it would cause. (*Ken Ellis*)

problem with lubricating express engines became apparent with subsequent boiler modifications. After the war, the advantages of increased superheat were temporarily offset by increased carbonisation. This was when the oil reached high temperatures in the cylinders and formed deposits. A mechanical lubricator was designed which delivered oil independent of the steam supply; this, together with an improved type of oil, minimised the problem.

Tyres and rails were completely smooth, so locomotives needed good adhesion. In dry weather the wheels would slip if the circumferential force exceeded the load by more than about 1 to 6. Engines hauling the heaviest loads on the 'Western' were designed so that almost their entire weight was supported by eight coupled wheels. This increased adhesion and, with careful acceleration to avoid 'snatching' the couplings, would get a heavy goods train moving sure-footedly. A long fixed wheelbase did, however, restrict route availability because it was likely to derail on secondary routes with tighter curves. To offset this somewhat, tyres with thin flanges were fitted to one or two sets of coupled wheels on all classes. Some provision for side play was also built into the coupling rods and axleboxes. The tyre profile had been altered in the late 1920s, giving more contact with the rail, particularly on curves and where any drop occurred in the track.

The 'chief' at Swindon from 1902 to 1921 was G. J. Churchward. He designed and had installed at Swindon an engine testing plant for evaluation of locomotive power, water and fuel consumption at varying speeds. Not all Mr Churchward's designs were successful but he developed a standard range of locomotives with several pioneering features, some of which he had studied in foreign designs. These he developed further and they were never superseded, such as: 1) Tapered boilers allowing better circulation of water and so-called 'free steaming', the ability of the boiler to supply adequate steam to the cylinders; 2) Long travel valves which regulated the admission of steam in and out of the cylinders, giving greater versatility to their adjustment (cut off) when running; 3) The Belpaire firebox which provided the largest possible steam space and area for the water in the barrel to be heated at the firebox end, the hottest area in the boiler; 4) Water added to the boiler by 'top feed' which preheated it reducing thermal shock and extending boiler life; 5) He developed a smooth running four cylinder design from studying French engines and gave it a modified inside Walschaerts' valve gear. The latter was very efficient for steam distribution: it was lighter, with fewer moving parts, and had improved reverse action. In the event of a breakdown, the gear on the defective side could be disconnected and the locomotive worked back to a depot under its own steam. The only other types of valve gear used on the GWR then and subsequently was the Stephenson gear for the two-cylinder engines.

A new design would start with the Chief Mechanical Engineer working out broadly what improvements he wanted over a previous design. As is well known, the CME, Mr Collett, simply fine tuned or enlarged Churchward's, and in some cases Dean's, designs. A team of draughtsmen would be responsible for producing the general arrangement and detail drawings, with the chief draughtsman overseeing the work. They would then, together with the Loco Works Manager, have to deal with anticipated production problems. Mr Hawksworth is known to have had considerable influence over several successful new designs up to 1932 while he was chief draughtsman. Once in traffic, the running department inspectors would compile reports from drivers and experience the performances of new locomotive types for themselves. The Locomotive Running Superintendent would liaise with the draughtsman concerned regarding any major problem; they too would probably want to ride on the footplate to clarify a diagnosis. Faults were of two main types, either failure of a component or poor performance, with perhaps excessive vibration at certain speeds. What the investigators were looking for were trends. If similar faults occurred on several engines, there may well be a design fault, at which stage the CME himself would have taken an interest.

In broad terms, locomotive development reached a plateau by the time Mr Churchward retired, allowing the workshops to 'tool up' for mass production. The A Shop had been extended and re-equipped and in the early 1930s stripping and erecting engines was being done on a 'circuit'. This meant passing the engine along at each stage of building, from one gang to the next. One of the advantages of this was that tool equipment became the property of the relevant gang and suffered less misuse. The extra lifting, however, increased the risk of cracks at the weakest points of the frames – the corners of the horn gaps. By now, the GWR fleet was made up of a smaller range of standardised types with many interchangeable parts. These parts were now being machined quicker using automatic machine tools, jigs, and fixtures, although engines brought in for repair still had to have their worn working parts machined and replaced to suit. By the 1930s, the CME Department were keeping pace with the ever-increasing demands of the Traffic Department.

The company now had a large number of new 0-6-2 tank engines – the 56xx class, for the South Wales coal traffic. This was part of a programme to replace numerous

Laying out new locomotive frames in the Erecting Shop, the first stage of assembly. The frames have been temporarily bolted together with cross stays and stiffeners and horizontally jig-drilled. The next stage would be lining them up. Note the hydraulic riveter suspended from above. The engine in the background is Hall Class 5946, built in March 1935. (*Author's collection*)

types taken on at the absorption of the minor railways and the grouping of the principal ones in 1923. The standardisation of pannier tanks continued in 1929 with the introduction of an 0-6-0 PT: the 57xx class. Large numbers of these were eventually built, with variations for goods, empty stock, passenger and working over the Metropolitan electrified lines in London. Most of the early batches were being contracted out to other locomotive builders, twenty-five at a time. The company magazine said this unusual occurrence was due to 'the company's policy of helping revival of trade.' Certainly the Works' own locomotive building programme was not particularly heavy during the period 1929–31. The magazine goes on to say of the order for 100 subcontracted engines placed in May 1930: 'The total value of these orders exceeds £250,000.'

In the 1920s, the company only had the excellent but ageing Armstrong and Dean 0-6-0 tender engines to work 'pick up' goods trains on longer branch lines and cross country routes. They had just inherited more of these routes at the Grouping of 1921 as well as the substandard locomotives that came with them. This made the need for a new design even more urgent. The result was the 2251 class, which first appeared in 1930. Mr Collett's department continued to build Churchward's 2-6-0 tender engines for mixed traffic work, with improvements to the 1932 batch. Other types suitable for suburban passenger, branch line work and heavy goods already mentioned also continued to be produced with modifications. These new and not so new designs being built in the 1920s and 1930s would, although not realised at the time, last until the end of steam on the WR three decades later.

The GWR alone built all their mainline engines at their principal locomotive works. The team under Collett had redesigned a 4-6-0 Saint to run with smaller wheels. Its suitability for both fast fitted freights and passenger services was far in excess of anything available up until that time. Based on this, large batches of Hall class engines were ordered from 1928 onwards. The two latest express passenger types were simply enlarged versions of the Churchward Stars and Saints. It was with these, the Castles and Kings, that the problem of lubricating the big ends began to show up, using the old worsted yarn. Someone at Swindon then came up with the idea of a felt pad pressed into a recess cut into the connecting rod bushes. This controlled the flow from the oil bath above and admitted the oil evenly and sparingly.

All remaining locomotives and routes on the Great Western were fitted for Automatic Train Control by the 1930s. This was a superior system designed by the company to ensure that their trains did not pass signals at caution or danger due to driver error. By means of contact between a ramp on the track and a shoe on the engine, audible signals sounded in the cab. If the driver did not cancel a warning signal, the brakes were automatically applied. The ATC apparatus was supplied by signalling contractors and fitted in the Works. Express locomotives had been fitted with ATC as they were built and now smaller engines that worked on main lines were being dealt with at overhaul. Unlike similar equipment used elsewhere, if the GWR system failed it would bring the train to a stand.

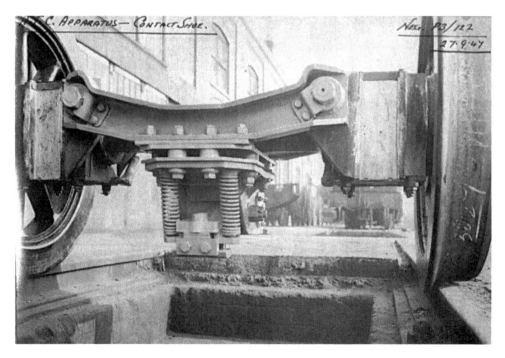

This official photograph for use in the Drawing Office shows the Automatic Train Control contact shoe attached to a pony truck wheelset. When the train approached a distant signal, the spring-loaded shoe was lifted by a ramp on the track. The contact activated audible signals in the cab: a bell for 'all clear' or a siren if the distant signal was 'at caution'. Ray Lewis from Linslade Street made up the ATC shoe assemblies in the 1950s. He was the most highly regarded of fitters in R Shop.

Another desirable feature of locomotive design was ease of carrying out maintenance and running repairs. Occasionally, working parts associated with valves, valve gear, pistons and cylinders would fail without warning out on the road. After the enginemen had disabled the offending parts, the loco could usually be driven back to a depot under its own steam. There, a repair could usually be done without sending it back to Swindon. A hot axlebox would require the wheels to be run out; the larger motive power depots had lifting facilities or a wheel drop pit to do this. Then, the bearing and axlebox could be repaired or a replacement sent from Swindon. During its heyday locomotive work accounted for about 50 per cent of the activity at Swindon Works and required the best engineering methods available. Great emphasis was placed on determining the best materials and producing working parts to fine tolerances.

K. J. Cook, OBE was Mechanical and Electrical Engineer – Western Region in 1950–1. He spoke of the need for accuracy of the working parts of the locomotive at his presidential address to the Institution of Locomotive Engineers in 1955:

Concentrated power is transmitted between the axles by rigid couplings subject to rotating and alternating tensional and compressive forces. These movements, caused from within the locomotive by its direct or induced forces and from without by irregularities of the track, have an effect upon the dimensions between axle centres and argument may therefore develop as to whether extreme basic accuracy is necessary. It is true that if there are errors in original setting, the movement of axles during motion and power transmission may tend to cancel them out, but they may equally add to the error and also to the stresses set up. It is therefore fairly clear that the greater the original accuracy the lower will be the maximum stresses set up in components and it also enables initial tolerances of working parts to be reduced to a minimum, which in itself reduces hammering effects in bearings and the rate at which wear and slackness develop.

Until the early 1930s, the 'lining up' of the locomotive frames was not particularly accurate over their entire length, giving rise to the 'maximum stresses' in the interaction of the working parts that Mr Cook spoke of. The GWR invested in a German system which could measure these distances to within a thousandth of an inch and establish absolute right angles. This did away with the deflection and sag in their old method, using fine cord through the same planes.

The Zeiss optical alignment system used a self-centering telescope placed inside the cylinder, the cylinder block having been refitted to the frames. A length gauge and dial indicator was used in conjunction with the telescope. This would establish the distance from the front cylinder face to the centres of the horn ways: the cut outs which would carry the axleboxes. To determine the right angle axis of each set of horns, the telescope, which was set parallel to the centre line of the engine, and a distant optical collimator were used. When these measurements were known, final machining of the horn cheeks was done using a transversing grinding machine with oscillating arm. This was also introduced at the same time as the optical equipment (1934). Accuracy in the frames would allow the coupling and connecting rods to turn the coupled wheels with minimal and even wear and movement on the bushes, crank pins

The Zeiss telescope
positioned in the cylinder
bellmouth so that the
zero could be set at the
cylinder face. (*GWR*)

and axleboxes. This resulted in significantly increased mileage of locomotive between repairs. Now supporters of the GWR could, and did, say that their locomotives arrived for shopping in the same condition other companies' Works were sending engines out after overhaul. The time taken to 'Zeiss' a locomotive frame was about two and a half hours. The Pooley scales used with the weigh-table were also calibrated using the Zeiss equipment once a year. Large jigs too could be checked for accuracy during manufacture using this method. Calibration of the Zeiss equipment was done in the Works Tool Room.

The total locomotive stock was fixed at around 3,600, increasing to about 3,800 after the war. About 1,000 locomotives went through Swindon annually, while the smaller Works also took in a share of the workload. Wolverhampton, Worcester, Caerphilly and Newton Abbot dealt with some planned maintenance, mainly on smaller types. They too were under the control of the Loco Works Manager's office, Swindon. By the mid-1930s, most of the locomotives taken on from the constituent companies were either scrapped or rebuilt. The longer an engine was in service, the higher the costs due to repairs and availability. This was because the working parts were gradually being replaced by mainly reconditioned parts. The main frames would require strengthening and if extension frames were fitted, they would need repairs or replacement.

More was expected of the Western's King class 4-6-0s than of any other type. They hauled the heaviest trains to the fastest timings for 30 years but with restricted route availability, only thirty were ever built. When the Kings had been in service for between 20 and 25 years, they were averaging about 50,000 miles a year each and receiving heavy repairs at Swindon about every 19 months. They spent more time under repair at their home depot than in the Works. These engines in particular were not held at Swindon Works any longer than necessary and a reconditioned boiler was kept ready. Jim Lowe said that they tried where possible to bring more of them in during the period of the winter timetable in the 1950s. The reason why new engines

On either side of the frames a purpose-built grinding machine would skim the horn ways at right angles during their alignment. Later, in the 1940s, the frames were lowered onto an adjustable jig which held them rigid at this stage. (*GWR*)

were not built to replace or supplement the Kings after the war is not clear. As a compromise, the Works were allowed to redesign and rebuild them because, when they were available, the ageing Kings still performed well.

Modifications were made to improve the steaming based on comparisons with French practice. Stationary plant and road testing was undertaken by the research and development section of the Drawing Office. The main changes took ten years to complete; work would have started earlier but for the war. Firstly, a larger superheater was fitted in 1948; then, rebuilt boilers were fitted as they came through the Works. The R&D section under Sam Ell also redesigned the draught arrangement to improve the rate of combustion. Then, to clear the exhaust away quicker and reduce back pressure, a double blastpipe and chimney was developed. Now the performance of these so-called 'free steaming' Kings was improved considerably over the pre-war version and many of the 'Castles' also received the expensive rebuilding. Amazingly, seventeen of the latter were completed as late as 1961, well into the period when some of the class were being withdrawn due to dieselisation – a good example of Swindon being a law unto itself. One proposed modification, however, was not completed due to the coming of the diesels despite drawings being ready by 1956. Jim Lowe remembers two sets of roller bearings arriving from Timken for fitting

The other Erecting Shop, BE Shop, looking east towards the tender section in the background. Here they normally dealt with smaller engines than this Bulldog class 4-4-0. The date could be anytime between the fitting of this class with ATC shoes (seen below the buffer beam) in 1928 and 3417's withdrawal in 1948. Engines normally spent 17 or 18 working days and nights being overhauled. The Works were expected to keep no more than 5 per cent of the locomotive stock out of service at any one time, with around 6 per cent stopped elsewhere. (*Author's collection*)

to two of the Kings; they remained in the AE Shop new work stores, never to be used.

To get the best out of an ageing locomotive stock, minor modifications were constantly being tried and tested. There were then bound to be failures and even bad practice but little of this ever became known outside the industry, so it is worth recording an incident here. Swindon had always remained largely independent of the head office at Paddington but once the railway became nationalised in 1948, the new regime had other ideas. Even so, Research and Development, formerly the 'experimental section', undertook a series of experiments on locomotives, mainly ex-GW passenger types. Even after the diesels started to be introduced, the experiments continued.

One series of errors was described to me by Ken Ellis, with additional details added by Richard Woodley, an authority on Western Region steam locomotives. Twenty Hall class 4-6-0s were subjected to experiment No. W/SW/L/139, authorised in March 1957; this involved fitting BR standard type piston valve heads and steam chest liners instead of the GW types. On some test runs, high-frequency vibration was reported on the footplate, but not always. At the end of August the experiment was tried on one of the King class engines, 6010 *King Charles I*. During the factory trials between Swindon, Didcot and Reading the King encountered the same problems that had occurred with some of the Halls, only worse. It was reported that 'high frequency vibration was experienced when running at speed but was most severe when coasting.'

Driver Hayden and fireman Lye on the running plate of the recently streamlined King class locomotive 6014. This is a press photo taken at Bristol Temple Meads station on either 13 or 14 March 1935. It shows very clearly that the hemispherical front casing was the most disfiguring of the additional fairings. The locomotive, with two coaches (a 'B' set), was working 'running in' turns between Swindon and Bristol at this time. On the run on the 14th it was reported that 'high speeds were being reached'. Joseph 'Charlie' Hayden retired in 1949; he was well known at Swindon Shed for his fast running. Gordon Shurmer, a fireman there from the late 1940s, said his nickname was 'Kay Don', after a famous racing driver of the period. Charlie Lye also became a 'top link' driver at Swindon, in the 1950s.

Swindon was among the very first to attempt to streamline their express locomotives but it remains a source of speculation as to why they never took the idea seriously, especially as the other railway companies were soon showing how successful it could be, albeit with locomotives where the streamlining was part of the original design. Presumably they thought the reduction in wind resistance did not affect the speed and coal consumption significantly enough. Two GWR locomotives were altered in the centenary year of 1935: 5005 *Manorbier Castle* and 6014 *King Henry VII*. Nothing official has come from Swindon Works on the matter and it is generally agreed that the Chief Mechanical Engineer was not interested from the start. The idea seems to have originated from the Board at Paddington, who wanted something to impress the public for the company's centenary. It is said that the CME moulded some Plasticine around a model of a locomotive and asked the Drawing Office to come up with modification drawings. Steel plate fairings and cowlings were the result: they were to deflect the air around and away, thus reducing drag. The company intended to obtain much publicity out of it and had plenty of photographs taken.

Some of the modifications lasted less than a year. Cowlings over the outside cylinders, front steam chests and outside steam pipes were the first to be permanently removed: they caused overheating and made maintenance difficult. During the war both engines had most of the rest of the streamlining removed. Eventually, only the special snifting valves, oilboxes (added to counteract problems with the oil feed now getting too hot) and the V-shaped cab front on the King survived. In 1937 *The Locomotive* magazine claimed Collett said: 'Streamlining is really only effective for speeds over 70 mph, and then it largely depends on the direction of the wind.'

The screw reverser and other controls in the loco cab could not be handled because of the shake. Ken said: 'The 'backroom boys' at Swindon spent a lot of time trying to find out why the new valves and liners would not run on 'sixty ten'.' They could not ascertain the problem and Ernie Nutty the Senior Technical Assistant reported this to his boss Sam Ell. For some reason Mr Ell was a bit short with him over the protracted problem and said: 'Take it away I've finished with it.' Someone other than Mr Nutty interpreted this as return it to traffic and 6010 turned up at Old Oak Common about 12 September, supposedly okay.

The shedmaster at Old Oak decided to return the engine to Laira, its home shed, on the down Cornish Riviera Express the following morning. Whether he knew of the problem and was making a point is not known. This train was the pride of the WR and its schedule and load required an engine in very good condition. When news reached Swindon that the train arrived 35 minutes late at North Road station, Plymouth, Ernie Nutty was furious. Needless to say, the locomotive was back in the factory for a 'light casual' repair in about a week or so. No doubt the 10-inch semi-plug piston valves that had worked perfectly well for many years were refitted. The engine would have gone to Harold Rayer's 'light repairs' section in A Shop and not entered the overhaul circuit.

In theory, locomotives of the same class should perform similarly, but they had varying reputations. Even after several overhauls, the men who worked with them say certain engines remained 'good uns' or 'bad uns'. Ken Ellis, a technical assistant at Swindon in the 1950s, told me: 'Despite the episode with 6010, Ernie Nutty always said she was the best 'King'; most of us in the office thought 6025 *King Henry III* was the best of the class.'

C. B. Collett was head of the department which dealt with all the mechanical and electrical work of a large railway company as well as its docks. As CME, he was directly responsible to the General Manager and to the Directors at Paddington. Mr Collett joined the company in 1893 in the Swindon Drawing Office and soon showed particular initiative and ability and was promoted to ever more important positions. During the First World War he was awarded an OBE for organising munitions work done by his department. Most of his shop floor experience was gained before he took over at the top and he was rarely seen around the factory or even in the Drawing Office. With so many fine engineers from the shop floor up, it is misleading to attribute all the mechanical developments to the 'chief' directly. Indeed, there are historians who claim the CMEs after Mr Churchward were no more than figureheads. However, as head of department it was he who would have the final say as to whether new designs or modifications went ahead. In that sense at least, Mr Collett can take the credit for the developments during his term of office.

All the senior staff in the CME Department except the divisional engineers were based at Swindon Works and all were subordinate to Mr Collett as CME. In the 1930s, his immediate staff were: Mr Auld, Principal Assistant to the CME, who had taken over as No. 2 when Mr Stanier was poached to become CME on the LMS in 1932; Mr Hawksworth became Assistant to the CME, again due to the reorganisation caused by Stanier's departure; Mr Hall succeeded Mr Crump as Locomotive Running Superintendent and Outdoor Assistant to the CME when the latter retired in 1931

Charles Benjamin Collett, Chief Mechanical Engineer for the GWR throughout the 1930s and the first part of the Second World War.

One of the last Swindon designs was this 0-6-0 pannier tank, the 1500 class, introduced in 1949. Only ten were built, probably because the diesel equivalent was proving successful. The 1500s were to be a 'no nonsense 24 hour shunting engine' with a short coupled wheelbase for sharp curves in and out of sidings. The cylinders and valve gear were on the outside, a departure from the GW practice of concealing the clutter for aesthetic reasons. This, together with the absence of footplating along the sides, allowed better accessibility for maintenance and oiling of the moving parts. The 1500 class would be used for empty coaching stock movements between Old Oak carriage sidings and Paddington, or similar work elsewhere. (*GWR*)

– his assistant was Mr Simpson; Mr Hannington was succeeded by Mr Cook as Locomotive Works Manager following the former's fatal accident in 1937. Assistant Loco Works Managers were Mr H. Johnson, Mr Lawson, Mr Cuss and Mr Grainge, who was Electrical Assistant. Mr Evans was the long-serving Carriage and Wagon Works Manager; his assistants were Mr Dawson, Mr Randle and Mr Hurle; the latter was also responsible for train lighting. The Chief Clerk was Mr Kelynack; the Chief Draughtsman, Mr Smith; Assistant Chief Draughtsman, Mr Woolacott; and the Chief Chemist, Mr Dawe; all reported directly to the CME.

Unlike Swindon, the other railway companies watched outside developments and quite naturally adopted some of the superior GWR ideas themselves. One exception was the other companies' move towards increased superheat to improve locomotive performance in the 1930s; the Great Western did not. With the problem of burning oil in the cylinders in mind, Mr Collett stayed with his predecessor's low degree of superheat (Later, because of inferior coal, Mr Collett's successor reluctantly reversed this decision). Collett seemed quite happy to sit back and consolidate his position in the mid-1930s while the other companies designed new express locomotives and more than closed the gap left by Mr Churchward; however, few writers criticise him over this. Covering every type of haulage requirement with a minimum of locomotive designs was essential for the Works, who had to build and maintain them. It was Mr Churchward who first set about a standardisation of locomotive classes. However, his successor, C. B. Collett, was the one able to fully exploit it because the period of evolution was over. When he retired in 1941, Mr Collett had reduced GWR locomotive types down to thirteen, defined by wheel arrangements and whether they were tank or tender engines, and thirty-seven classes. He revived the old Victorian 0-4-2 tank and 0-6-0 pannier tank designs with, of course, recent improvements and produced some fine engines. The building of the excellent Earl class 4-4-0s for secondary passenger work from parts of the Duke and Bulldog classes was brilliantly unconventional.

Sir Nigel Gresley on the LNER had been trying to get the other CMEs interested in a national locomotive testing laboratory. Mr Collett predictably showed little enthusiasm but then quietly had the Swindon Test Plant (the only one in the country until 1948) rebuilt in 1936–7. He also played a big part in the development of Automatic Train Control and equipping the GWR with it. The upgrading of the running sheds around the system was the responsibility of the CME, but again Mr Collett had little to do to improve or enlarge upon Churchward's work. He found out about copper welding techniques being perfected on the continent and sent the Works Manager to investigate. This led to the development at Swindon of welded seams on the copper firebox inner wrapper, hastened by the need to reduce the heavy maintenance of inaccessible lapped and riveted joints. There was a lot of scepticism as to the strength of welded firebox seams at first but Collett's faith in them was proven.

CHAPTER 5

Steam Locomotive Repair and Overhaul in the 1950s

An account of locomotives passing through A Shop compiled mainly from information supplied by a former locomotive erector in the AE Shop, Jim Lowe.

All engines had a 'tentative date', the date they would next be expected to need Works attention; this varied depending on the class. Prior to this date, a report of its condition was sent to 'shopping control' at Paddington from the division covering the loco's home depot; the report was known as a 'shopping proposal'. Taking a locomotive out of traffic and through the works was very expensive, therefore the stage at which it was no longer to be 'patched up' had to be based on several factors: mileage run since last overhaul; repairs carried out at sheds and recorded on the engine's 'tickler card'; and boiler and mechanical inspector's reports. Detailed information also allowed the authorities to ascertain what work would be required in advance, saving time later. Before acceptance into Swindon Works, locomotives would arrive at the reception sidings at the east end of the Loco Works from their home depots. This was recorded as entering the 'factory pool' on the engine history. All the engine preparation in and out of the Works came under the control of foreman Stan Morris; when he retired in the 1950s, his replacement was a Mr Tucker from the progress/work study section.

There were three Works pilot turns and three sets of enginemen to move locomotives to and from the Erecting Shop traversers. One turn involved bringing locomotives from the reception sidings to the Reception Shed, officially known as the BSE. Another turn dealt with small 0-6-0 tender engines, tank engines and all tender movements in and out of B Shed. A third turn moved engines that had been pushed through the BSE Shed, ready to go into A Shop, and took their ex-Works engines away. The B Shed pilot had other duties too. They took wagons of sand and supplies to and from the foundries: track chairs from the Chair Foundry and turnings from R Shop via the short traversing table between the Iron Foundry and B Shed.

Four or five withdrawn but not yet condemned tank engines were kept for Works pilot duties until their boiler certificates ran out. The V Shop boiler inspector, Brian Carter, checked the continued worthiness of these engines after boiler washouts. They could be seen stabled on the turntable roads with their shunters' trucks when not required, as they and their crews were allocated to the Works and not the Running Shed. The many other Works pilot engines and their crews working the yards around the 'factory' were based at the Running Shed. The accompanying shunters' truck carried tools such as shunting poles, brake sticks, jacks, packing and a long rerailing

4901 *Adderley Hall* in the Reception Shed, apparently being prepared for the Erecting Shop. This engine is recorded as having been withdrawn two months before this picture was taken, in September 1960. These dates were known to be inaccurate in some cases, as seems to be the case here. Jim Lowe told me that these early withdrawals sometimes made it into the Works before a decision was made as to their future. (*R. Grainger*)

The traverser at the east end of A Shop. Two pilot engines and a match truck are on the left on one of the turntable roads. The pile of ash on the ground suggests that the nearest one has had its fire emptied. This would normally be done at the shed but A and B Shop pilots never went there. Note the rope winch box and capstan in front of the two engines waiting to go into the shop.

tool; all had been made 'inside'. According to *The Railway Magazine* for December 1951, a visitor to Swindon Works noted ex-Barry Rly 0-6-2 tanks (258, 269, 272) and an 0-6-0 (1709) still working more than a year after withdrawal. The last of the engines absorbed from railway companies in South Wales and rebuilt was used in 1957. After that, the Western Region used GWR shunting engines displaced by new diesel equivalents. The footplatemen had a large corrugated shed by the turntable which they shared with others who worked at the Reception Shed. Only if one of them were off sick did the Running Shed supply a driver or fireman. Pay was, however, collected with their colleagues round at the shed. The A and B Shop pilot drivers would have been taken off main line work for disciplinary or more likely health reasons (green card men); the firemen would be men from the lower links. With continual engine movement in and out of A and B Shops, the occasional derailments had to be dealt with quickly.

The purpose-built Reception Shed came into use in 1944; it was sited between A Shop and the main line. Incoming locomotives had their smokeboxes cleared; fires and brick arches dropped; water drained from their boilers and tanks or tenders. The latter were now detached to be dealt with separately in B Shed. Here too the coal was taken out and ash was put into hoppers and dropped into wagons by overhead crane. The Running Department tried not to send in locomotives with very much coal as they were charged for it. Coal taken from incoming engines was recorded and taken into account when refilling later. Until 1956, some smaller locos as well as tenders were dealt with in the original Erecting Shop in B Shed; they would be parked on one of the two roads east of the Telephone Exchange until taken inside. Travelling cranes were also repaired in B Shop and they were parked on the curve of the Gloucester branch. All other locomotives for planned overhaul were taken into A Shop. From 1956, when the rail car diesel repair section was set up, B Shop had to stop taking steam locomotives. The names of the repair classifications were changed after nationalisation; there were three types of overhauls, now called 'general', 'heavy' and 'intermediate'. Erecting Shop foreman Sid Abrams would chalk the type of classified repair or overhaul to be undertaken on the side of each locomotive while it was in the Reception Shed.

It was claimed that about ten engines per week were overhauled at Swindon in the late 1940s. Lesser repairs, where the boiler did not come off, were either 'light' or 'casual' and could also be carried out at the larger running sheds after notifying shopping control first. The annual figure for 1956 was: 368 engines had 'heavy' or 'general' overhauls and 255 had 'intermediate' repairs; another twenty-six had 'casual' repairs. These figures were significantly lower than those of 1936, due in part to improved facilities at other works and Running Sheds.

Chargeman Harold Rayer's gang dealt with 'casual' or 'light' repairs. The defects might have been caused by collision, breakdown (including a hot axlebox) or occasionally misuse. Two Wolverhampton Kings came into Rayer's section in 1956 with damaged fireboxes. They had both been fitted with Alfloc water treatment equipment which should have, by this date, been causing no problems; perhaps the wrong concentration was used, or the boilers were filled with soft water at another running shed. Despite claims that the boilers had been washed out thoroughly, it was found that a large patches of sludge had caused the inner fireboxes to bulge. Jim said:

Two Manor class engines, 7809 and 7815, have been stripped down, leaving only the frames, the cabsides and the combined cylinder block and smokebox saddles. This photograph is dated 23 April 1963. (*R. Grainger*)

The stays would have to come out and the affected plates flattened. It is likely that these defects were below the footplating so the boilers had to come out and that's why they came to the Works. These situations would lead to a heated discussion between Paddington and the shedmaster at the home depot.

There were two sections for the light repairs (see diagram); the one at the back of A Shop was for work where the boiler or wheels needed to come out. Regardless of whether the boiler needed attention, the opportunity was taken by the Boiler Shop inspector to check it. Engines for light repairs outside the overhaul circuit were cleaned (with white spirit and oil) after the work was completed, so it could be dirty work. These engines would still require a trial afterwards.

Erecting was heavy work and, in the case of stripping, would sometimes require a hammer and chisel to shift nuts and certainly a hammer to remove bolts. If they still wouldn't budge, 'Ernie the burner' was summoned to cut off ceased and rounded nuts by oxy-acetylene torch. The procedures for stripping and rebuilding locomotives at Swindon were little changed since the 1930s and, in many aspects, since before the First World War. The main changes were the A Shop circuit, which was worked out and introduced by the chief erecting shops' foreman, Mr Millard. He also made it clear in a paper presented to the Swindon Engineering Society in 1928 that the best methods available for this work were not always those used in Swindon Works. Therefore, I assume that he was the main instigator of improvements in tooling, jigs and plant during his term of office (until 1954).

0-6-0 Pannier Tank No. 6705, built by W. G. Bagnall in 1930, receives attention in B Shop on 18 September 1941. (*Author's collection*)

Unlike the manufacturing shops, the erecting shops relied solely on incoming parts and those parts arriving ahead of schedule. Rebuilding a locomotive had to be done in a set order; if parts were unavailable, little or nothing could be done until they were. Production meetings took place every morning to discuss the availability of parts, gauges and specialist tools to complete the next stages of each engine being worked on. Progress chasers reported back to the Engine Progress Office, who then either notified the 'chaser' involved with the production of parts from other workshops or enquired as to stores availability. All progress staff had been chosen from among the tradesmen so they would understand production workshop routines and priorities. The head of the A Shop progress office was Reg Thatcher and his 'chaser' at this time was Frank Soper. The progress of engines passing through or being built in the AE Shop was tracked using a board upstairs in the chief foreman's office. As completed work slips were received from the shop floor and endorsed by the inspector, so the engine's progress card moved across the board towards completion. Mr (Ernie) Simpkins became chief A Shop foreman in 1954; Mr (Jim) Owen remained as assistant chief foreman. Section foremen in the 'AE' in the mid to late 1950s were: Mr (Dennis) Cole, Mr G. Gardiner, Mr (Arthur) Graham, Mr (Pat) Keefe and Mr (Sid) Maslin. The latter two worked a fortnight 'about' on nights, said Jim.

The work of stripping and rebuilding during major overhauls was divided up into four stages, with a gang of men permanently allocated to each. The sequence used in the A Erecting Shop is summarised as follows.

The locomotive was taken into the Erecting Shop facing east, by a traversing table. When adjacent to the chosen stripping pit road, it was winched across by capstan and cable and dismantled in a set order. The sixty pits in the A2 bays were served by

2-6-2 passenger tank engine No. 4144 is in AE Shop undergoing repairs. (*R. Grainger*)

100-ton overhead cranes which could lift the largest steam locomotives complete and move them anywhere along the bay. The eighty pit roads in the A1 bays were used for erecting the smaller classes up to the capacity of the 50-ton overhead crane. The AV Shop (boiler repairs) was between A1 and A2 (see diagram). A short travel crane was installed high up in the raised roof of the boiler bay; it was primarily used to suspend upended boiler barrels while their firebox and smokebox were riveted on. The bays in A2 were used for the larger engines and each road was long enough to take a smaller engine too, perhaps a 42XX or a 41XX type, and frequently did. There were two or three stripping pits in A1 and four in A2.

First, the connecting rods, coupling rods and horn ties were removed, then the rest of the valve gear, and it was all put onto a bosh trolley which stood at the end of the pit nearest to the traverser. The loco was then lifted sufficient for the wheels to be run out. Any work in the pits underneath would require electric lamps for illumination; electric and compressed air points had been fitted in the pits and this did away with the need for dangerous flare lamps. Some men kept candles to use as it saved time getting lamps from the stores.

The operations to overhaul driving wheels in the AW Shop were lengthy and this work had to be started as soon as possible. Although the loco was rebuilt using wheels and other parts from stock, those removed had to be made serviceable within a strict period of time to maintain the pool of spares. Used wheels were dealt with as a set; depending on their state, they were either skimmed back to true on a heavy-duty wheel lathe or new tyres were fitted then skimmed. If they didn't need replacing, the

Wheeling a locomotive was tricky and labour-intensive because of having to 'jump' the axleboxes simultaneously. The horn gaps had to slide down into position as the loco was slowly lowered by overhead crane. Here an unknown type, possibly a diesel shunter, was being wheeled. (*Author's collection*)

crank pin bearing surfaces were usually lightly machined. Replacing a pin was a fairly major undertaking as it meant taking the wheel set apart. Finished wheels would go onto a balancing machine before leaving. A lot of locomotive wheels were received into the A Wheel Shop from the home depots. One reason might be damaged crank pins due to violent slipping, in which case the rods would also be damaged. They too got prompt attention because they left a serviceable engine standing idle.

With the frames lowered onto baulks of timber or jacks, the coppersmiths removed all steam and water pipework; the cylinder casings were occasionally removed (by tinsmiths), but only if the K Shop inspector agreed. The cab roof was taken off by boilermakers. The boiler was unfastened, lifted out and lowered onto a trolley to be towed outside to the 'Barn', where it was inspected and the flue tubes removed. Then as much sludge and scale was raked out as possible before it went to the Boiler Shop. The Barn gang were the only men to get as dirty as the stripping gangs; nobody envied the men on either type of work but most of them didn't ever want to move. The bogies and pony trucks were sent for repair in the A1 Bay on Fred Dingley's section; this section later assembled the D800 bogies. The bosh trolley ran on the rails and was fitted with upright posts (stanchions) to hold the long motion parts. They could then be taken to the bosh for cleaning via the traversing tables. All the dismantled parts were degreased and cleaned (boshed) in boiling caustic solution and rinsed. Inspectors then marked each part with a strip of paint; the colour depended on whether they were reusable, repairable or scrap. Apart from the latter, they were then sent to various repair workshop gangs and put into a refurbishment cycle. After 'boshing', all the bolts and nuts were checked by the 'green card' men of the reclamation gang. It was usually the large 'turned bolts', which were hydraulically pressed into hornblocks and used for securing cylinder castings to the frames, which were damaged and thrown out. The smaller 'soft' or 'black' bolts for holding fittings other than motion parts were usually salvageable. Two days were allowed for stripping a locomotive down and dispersing the parts.

The frames, with only the cab sides left in position, were cleaned by hand and then taken by crane to the 'frame rectification section'. This was chargeman Georgie Gardner's gang; when he became foreman, Ron Glass took over. Ron had several relatives in the shop, including Reg Glass, chargeman of the connecting rod gang in AM Shop. On Gardner's gang the frames were inspected for fractures and loose bolts and rivets, etc and with long chisels, carbon deposits were removed from the steam passages and cylinder ports (the reasons for carbon build-up are discussed in chapter 4). Depending on the locomotive type, such things as the overhauled cylinder block, cylinder and motion plate castings and smokebox saddle were refitted. In service the bolts holding the cylinders invariably became distorted due to the forces of the motion against the rigid frame. So, before refitting, the holes would be broached and oversized bolts drawn from the shop stores. Now, with screw jacks at the back end, the frames were levelled and optically surveyed. With the measurements obtained, the hornways and cylinders would be machined relative to each other to bring them back into alignment. A homemade grinding machine would skim the hornways at right angles with oscillating arms. Next, a purpose-made machine powered by compressed air was attached to the cylinders and slowly rebored them using tipped tools. The sizes of the rebored cylinders were sent over to the machine section so that pistons and piston valves could be made to suit. If the rebored cylinder had reached its limit, a cast iron liner could be made. This was cooled in a tank of liquid carbon dioxide and inserted; as the liner returned to normal temperature it expanded and held fast. Where there was a choice, cooling had the advantage over heating in that it did not change the metal's properties so much. With the frames 'lined up', there was no need to machine the axleboxes out of centre and out of square to suit.

During the five days in the next section, in the care of Frank Comley's gang, an overhauled boiler was fitted back into the frames and the engine 'wheeled'. All parts were received from the shops where they had been overhauled, or from the Stores; the latter would have been undercoated, oiled or greased to prevent surface rust in storage. Inspectors had to pass each stage of the refitting. The engine was lifted up and carefully lowered onto the driving wheels, which had been positioned underneath. With the crane driver receiving signals from the 'slinger' on the ground, the axleboxes were jumped (levered) into the descending horn gaps. This done, the horn ties were fitted and the engine lifted again so that the wheels could be turned, the cranks lined up and coupling rods fitted. The heavy rods were manhandled and would require some force to get the bushes over the crank pins, so other fitters were summoned to help. Then the springs were put up and slide bars fitted; the screw or lever reverse, the valve gear rockers, brake hanger brackets and cylinder drain cocks were all fitted in

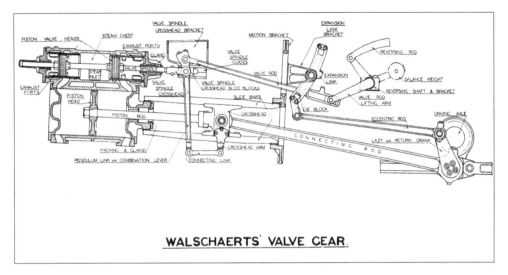

WALSCHAERTS' VALVE GEAR.

Outside Walschaerts valve gear, as used on the 1500 class and inside on the GW four cylinder locomotives. Locomotive valves allowed steam in and out of the cylinders by sliding back and forward across ports. The valve setting plant in A Shop was designed and built at Swindon. The locomotive was lowered onto adjustable rollers; those in contact with the big end driving wheels were driven by an electric motor. The operator could start, stop, reverse and inch the rollers round, which moved the wheels and valve gear very precisely. A second man would check the position of the piston valves in relation to the cranks. Adjustments to the eccentric rods were worked out and minor alterations up to 1/16th of an inch could be made by the setters. Anything more required the blacksmith to 'draw' (lengthen) or 'jump' (shorten) the rod. Jim Lowe remembers that Bob Jarvis and his mate Hubert Keen were two setters in the 1950s and that chargehand Tom Weaver and a mate usually did the smiths' work for the erectors. The apprentices would often remark that the skills of valve setting were not readily passed on.

The tank engine bays in A and B Shops had a simplified plant with rollers powered by compressed air. This did away with the laborious method of moving the loco with a pinch bar under the wheels along a section of track, steam cranes excepted. The wheels needed to be inched round so as to bring the cranks into certain positions while measuring the corresponding valve events (positions). Some Running Sheds adjusted the valves and they had to do it the hard way.

Valve gear on GWR locomotives worked via eccentric sheaves attached to one of the driving wheel axles, or via outside cranks as above. As the wheel turned, the eccentrics pulled rods forward and back (see illustration above). This movement was transferred to the valves via an expansion link through which the die block could be moved by the driver to alter the length of travel of the valve spindle; when accelerating, it was progressively shortened (expressed as percentage cut off) by the engine driver. This in turn produced the shorter and more frequent bursts of steam required to maintain a working piston which was by then assisted by the momentum of the locomotive/train. On four-cylinder engines the valve gear was connected to the inside cylinders, the outside gear only requiring a rocking lever (not visible here) connected to the inside valve spindle at the front end. The cylinders moved the connecting rods: the two inside rods drove the leading coupled wheels and the two outside drove the intermediate or middle sets of wheels. From a standing start the reversing gear could be put into 'back gear' and the mechanism would move the locomotive in the opposite direction.

turn. The latter two were done by men who did nothing else, possibly 'green card men' who were disabled in some way. Spectacle plates (window glasses) were put back in the cab if they had been removed.

The steel boiler, with its copper firebox, had been overhauled in V Shop by the boilermakers. The Works also did repairs to boilers in A and, before the war, B Shops; Wolverhampton and Caerphilly Works also had facilities for boiler repairs. On its way back to the Erecting Shop, the boiler had safety valves, regulator valves and water gauges etc fitted so that the boiler test could be carried out; this was all done in the P1 Shop. Here in the 1940s a standard No. 15 boiler designed for the County class was used to provide steam of sufficient pressure for a hydraulic test followed by a steam test, thus avoiding the need for a fire in each firebox. Whether it had replaced an earlier static boiler I do not know. Before leaving 'P1', the boiler was moved to a fixture where it was plastered with a two to three-inch layer of asbestos. The insulation was dried while the boiler was hot using steam from a central supply. Cleating with galvanised steel sheets then followed; some had to be put through tapered rollers to produce cone-shaped sheets to cover the tapered part of the boiler – this was a tinsmith's job.

The last four days that the loco was 'inside' were spent in Stan Lewington's 'finishing off' bays (when Stan retired, his replacement was Jack Steward from B Shop). The first job was to blow out the smokebox, steam chests and passages with a compressed air line and check they were clear of nuts and bolts etc, using small mirrors on rods. 'Finishing off' saw the motion, con rods, crossheads and wooden footplating refitted (see also Alan Lambourn's memories of loco erecting as an apprentice). Carpenters from D Shop fitted the cab flooring; one was always Bill Hurst and the other was often Pete Pragnell. The valves and pistons were inserted and injectors and cock gear were 'put up' so that the coppersmiths could fit the associated pipework. Moving parts would be lubricated prior to fitting and a gang of about three men made sure wicks, corks and oil were placed correctly in the oilboxes. Fitters were responsible for fitting all oil-soaked pads during assembly. The locomotive would be painted and varnished simultaneously with the final refitting work. If it was a larger, named engine, its two nameplates, which had been repainted, were also now refitted (for details of locomotive painting see chapter 7). With all the glass in the roof, A Shop could be uncomfortably hot in the middle of a summer's day as neither side of the locomotive was in the shade.

Des Griffiths remembers that if a man stood about while his mates earned the piecework, he was likely to be a marked man: 'Someone in the pit was likely to paint the back of his shoes red while he was leaning against the locomotive [red was the colour the inspector used to mark dismantled parts that could not be reused]. To the amusement of his mates he would unknowingly be classed as unserviceable for the rest of the day.' All the wages grades in the shop were on piecework. Gilbert King was the piecework chargeman in A1 bay, and Alfie Bown in A2; they calculated the fortnightly figures to be forwarded to the wages office via the group office. Jim can't remember the other piecework chargemen but did recall the inspector, Maurice Smith.

The next stage in the locomotive's circuit involved lifting it along and onto the valve setting machinery. The wheels were lowered onto adjustable rollers; those in contact with the big end driving wheels were driven by an electric motor. The operator could start, stop, reverse and inch the rollers round, which in turn moved the loco wheels and valve gear very precisely. A second man would check the position of the piston valves in relation to the cranks. Minor adjustments could be made by the setters but Stan Lewington would be asked to send the erector concerned over if the eccentric rod needed altering. He would take it to the blacksmiths' section in the shop with instructions to 'jump' or 'draw' (shorten or lengthen) it, usually no more than about 1/16th of an inch. Jim remembers Bob Jarvis and his mate Hubert Keen were the valve setters; apprentices said their skills were not readily passed on. Driving wheels from the AW Shop that were going back onto locomotives were put next to the valve setting plant. Nearby, eccentric sheaves and straps together with their whitemetal liners were stacked, having arrived from Colin Wood's section in the AM Shop. When he was not assisting the valve setter, Hue would fit the sheaves to the axles of the wheelsets and clamp them together with the two halves of the strap. While the engine was having its valves set, the 'finishing off' gang who had been allocated to it would work on another engine, perhaps putting up brake gear. When the engine returned, and before it was lowered for the last time, the fitter 'pulled on' (tightened up) the nuts on the spring hangers until they were slightly too tight. This was achieved by knowing the pre-determined length and the number of threads showing on the bolt end. Now it was lowered and if a bogie or pony truck was to be fitted, it was placed in position on the pit underneath. Inspectors Norman Jarvis or Jim Cole checked the finishing work; later, when the engine was in steam, one of them would also check its ability to create sufficient vacuum and retain it.

Locomotives spent up to 17 or 18 working days and nights being overhauled and the Works were expected to keep no more than 5 per cent of the total stock out of service at any one time. In the 1950s there was an expanding number of services that required heavier and faster trains. At the same time, the majority of suitable locomotives, the four-cylinder Castles and Kings, were of an age where maintenance and repairs at the depots was increasing and availability was decreasing. For this reason these express passenger types were not held at the Works, out of traffic, any longer than absolutely necessary. They would be worked on day and night. The day foreman would leave instructions as to the work to be undertaken by the night shift and check with the stores that all parts and tool equipment would be available. Certain jobs were traditionally done at night, such as the stripping down. In the later stages, if the engine schedule allowed it, putting up the inside motion or fitting the inside valves and pistons was often left for a night gang, as was fitting the crosshead slide (or motion) bars. There were two upstairs mess rooms in the A Shop where some of the night workers spent their hour break playing cards or putting their feet up and having a doze.

Erecting the 'new builds' was done on special narrow pits in the north-west corner of A Shop; the chargeman here was Ernie Slade. These pits had steel machined tops and were perfectly level. The new frame members came separately from W Shop on specially adapted trailers hauled by a Fordson tractor. They were then laid out, jig drilled and reamed and cross members bolted on. The two main longitudinal frame plates were stood upright on jacks and secured by cross stays and temporarily bolted up, next they aligned with each other using frame stretchers. The 'new build' section had their own circuit over two or three pits but used the same valve setting facilities. From now on building new locomotives followed almost the same sequence as for the rebuilding.

Visitors didn't usually get to see engines coming in and out on the traversers and therefore such photos are unusual. Here, 5028 *Llantilio Castle* starts its journey out of the A Erecting Shop after overhaul. The photo was taken by erector Ted Baden in early Western Region days. (*Jean Moulding*)

One of the 50-ton overhead cranes in what became known as the A Shop 'bosh bay'. It was built into the original part of the building just after 1900. These cranes travelled above the pit roads, powered by Swindon-built electric motors. The hydraulic hoists seen here were also made at the Works. Harold Smith was chargeman of the cranemen, the traversing table men and associated labourers in the 1950s. (*BRW*)

The first job when the new or overhauled locomotives were moved outside was to tow them back to the Reception Shed. Matching tenders were brought up from B Shop as required; the pilot also brought up the tank engines overhauled there. The tender or bunker was coaled and watered and the boiler too was filled with water. Ray Gwillam says in his book, *A Loco Fireman Looks Back*, that measured amounts of coal were dropped back in, but Jim Lowe said no, there would be no reason for this. Steaming the engine was not usually done until the day following its departure from the shop. A gang of men under chargeman Jack Rogers raised the steam; they were unskilled but the NUR had negotiated more than the labourers' rate for them. Jack had been a Swindon 82C driver. The fire was lit using oily rags and timber that was stacked on the footplate beforehand. Scrap offcuts of wood for 'lighting up' came from the carriage side, in wagons. At least two open goods wagons could usually be found on the turntable roads from which the firelighters barrowed the wood to the locomotives.

With sufficient steam pressure on the gauge, Jack Rogers' gang were allowed to move engines along the reception shed as long as they did not go over any points. They handed

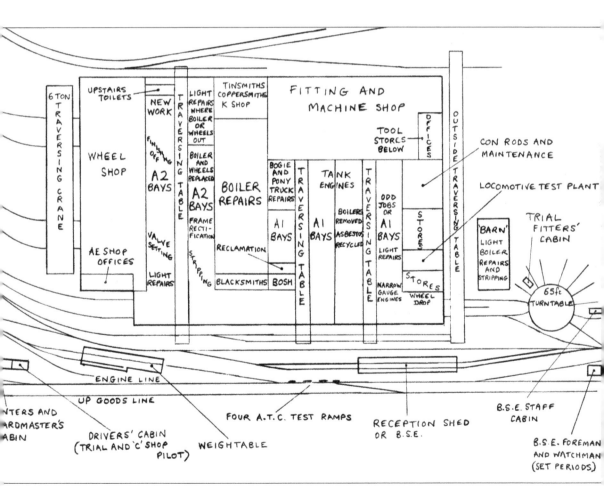

The layout of A Shop and associated buildings just prior to the reorganisation for building the first mainline diesels.

over to the trials crew, who continued to raise steam, oil round and top up the axlebox keeps and big end oilboxes. Enginemen were divided into various links. Light engine trials were part of the duties of men in No. 8 link; they were neither the most experienced nor the most junior. Their cabin was on the west side of the Works weigh table and was shared with the Con Yard and Sawmills pilot crews. The 'trial fitters' had a cabin near the turntable and they dealt with any faults developing prior to the light engine trial. Gradually, as the coal was added and the boiler pressure increased, the pressure gauge needle would start to move. The large injector was opened and closed to check that the vacuum that released the brakes was holding. A boiler inspector, often Brian Carter, was on hand to see that the boiler was functioning normally as steam was raised.

The locomotive, and tender if applicable, was then moved to the Weigh House to have the springs adjusted to obtain the correct loads for each axle. Fred Drinkwater was chargeman here, like his father before him. If Fred was not there, one of the fitters would deputise for him. The Weigh House had new machinery installed in 1929–30, consisting of six balancing tables on 7-foot lengths of track, each capable of measuring axle loads up to 13 tons. It was purpose-made for the company by Henry Pooley & Sons Ltd of Birmingham. Because of the lack of activity during the annual holiday shutdown in July, the balancing pans could be cleaned and calibrated. Jim remembers: 'A firm called W&T Avery (who had subsequently bought out Pooley) were contracted to complete this before the Works reopened two weeks later.' After recording the weights, the locomotive was moved over the pit and fitters' mates would tighten or slacken each leaf spring nut underneath according to Mr Drinkwater's instructions. Because the spring hanger nuts had been deliberately over-tightened in the Erecting Shop, it was now much easier to 'pull off' (slacken) than to 'pull on' with the weight bearing down on the springs. The engine was then driven back over the scales and rechecked.

Outside the other end of the Weigh House was a rail joint with a drop of three quarters of an inch. The engine and tender, if applicable, was taken over this step and back again to 'unsettle' the springs, which were now carrying their working weight. If this road was occupied, large washers could be used instead. After checking the loading once more on the scales and topping the tender up with water, the engine was ready for its trial trip. Jim said that the method of adjusting the loading on BR Standards was by using shims of different thicknesses. The load on the spring could be taken off using a small hydraulic jack, which allowed shims to be added or taken away.

Jack Leonard was the running inspector in the 1950s; he lived in Wootton Bassett. He would give the driver any special instructions about the trial. The Running Deparment was part of the CME's Department but separate from the Works; therefore, all running inspectors came under the Divisional Locomotive Superintendent at Bristol, not the Works Manager. The fire was managed so that the safety valves lifted outside after weighing, at which point the inspector checked the reading showing on the pressure gauge. When he was happy, the fireman rang the signalman at Rodbourne Lane to ask to cross over to the down main line. The engine was usually taken down to Dauntsey on the original main line to Bristol, a distance of 10 miles. All but the smallest classes went to Dauntsey unless the occupancy of the line was very high. Then all but the largest locos, those without speedometers, went to Little Somerford, 12½ miles out on

Narrow gauge engine *Prince of Wales* is seen outside the south-east corner of A Shop in March 1960. It had just been overhauled and for this a narrow gauge section of track was laid on timber baulks over a pit. It has recently been steamed to check that all was steamtight, but not road-tested. This would be done back home, between Aberystwyth and Devil's Bridge on the Vale of Rheidol Railway. Now for the long ride back to west Wales chained to its trolley wagon. The Works had been maintaining this locomotive and her sisters since the 1920s. (*Ken Ellis*)

the South Wales line. Sometimes, on special main line trials, this route was preferred. The outward journey was taken fairly leisurely in case there were any major problems. With so many working parts and joints needing to be steamtight, it was expected that adjustments would be necessary. Ronny Hinder and Colin Benfield were the two fitters on the 'trials gang'; both had fathers who were drivers. Going out, one of the fitters sometimes rode on the front or rather the back, as the engine was running tender first. Ronnie was particularly fond of doing this: 'Presumably he could diagnose problems with the motion by listening to it from there,' said Jim. Apprentices allocated to the 'trials gang' also went out, so it could get a bit crowded on the footplate. In the siding at Dauntsey Station the bearings and bushes were checked for overheating and oil penetration.

Some delay was normal while waiting for a clear road back to Swindon. On the return journey the engine was worked up to 30 mph at the first milepost. The inspector checked the speed with a stopwatch against the mileposts that were ¼ mile apart; if there was a speedometer fitted, that would be checked at the same time. At the top of Dauntsey Bank, the engine had to be doing 60 mph and assuming Wootton Bassett distant signal was off, the driver would 'open her up' passing Tockenham signal box.

When back at the Works, the engine was parked on one of the turntable roads and the inspector handed the 'trial fitters' a snag list of things to check or attend to. They dealt with the mechanical faults but a boilermaker, tinsmith or coppersmith might be needed if other problems arose; anything major might require the engine to go back 'inside'. When the inspector was satisfied, he released the locomotive to 82C, the BR code for Swindon shed.

The trials of smaller engines stripped and rebuilt in B Shed took place between the Weigh House and the Triangle, outside the Works, a distance of three quarters of a mile. The engine made two or three passes up and down this the 'engine line'. If there were no major problems, the locomotive was, like the A Shop engines, taken to shed by the trials crew before knocking off. Shed fitter Ellis Millard and a mate who were actually A Shop personnel would attend to any mechanical adjustments and repairs that arose while here. The shed foreman would allocate ex-Works engines to stopping passenger train services with three or four coaches, which Swindon shed covered, services such as the 7.20 a.m. all stations to Bristol Temple Meads, the 9.20 to Gloucester and the 10.10 a.m. Didcot stopping train. Another 82C turn was an early morning stopper to Frome. This was possibly a newspaper/parcels train and was often a 'running in' turn for a 2-6-2 tank engine which returned later with a two-coach train. Smaller ex-Works engines might also be used for local shunting duties. Each class of engine would have to do so many miles 'running in' while remaining under Works control. They would then work a service which would get them back to their own depot, tank engines excepted. They usually went home light engine.

Steam locomotives were continually being superseded by improved designs. Jim Lowe said:

An overhauled 28XX heavy freight locomotive parked on a turntable road just before or just after its trial run. The large corrugated cabin behind was used by the A and B Shop pilot enginemen as well as the gangs who worked in the Reception Shed. (*Author's collection*)

After the war it was the responsibility of Shopping Control at Paddington to decide which engines were withdrawn. They took into account: regional requirements, the age of the engine and the mechanical state upon inspection prior to overhaul. The latter might be carried out at Swindon or other smaller works in the CME's Department such as Wolverhampton, Worcester, Newton Abbot or Caerphilly.

When the main line diesels were first put into service in the late 1950s, engines of the Castle and Hall classes began to be withdrawn. At first, the rate of withdrawal was very slow because of teething problems with the new engines and a certain amount of relegating steam to lesser work. Only steam locos requiring major repairs between overhauls were taken out of service; this included those involved in accidents. When the Western and Hymek diesels were also introduced, the rate of replacement was speeded up considerably. From the start of 1962, Castles in particular and Halls were being withdrawn upon application of their normal 'shopping proposal'. However, the selection could be inconsistent; why some were selected while others received overhauls and major modifications is a bit of a mystery.

Written on the back of this snapshot is: 'Taken from an overbridge between Swindon and Uffington.' There is more but the anonymous writer, and perhaps the photographer too, admits he was speculating on what was going on. A 48XX class 0.4.2T locomotive has become derailed by catch points at the end of an up goods loop while running from Swindon to work on the Faringdon branch. It was not unusual for the Works to send out a loco which was still 'on test' after repairs or overhaul with the breakdown vans, which might explain why a Castle and not something smaller was sent. A steel cable can be seen attached, ready to pull the 48XX back onto the catch point stub once the breakdown crew have prepared the trailing wheels. The ballast will have been dug out to 'bed in' the traversing jacks.

The breakdown vans were normally kept parked outside the south-west corner of A Shop and men from that shop were sent out with them when required. This was done on occasions when there was no need of the breakdown train complete with its travelling crane, said Jim Lowe. Jim also told me that he thought the vans and crew became the responsibility of the running shed in the late 1950s. (*Author's collection*)

CHAPTER 6

FT&E Apprenticeships and other Recognised Training

Tradesmen or journeymen (a word of French origin, meaning skilled men paid by the day) who built locomotives could be boilersmiths, coppersmiths, blacksmiths and tinsmiths among others. Most, however, were trained in what was called 'fitting, turning and locomotive erecting'. When these young men were asked what trade they were learning 'inside', the accent was on the 'erecting', which set them apart from the less glamorous carriage fitter and turner. Fitting, turning and erecting, still sometimes called 'engine fitting and turning' until the 1930s, was a primary trade on the loco side along with patternmaking, just as coach builders and finishers were, on the 'carriage side'. The pay scales for these primary trades were, however, no better than some other trades such as bricklayers, boilersmiths, carpenters and tinsmiths. In 1945 it was said that there were 160 apprenticeships of various kinds given at the Works, all spanning a full five years. It is a myth that they always started on the sixteenth birthday; of the thirty-four apprentices taken to learn the craft of the coppersmith between April 1934 and the start of the war, only fourteen commenced the day they reached sixteen years.

First sons of men employed 'inside' often got 'free passage' but the company recouped the costs of schooling and administration from premium apprentices. Those applying for the 'premium' training in the CME Department during the 1930s received a short letter, an application form, a memorandum of regulations for either the Locomotive or Carriage Departments, a notice listing the recognised school examinations that the candidate needed (see illustrations), and another listing the courses of study undertaken before and after acceptance. The 'memorandum of regulations' under which apprentices were employed made sober reading. The regulation 'Notice to leave the Company's service will be given on completion of apprenticeship' was more likely to be enforced for locomotive than for carriage apprentices out of their time.

Ian Sawyer was 'offered a start' in the Works in 1947. He had no relatives there so he and his mother went to see the Locomotive Works Manager, Mr Cook, and it was arranged that Ian would become a premium apprentice. An office boy then took him to see some of the areas where he would be working: 'The noise and frantic activity of the R Shop automatic machines and the thought of having to become part of it, frightened me half to death.' Ian's mother paid 2s 6d to register his indentures and was invoiced every six months for £10 (see letter); with it she was given a report on his progress and punctuality. Six months' notice of termination of the employment was required either way. It seems some premium apprentices even got concessions:

GREAT WESTERN RAILWAY.
CHIEF MECHANICAL ENGINEER'S DEPARTMENT,
SWINDON.

Memorandum for the guidance of prospective Premium Apprentices.

It is desirable that before commencing their practical training, all prospective apprentices should have obtained one of the recognised School certificates awarded to boys of about the age of 16 years, reaching what is known as the Credit standard in the English Group, in one foreign language, in Mathematics, and in one subject in Science.

The examinations now generally accepted as standards are shewn below :—

1. Oxford Local School Certificate Examination.
2. Cambridge Local School Certificate Examination.
3. Oxford and Cambridge Joint Board School Certificate Examination.
4. University of Durham School Certificate Examination.
5. University of London General School Examination.
6. School Certificate Examination of the Joint Matriculation Board of the Universities of Manchester, Liverpool, Leeds, Sheffield and Birmingham.
7. University of Bristol First School Certificate Examination.
8. Senior Certificate Examination of the Central Welsh Board.
9. Leaving Certificate Examination of the Scottish Educational Department.

THE FOLLOWING ARE ALSO RECOGNISED :—

Preliminary Examination of the Institution of Civil Engineers.

Studentship Examination of the Institution of Mechanical Engineers.

Ordinary Matriculation Examinations of the British Universities, provided the candidate passes in the subjects enumerated above.

Apprentices are required to attend specialized Engineering Courses at the College, Swindon, immediately they commence their term.

These courses serve as a good preparation for Associate Membership of the Institution of Civil Engineers, for Associate Membership of the Institution of Mechanical Engineers, or for the Engineering Degree Examinations of the various Universities. In this connection it should be remembered that a certificate must first be furnished as a proof of the attainment of a good standard of general education, and this certificate may be obtained by passing one of the examinations indicated above.

It should also be noticed that unless an apprentice has reached this standard of education, he cannot hope to secure the full benefit of the specialized Engineering Courses arranged at Swindon.

C. B. COLLETT,
Chief Mechanical Engineer.

November, 1936.

'One new starter was allowed to arrive late every Monday morning from his home in Berkshire. The resentment felt by his colleagues subsided somewhat after they heard he had fallen asleep on one down journey and awoke to see the red cliffs of Dawlish flashing by,' said Ian.

Buying your training at Swindon Locomotive Works ceased in 1950 and overpayments were refunded. By now, the Works was finding it increasingly difficult to attract and retain apprentices of the required standard. George Connell said that of the eight lads that started with him in 1949, six went elsewhere before completing their time. Before starting his training as fitter, turner and erector, Ian had a month in B Shop working on tenders: 'I was put with fitter Fred Wiltshire repairing water scoops on the 'water road'; this was my probationary period. Later I would work with Fred's brother Stan who was chargeman on the AM axlebox gang.'

Jim Lowe was apprenticed to FT&E at Swindon from July 1951. He was what was unofficially known as an 'outstation apprentice' because he came from outside the area. In the past, 'premium apprentices' had also usually originated from outside the area. Local apprentices invariably had a father in the Works, entitling them to free 'passage'. Jim was living in South Shields and was interested in working with locomotives. He had done a pre-apprentice course at his local college, learning the basics of fitting and machining.

> The only work I was offered was rivet hotting in the shipyards or working down the coalmines. Gateshead Railway Works was rumoured to be closing and they suggested I apply for a craft apprenticeship at Swindon. My father said: 'You'll be alright there' so I did, and was accepted subject to a medical at Park House. At the labour exchange they gave me the name of someone 'inside': a springmaker from Manchester Road who wanted a lodger. Three other 'outstation apprentices' started with me: John Cole from Totnes [a friend from his home town, Michael Kingdon, had started the year before], Brian Wilson also from Devon and Keith Greenland from Westbury. We always felt separate from the local lads who trained with us. I liked Swindon, it still seemed more like a market town compared with the industrial towns in the north; I was not homesick. During those early days my wages went on rent and a privilege ticket to stay with his family in Uxbridge at the weekends. Discounted privilege tickets were available to those whose home was some distance away, after just one week of work. New starters from nearer home had to work a longer period before entitlement. The landlady would cook for me and do some washing but if I stayed there weekends I had to pay more.

Certain sections within the Loco Works were better suited to the novice and apprentices would all visit a number of them. Therefore, they could make a calculated guess as to where the next placement might be. Until the early 1960s, the apprentice 'inside' had no training school with specially trained instructors. They were not required to produce test pieces or make their own tools, traditions that were often associated with men learning a craft. The first two years were spent turning, the next eighteen months fitting and the final eighteen months erecting. Each placement lasted about three months, with premium apprentices more likely to stick to the schedule. A

GREAT WESTERN RAILWAY.

F. W. HAWKSWORTH.
Chief Mechanical Engineer.

Chief Mechanical Engineer's Department,

SWINDON, WILTS.

Telegrams
LOCO. SWINDON.

Telephone:
SWINDON 2611 : Ext. 107.

Friday, 30th May, 1947.

Your reference :—

Please quote this reference :—

S21050
13/6

Dear Madam,

With reference to our previous correspondence, your son has now completed a satisfactory probationary period and I am prepared to accept him as a premium apprentice to Fitting, Turning and Locomotive Erecting in these Works.

I shall be glad if you will send me a cheque or money order for £10. 0. 0d. made payable to the Great Western Railway Company in settlement of the first instalment of the premium. A postal order for 2/6d. left blank, will also be required in connection with the registration of the apprenticeship documents.

Yours truly,

For F. W. HAWKSWORTH

Mrs. W.K. Sawyers,
356, Cricklade Road,
SWINDON, Wilts.

The company was well known for using up old stationery. A similar letter sent to Mrs Sawyer in 1950 still had Mr Collett's and the company's name upon it, crossed through.

(2428-1)

GREAT WESTERN RAILWAY.

CHIEF MECHANICAL ENGINEER'S DEPT., SWINDON.

No. 5627

Thursday, 5th June 1947

The sum of

RECEIVED *from*

£10. 2. 6d.

Mrs. W.K. Sawyer,

356, Cricklade Road,

SWINDON, Wilts.

in payment for 1st instalment of apprenticeship fees and registration stamp.

in respect of Ian Melyn Sawyer 1852.

For F. W. HAWKSWORTH,
Chief Mechanical Engineer.

48 Bks., 120 lvs.—Est. 897—2-42.—(9).

A company receipt for Ian Sawyer's apprenticeship fees.

common complaint was: 'I was just getting used to the work and being accepted, when I would be on the move again.' Sending youngsters for a bucket of steam or a skyhook from the shop stores or from old Bill over there, was tried on the unsuspecting. Some had heard about the practice in advance and the jokers had to come up with ever more plausible sounding requests. Bob Grainger was sent for some 'tarred yarn'; the only reason he went was because he couldn't imagine the man was capable of a practical joke.

Before the start of first term, the student would have to register at the College to undertake 'technical instruction', which would run concurrently with his practical work. By the 1930s there were part-time day and evening college courses available for most engineering trades. For students on the 'carriage and wagon side', there were courses for trimming and upholstery, coach finishing, bodymaking, wood wagon building and wheelwrights. Trades available for both sides of the Works were for electricians, welders, carpenters and blacksmiths. Sessions were held on three evenings a week from 7.15 p.m. to 9.15 or 9.30 p.m., with some homework as well. Examinations could not be taken unless the attendance over the year was at least 75 per cent.

Before the war, engineering classes were made up almost entirely of students from the Works studying the National Certificate Scheme. On the 'carriage side' they took the City and Guilds of London Institute diploma for railway carriage building. To further stimulate apprentices to give their best, the chairman of the GWR awarded a £10 prize each year for the highest marks in the local engineering examinations. A complete valve gear and motion from the broad gauge locomotive *Lord of the Isles* was laid out in the Technical College. Railway students could pull the reversing lever and see the action instead of trying to imagine it with diagrams. Later, when the classes were made up of apprentices from Vickers Armstrong, Garrards, Plessey's and Marine Mountings as well, the valve gear was removed.

A City and Guilds mechanical engineering course was started after the war alongside the Ordinary National Certificate. Before leaving school the careers master would recommend boys for one or the other. Those holding the School Certificate to credit standard could register for either course, the ONC being more suited to the academic. C&G apprentices were taught at the ex-army buildings in the old Goddard's estate. A small fitting and machine workshop was installed here temporarily. This course was more about craft practice, but included basic mathematics and engineering formulae, metallurgy and some electrics.

The ONC syllabus was split between three main subjects, each taken on a separate evening. They were mathematics, machine drawing and engineering science, with an end of term examination set for each. After successfully completing the three-year course, some went on to study for the Higher National Certificate in the remaining two years. At the end of the third or fourth year, apprentices that had passed the evening course with credit could go on to a 'day studentship'. They would attend college one day a week, for which the company paid their normal day's wages, and one other evening. These classes were held from October until April for four years and were equivalent to a degree course. This scheme was replaced in the 1950s with a five-year sandwich course in Mechanical Engineering; the apprentice alternated between six

CHIEF MECHANICAL ENGINEER'S DEPARTMENT.

GREAT WESTERN RAILWAY. $\left(\begin{smallmatrix}4049\\A\end{smallmatrix}\right)$

Memorandum

OF

regulations under which APPRENTICES are employed

IN THE

LOCOMOTIVE WORKS,

1.—Apprentices are taken in the Locomotive Works, as vacancies arise, to the Trades of Engine Fitting and Turning.

2.—An Apprentice should serve a term of 5 years in order to be considered a fully qualified mechanic, but the engagement may be terminated on either side at the end of any six-monthly period. In this event the time served cannot be regarded as a complete apprenticeship.

3.—A Premium of £10 is payable in advance for each period of six months. 2s. 6d. Stamp Duty is payable on the registration of the application form.

4.—Apprentices are generally taken at the age of 16 years. It is particularly requested that no application be made on behalf of a youth who is not of sound constitution and of good bodily health and strength, as otherwise he would not be able to carry out satisfactorily the obligations specified in this Memorandum.

5.—Before a youth is accepted as an Apprentice he will be employed in the Workshops on probation for one month without wages. During this time he will be required to work the ordinary hours of duty as given in paragraph 11. At the expiration of the probationary period, if his conduct and ability are found to be satisfactory, he will be entered on the Register of Apprentices, and receive wages under the conditions stated in paragraph 10.

6.—Every registered applicant must produce a certificate of registration of birth before commencing the month's probation, also a medical certificate of his suitability for following the employment.

7.—During the month's probation it is desired that the probationer, will make himself thoroughly familiar with the significance of these Regulations, and if at the end of the month he is not satisfied with the conditions laid down, or if he has any doubt of his ability to comply strictly with the requirements specified, it is expected that his application to be entered as an Apprentice will be withdrawn.

8.—Apprentices are subject to the Rules and Regulations in force as to the management of the Workshops in which they may be employed. Great importance is attached to regular and punctual attendance.
In the absence of a justifiable reason, an apprentice will be liable to dismissal if he fails to make full time regularly, or if he misconducts himself in any other way.

9.—It must be understood that Apprentices being in receipt of wages for work performed, must necessarily be kept for some considerable time upon work in which they have become tolerably proficient. Variety of work will be given to Apprentices from time to time so far as the general arrangement of the Workshops will permit, but it is impracticable to remove them frequently from one class of work to another.

10.—Apprentices will be paid wages according to the scale in force, but the yearly increments will be dependent on good conduct. Should there be any ground for complaint in regard to timekeeping or any other respect, the advances may be withheld.

11.—A normal working week consists of 47 hours. Payment is made for the number of hours actually worked and for one week's leave per annum after 12 months service.
All Apprentices are required to commence work punctually, and to make full time.
No Apprentice is allowed to work when the Works are closed, except under special authority.

12.—Apprentices are not bound by Indenture, but those who complete satisfactorily the full term of apprenticeship will at the end of the term receive a certificate stating the class of work on which they have been employed, and their ability and general character. A record of any time that may have been lost during the Apprenticeship will be kept in the following form :—

YEAR ENDED	HOURS WORKS OPEN	HOURS WORKED	TIME LOST (HOURS)			
			SPECIAL LEAVE	ILLNESS	WITHOUT LEAVE	TOTAL
TOTAL FOR 5 YEARS						

13.—The usual holidays are as follows :—
Easter, 3 or 4 days ; Annual Works Holiday, about July, 7 days ; Christmas, from 4 to 7 days. The holidays may be extended by one week at Christmas, and by one week at the Annual Works Holiday, provided that written application is previously made by the parents or guardian. No extension beyond this will be allowed unless the circumstances are exceptional.

14.—Every Apprentice is required to attend the Engineering Classes at the Technical School during the Winter session, and to take the course of theoretical instruction which will be prescribed for him.

Swindon,
April, 1937.

C. B. COLLETT,
Chief Mechanical Engineer,
G.W.R.

200—N.B./8—1989—(26)

NOTE.—It must be clearly understood that notice to leave the Company's service will be given on completion of Apprenticeship.

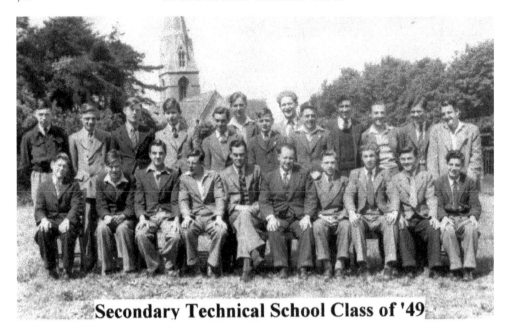

Secondary Technical School Class of '49

In the grounds of the Lawn estate a number of military prefab buildings were converted for use as a secondary technical school after the war. The pupils seen here took junior engineering or building courses as further education between 1947 and 1949. Six of this group went on to do fitting, turning and erecting apprenticeships in the Works. Junior commercial classes were available here too and no doubt some of those girls and boys went on to take up clerical positions 'inside'. (*George Connell*)

months at the Bristol College of Technology and six months in the Works. Incidentally, some short courses were run in 'the factory' for schoolboys on placements from public schools; I have not been able to find details of this scheme.

In the Locomotive Works, apprentices began their training in an area attached to R Shop known as 'the scraggery'. Work done there included facing (scragging), chamfering and threading blank nuts on horizontal and vertical spindle machines. The formidable Harry Turner was the chargeman most apprentices remember here in the 1950s. He would position himself so that you didn't notice a pair of eyes above the back of machines and below his cap. The senior person in any gang of workmen was made up to chargeman. He had a small partitioned area in the shop called a 'box' where he compiled the piecework figures and material slips, etc relating to his gang. Some chargemen took this work home with them where it was quieter.

Having got a feel for basic machine production work, the next move would be onto centre lathes with Reg Hancock's gang. They would machine such things as safety valve spindles and wagon screw couplings. Many older machines in R Shop still had overhead belt and countershaft drives and these were often the ones to be allocated to newcomers. Although many types of machine work were carried out in this shop, apprentices remember it best for two rows of twelve automatic turret lathes with bar capacities of 7/8 inches up to 2 5/8 inches. Reg Emmons' gang worked the R Shop 'autos'. Apprentices would look after two, three or four 'autos' depending on the type. They fed the bar in, kept the coolant topped up and saw they functioned

Mike Farrell producing firebox crown staybolts in the 1940s; he is using a Ward No. 7 combination turret lathe in R Shop. (*BRW*)

correctly but were not responsible for the tooling. The machines were fitted with a special attachment for manufacturing of short or long staybolts that held the inner locomotive firebox to the outer. These were produced in large numbers and although inspected in the shop, a sample would be checked in the Tool Room every week to see that the thread form and minimum diameter were within limits. Other automatic lathes were 'tooled up' to produce large numbers of bright steel hexagon lock nuts, of which some were subsequently castellated. All sorts of other parts were produced on the automatics, from heavy handrail pillars to small collared studs threaded using dieheads. Ian said that in 1947 there were still a couple of women working here who had been taken on during the war. They had to keep their hair covered so as not to catch it in the moving machinery. The unions had negotiated that as female labour left the workshops, they should be replaced by men.

Soluble cutting oil was used in large quantities for lubricating and cooling cutting tools in the machine shops. One of the worst things about turning, until you learnt how to avoid it, was getting this cutting fluid all over you. It could leave a rash on the skin and you couldn't get rid of the odour. It was a mixture of liquid soap, machine oil and water and was recirculated through the machine tool. Jim remembers removing the swarf (the sharp metal strands produced after each cut) and taking it in metal containers to Mr Pickett in the Oil House. Here, the residual oil was separated by centrifuge and drained into drums. The metal turnings were loaded into wagons and shunted up to the weigh table in the North Yard before being sold to contractors. Bert Pickering was the R Shop turners' foreman in 1951 and 'Algy' Evans was chief foreman.

The A Machine Shop was the other place apprentices spent time during the turning period, on machines such as surfacing and boring lathes. By now the work allocated was likely to be larger and they learned to load the chucks using a 5-cwt swinging jib. These were fixed overhead and strategically placed, often serving more than one machine. Sid Abrahams, the assistant chief foreman in A Shop, would allocate the apprentices here. One job he had apprentices doing was lightly skimming the new whitemetal faces of axlebox bearings on a 30-inch vertical borer in Wiltshire's axlebox gang. An elaborate production circuit was laid out here, with plant and conveyors for stripping, machining, whitemetalling and rebuilding the axleboxes.

Apprentice coppersmith Ray Eggleton outside K Shop; the Case Hardening Shop is in the background. By 1946, when this photograph was taken, Ray was in his fourth year and had worked in the A Shop coppersmiths' section, in the Boiler Mounting Shop with Frank Brooks, and in the Coppersmiths' Shop. Other apprentices who started with Ray at around the same time were Frank Goodenough, Gilbert Iles and Les Arman. (*Ray Eggleton collection*)

Some apprentices went to the machine section in T Shop, where they produced small brass items on capstan and turret lathes. There were machine tools in this shop that had arrived from Germany after the First World War as part of the reparations. Apprentices turned and thread chased mud plugs and fusible plugs on five spindle Wickman automatics. Other work done included non-ferrous engine and boiler mountings, Lambert valves and fire appliance fittings. Engine parts for repair were received from the AE Shop or from outstation; the latter needed cleaning in their own hot caustic bosh. As with all shops, newly manufactured items were retained for assembly as 'new builds' while repaired work was dispatched to the stores. Even W Shop, where most turning was done on large, heavy machinery, had apprentices allocated sometimes, but they only handled smaller work pieces, with 'leading hand' Bob Telling. By now some chargemen would trust apprentices to grind tungsten-carbide cutting tools and set up machines.

The V Shop took apprentices on its machine section, unofficially known as the 'monkey house'; here, they produced copper firebox stays among other things on 'single autos'. This was known as chargeman Shadwell's section; the leading hand was Dennis Bond in the early 1950s. Ivor Farr was the Boiler Mounting foreman in P1 Shop and the 'monkey house'. Most apprentices went to O Shop to learn machine tool maintenance in this, the Works Tool Room. 'The G Shop lathes were probably the most rewarding of all for me because we made one off nuts, bolts, eyebolts and valve bodies which were not available from stores stock,' said Jim Lowe.

The fitting period would include AM Shop bench fitting; apprentices were put on such things as pressing whitemetal bushes into valve gear straps and sheaves with a soft hammer. They would also work with fitters on axleboxes between machining operations, stripping, cleaning and rebuilding or replacing keeps, crown bearings and bolts, felt pads, bronze liners, spring buckles and keep filler pipes. Scraping surface plates by hand in O Shop was another character-building job. The middle tended to become worn with all the hardened instruments being slid across the face.

B Shop, sometimes referred to as B Shed, was visited by trainees as well. Being taller than average did not save Jim from what many apprentices were expected to do: crawl to the front of tender tanks to fit filters and do up nuts holding the floats and water level gauges. Bob Grainger remembers being lowered into and out of the side tanks of locomotives by the overhead crane. The 'slinger' would send signals to his mate the 'crane driver' when Bob agreed he was ready. Another job was to rough up the treads on the tender steps which had worn smooth using a cross cut chisel; the footplatemen would hammer them flat again because the edges wore their boots.

A large proportion of R Shop fitting work was repairing locomotive motion parts. Ian worked with fitter Wally Fisher, scraping regulator valves and fitting valve gear parts together. Ken Gibbs, who was to write a book about his apprentice days, was also here at this time (1948 or 9), said Ian. All the safety valves were manufactured and assembled by fitters in chargeman Marchment's (pronounced Marshman) gang. Apprentices would have to scrape and lap the valve seats to make the bearing surfaces steamtight. After assembly they were then tested hydraulically by the chargeman and then set by tightening or loosening the bolts holding down the coil springs, spindle and valve.

To go to G Shop and work with a fitter and his mate on routine maintenance or breakdown earned you valuable experience. Drain cocks and valves for the Works central steam supply were maintained by Dick Robinson, one of Harry White's fitting gang, with apprentices. G Shop factory maintenance covered most of the loco side and Harry's gang was based in a workshop next to the Hooter House and the hydraulic pumps. While Ian was an apprentice in G Shop, he stayed on one July during the Works shutdown, to assist with crane maintenance. Jessie Kibblewhite and Ian spent the fortnight high up in the roof of AV Shop working on the highest cranes in the factory. They laid planks across girders and changed cables, checked bearings and mechanisms and replaced worn parts where necessary. 'Jessie was a religious man, he called all apprentices John,' said Ian. The following year (1949 or 1950), Ian went to Scotland at 'Trip' and cycled around the Highlands with another apprentice, Dennis Harber. Apprentices could do overtime upon reaching 18 years and Ian went back to running the autos some evenings during his time on fitting.

The last period of the training was locomotive erecting. Most of the activity in the A Erecting Shop was with the various stages of overhaul; other sections were 'new work' and 'light repairs'. The work was invariably heavy as some parts had to be levered, prised and slung into position. Tools and gauges used by the erector were also large and heavy and had to be used in confined spaces. At the stripping stage, seized nuts and bolts had to be cut using heavy chisels and hammers. Only apprentices that had come to the attention of the foreman might be put on stripping. As well as being heavy, stripping engines down was dirty and not very exacting.

The young men would instinctively show respect to their elders but occasionally, some older hands would bully a submissive newcomer, safe in the knowledge that they would not be turned upon by those they had worked with for years. When Ian Sawyer was singled out, he refused to be intimidated. The journeyman fitter who Ian had stood up to called the chargeman, who also took exception to Ian's defiance, and the three of them went up to see the foreman, Jimmy Owen. While he sympathised with him, Mr Owen moved Ian to another gang and no more was said.

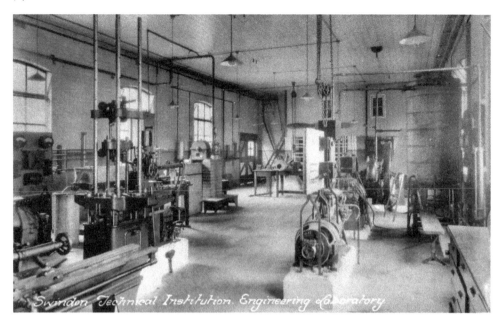

Some of the engineering facilities available to students in The College (North Wilts Technical Schools) in Victoria Road. Many young men from the Works would have received instruction here. These photographs were taken in the 1920s or 1930s. (*Swindon Museum collection*)

Former apprentice Alan Lambourn said:

My fascination with steam locomotives was never quite the same after working in AE Shop. When I first went there to work I was overawed by the noise and the vastness of the place. By this time [1957], erecting was no longer carried out in B Shop. I reported to Ron Glass the chargeman of the frame gang and handed him my allocation notice. Apprentices usually moved on at the same time and I was introduced to a fitter whose apprentice was going to his next placement. Locomotives came into the shop and were stripped down and all parts sent for cleaning. All except the frames and the cylinder castings or block/smokebox saddle which came to us. I would have to support a bar against the remains of the bolts holding the block, while the fitter knocked them out using a sledge hammer. The bolts had become twisted by the colossal alternating forces of the motion, and took some shifting. My mate assured me he wouldn't miss and knock my head off but I wasn't convinced. Next the frames were levelled and the cylinders rebored.

After a couple of months I moved to Frank Comley's gang where the first stages of rebuilding took place [See chapter 5]. Then I spent a couple of months with Harry Bown and his mate squaring up the frames using optical alignment equipment. There was no heavy work here and I didn't get any black finger or toe nails for a bit. [Typically, Alan did not work with all gangs on the A Shop circuit, nor did his allocations here follow the rebuilding sequence]

Following that I went to Stan Lewington's finishing off gang: he was feared by apprentices but I behaved myself and found him to be okay. Here a fitter, a labourer and an apprentice were allocated to each engine but, as always, you could call on others when necessary. We fitted springs and set them at the running height with an allowance for the weight of the water when the boiler was filled. Other men fitted the con rods, crossheads, wooden footplating, valves, pistons and the coppersmiths fitted their pipework.

(8802)

THE RAILWAY EXECUTIVE (WESTERN REGION)

MECHANICAL & ELECTRICAL ENGINEER'S DEPT.

PERMIT

ONE PERSON TO ENTER

SWINDON WORKS on Tues. 10th April 1951.

KEEP THIS PERMIT – Without it you may not be allowed to enter the Works.

GUIDES AT WORKS have numbered buttonhole badges. LOOK OUT FOR YOUR GUIDE WHOSE

BADGE NUMBER IS:- 8

Keep with your guide throughout the tour.

P.T.O.

Chief guide and watchman Bert Stratford is seen here with a private school tour posing with loco 4703 outside A Shop in 1953. The 'Western' knew that by encouraging the young to visit the Works, many would remain under its spell for life. Teachers accompanying schoolchildren over the age of 12 on tours by prior arrangement were popular until the 1960s. Large groups would be divided, with a guide to accompany each smaller group. Senior apprentices could act as additional guides and see that the visitors did not wander from the route. This was eagerly taken up by some lads as it was a welcome break from their normal work, although there was always a fear that some 'smart Alec' would ask an awkward question.

The route around the Locomotive Works covered the main workshops, the highlight being the A Erecting Shop. These schoolboys would be shown some of the more interesting workshop practises. No doubt a tyre being shrunk onto a wheel centre and a steam hammer in action were arranged. Before and after the war, parties and individuals arriving by train were not charged admission; otherwise, it was a shilling a head. On Wednesday afternoons, when the tour was open to the general public, the charge was sixpence but this was dropped in the 1950s. In 1956 the number of visitors to the Works was 16,300 and revenue raised by visitors' rail fares was £3,635. (*Author's collection*)

Apprentices generally did any fetching and carrying that their gang needed from other workshops and from the shop stores because their absence would not affect the piecework targets so much. For instance, when the length of a regulator rod needed adjustment, it was the apprentice that would take it over to blacksmith Tom Weaver in the Boiler Shop. Jim Lowe said you had to balance this long rod, equal to the length of the boiler which would receive it, on a sacktruck. It had to be pushed across to and through the P1 (boiler testing) Shop and down in the boiler lift and under Rodbourne Road, then up into the V Shop:

You had to negotiate some tight bends and hope that when you reached the doors, someone would hold them open for you. To 'draw' [lengthen] the rod, Tom and a mate would heat it and strike it a few times over an anvil; to 'jump' [shorten] it, he would use a foot operated electric hammer which effectively compressed it lengthways.

By the 1950s apprentices were assured of work 'inside' after serving their time but this had not always been the case. Before the war it was likely that at the end of the five years they would receive a letter stating 'Your services are no longer required.' Speaking of the situation during the Churchward period, Mr Holcroft, in his book *An Outline of G. W. Locomotive Practice 1847–1947*, said, 'Since vacancies had to be created to maintain the flow, many of these young men were 'birds of passage' as they either left of their own accord on finding employment elsewhere or were given a time limit to do so. The select few remained and were taken on to the permanent staff in the course of time.' No doubt this remained the policy up until the late 1930s. As Mr Holcroft points out, not all apprentices wanted to stay on anyway and many left after experiencing life in the Territorial Army or during national service. Being stuck in a dirty, noisy factory for the rest of their lives did not sit well with them. In common with skilled men trained by other respected British companies, many took advantage of the opportunities of having papers that were recognised with high regard the world over.

From the start of the war in 1939 the Works struggled to get enough skilled and unskilled labour and this situation continued throughout the post war period. After their training and reaching the age of 21 years, many ex-apprentices went straight on to do their national service. Others went in at 18, returning later to complete their time. Either way, government legislation after the war allowed them at least 12 months' work beyond their time. Ian Sawyer was 'called up' in 1952; he could have got exemption because his mother was widowed and Ian was the sole support. He did his two years' National Service and then reported to Mr Proudler in the loco side Staff Office to be given employment. Ian had found out about a vacancy in the AM Shop, bench fitting, but had also heard that the staff clerical officer was known for off-loading the worst jobs available first. Knowing they had to offer him work, he stood his ground and eventually got what he wanted.

Apprentices did not join a trade union but were approached to join soon after finishing their time. Terry 'Curly' French went to a union meeting when he was a first year FT&E apprentice in 1947: 'The men had been told that the forthcoming reduction in the working week to 44 hours meant that the afternoon tea break would go. It was therefore proposed and agreed that they would strike for that ten minute period each day. One way or the other, they continued to take the break.' There was no 'closed shop' arrangement until later but most did join the AEU; Gilbert King and Harold Bown were A Shop stewards who came round to collect the subs. Ian did join before he finished his time, quite illegally, through Tom Wheel, the AEU man in R Shop.

A plan of the proposed apprentice training school was received from the Chief Civil Engineer in 1956, together with estimates of the costs of building and mains services. Costs for machinery, forges and hand tools were prepared by the CME's Department at Swindon.

CHAPTER 7

'Loco Side' Work

Colin Bown lived in Bathampton Street in the GWR estate; his father was a semi-skilled metal machinist and his elder brother Roy was a blacksmith in F and F2 Shops. Colin's ancestors going back several generations had all been in the Works, like so many other locals; his great-grandfather was in the Rolling Mills. Colin only knew this because it was part of a story his mother told him. She said that her grandfather had emigrated to take up similar work in America and thought they might be ancestors of Judy Garland. 'I think this was fanciful thinking on her part because they had the same unusual surname as her, which was Gumm,' he said.

Colin wanted to work for the Parks Department of the Borough Council when he left school in 1945. His father said he must go 'inside' and after Christmas he went in as an office boy in MO 8, the Loco Works Manager's office. According to Education Committee statistics, ninety-three boys and fourteen girls went 'inside' during the 12 month period of 1945–6. There were four boys in MO 8 at any one time; the eldest was the senior and he kept an eye on the others. Delivering and collecting post kept three of them busy for most of the time; they each had a round and the boy on the long round had use of a bicycle. Collected post was taken back to the office, sorted and redistributed. Between them, they covered every office on the loco side: an area from the cutting up shop (originally called the 'refuse destructor house') down in the Concentration Yard to the CME office block, up to the Gas Works in the north and back via the machinery stores (known as Crystal Palace). This they did twice in the morning and twice in the afternoon. The fourth boy, the 'senior' or 'special boy', ran errands for the Loco Works Manager and his Assistants. Upon being summoned by an electric bell, he would collect and return drawings or documents for signing etc.

> Alfie Cowley from Redcliffe Street was one of the other 'office boys'. His older brother Bill was a coppersmith and taught at the College: later he emigrated to Australia and became a Professor of Geology.
>
> Six months before I was sixteen and the start of my apprenticeship I was sent to the factory's Gas Works as a fitters' mate. I remember working with Bert Smith and gas fitter 'Puddy' Moore amongst others; the foreman was Mr Ellison and his boss Mr Acroyd had the title of Gas Works Manager to the CME.

Jimmy Ellison's sister was Kathleen, whose experiences of the GW hospital as a child are told elsewhere in this book. By the late 1950s Mr Ellison's address was 'Gas

Silver first aid long service and gold 'one in a thousand' medals awarded to Bill Bown in 1932 and 1938. With regard to the latter, Bill's AM Shop team was one of five to win the all-line 'Freedom from Accident' competition in 1938. Points were awarded or deducted depending on injuries, or lack of them, at work. Places of work assessed to have similar potential for accidents were put into a league of fifty teams, each of twenty people. Therefore the gold medal awarded to the captain of the winning team was for one in a thousand.

Works, Iffley Road', so presumably he had become manager by then and lived in the house on-site which was provided for that situation.

William (Bill) Bown, Colin's father, worked in AM Shop; he had been president of the First Aid Movement and from 1951 was chairman of the Divisional Ambulance Committee. Earlier in his working life Mr Bown senior had been told his 'services were no longer required' not once but twice. William came from a large Gorse Hill family and consequently they were poorer than average. Being bright and lucky, he was given an assisted place at the Swindon and North Wilts Technical School and became a 'gentleman clerk' (a term used when 'lady clerks' first came into the Works). However, when he returned from service with the Royal Flying Corps in 1919, he was told there was no longer a position for him. He believed that the company did not expect as many men to return from the war and that the female clerks taken on to fill their places now kept them out. Bill was offered work as a machinist in the factory, which he had to accept, but was 'let go' at the start of the depression in 1929. Until he could get his job back 'inside', he went navvying, the only work available. He was laying flagstones in the newly built Shrivenham Road; Colin said his father's hands would be sore and bleeding when he got home.

Colin Bown started his apprenticeship as a sheet metal worker on 7 April 1947; the foreman at the time and throughout the 1940s was Mr House. Sheet metal men were still often referred to by the old name of tinsmiths or 'tinkers'. They cut, pressed, beat

The GWR standard locomotive headlamp, which until 1937 was painted red. One or two lamps were carried on the front of every engine in various positions to show what type of train it was working. The exception was the royal train, which carried a lamp in all four positions. 'The style of these and other train lamps, which were made in the sheet metal workers' shop, was simplified over the years to make them cheaper to produce. Outside firms started to undercut the Works on cost. We managed to stay competitive but were constantly told we may lose the order,' said Colin. The restricted supply of raw materials and labour in wartime prompted an appeal in the staff magazine. The company asked for more care to be taken with the handling of engine tools and lamps. They said: 'These lamps are now received in Swindon Works at the rate of 200 per week, of which a number are scrapped as being beyond repair.'

and rolled tinplate, steel, copper, brass, zinc and aluminium up to '8 plate' (or 8 gauge, which was just over an eighth of an inch thick), most of which was done by hand.

> We fabricated work by soldering or riveting it together; steel and aluminium were also welded. Flare lamps, hot water urns, steel lockers and cash boxes, time and pay checks as well as steel pay tins we made. Incidentally the Works signwriters used pay tins as paint pots. Apprentices produced the small copper and brass checks. We pressed them out and deburred them, then we dye-stamped the numbers in the centre and dipped them in aqua fortis (acid) to brighten them.
>
> I went to night school two evenings a week and on Saturday morning we had workshop practise as well as some theory. Our classrooms were in the former Nissen huts in the Goddard's estate just off the High Street. When you registered they told you what you would have to provide. It wasn't just pen, pencil and sharpener but equipment for 'mechanical drawing' as they called it: a compass, set square and a heavy wooden drawing board which you had to lug about. All this could be bought fairly easily second hand from ex-apprentices.

In those days we still had women in our shop who had started during the war. Most wore a bib and brace or a boiler suit but one or two preferred to wear a smock over a dress. With those in mind we placed highly reflective steel sheets in the walkways, one girl worked out what we were up to and wouldn't speak to us for ages. Normally you would go and do your national service when you reached 18 or at the end of your time aged 21. I had a touch of pneumonia and pleurisy so I got deferred.

One sheet metal gang went round the workshops replacing or repairing damaged machine guards. Every few weeks a journeyman and an apprentice went to Kemble pumping station to check the machinery guards were all in place and undamaged. Another gang looked after the cone covers and chimneys above the furnaces as well as workshop ventilation and extraction equipment. Our shop also made and repaired locomotive parts such as outside steam pipe casings, boiler mudhole covers and smokebox spark arresters. Guards lamps were made by outside firms but we repaired them. [Unlike train lamps, the three or four aspect lamps used by guards and signalmen were issued as personal property so were treated with more respect than the other portable lamps] Sidelights and taillights for brake vans, locomotive headlamps and gaugelamps were all made by the factory's tinsmiths; the headlamps were made up of 96 separate parts. We would get orders for 500 headlamps at a time but like all large orders, when less were required you started to worry that there was a general downturn in the industry. While there was enough work we would work nights a month about.

As an apprentice, Colin was sometimes sent to the Erecting Shop to remove the casings from locomotive elbow steam pipes. This would disturb the asbestos underneath but they didn't know the dangers then. If a worker died of respiratory disease, it was put down to tuberculosis or pneumonia. Links between asbestos particles and serious lung damage had been established by the medical profession but were not widely publicised and it continued to be used in industry for many more years to come. Swindon's medical officer gave a talk in the town in 1936, much of which was about silicosis, a condition very similar to asbestosis. He also said: 'No processes in the GWR Works produce disease-bearing dust with the exception of tool grinding in which proper precautions are taken.' Stan Leach said he saw men on the 'carriage side' put asbestos into their mouths, chew it into pellets and blow it out through lengths of conduit pipe.

Tinsmiths outside their workshop during the dinner break, in around 1950. From left to right, back row: Desmond Iles, Bob Turner, Alan Titcombe, Les King, Alan Gunter, Les Osbourne and Colin Bown. Front row: Gordon Staples, Bert Kewell, Roy Selwood and Vic Spackman. (C. Bown)

Des Griffiths from Morse Street left Sanford Street School in 1940. He worked as an errand boy for Cripps the Chemist in Victoria Road, then at the age of 15 he went 'inside'. Mr Proudler in the Staff Office gave Des the choice of either office boy or 'brush hand' until he could start his apprenticeship at 16. Des chose the latter, against his father's advice, and was escorted to a corrugated hut near the Works turntable. The gang under chargehand Bill Townsend stripped and blacked locomotive boiler cladding which had been taken from engines in for overhaul. This was done mainly by burning off the paint, oil and polish over an open fire, then wire brushing the surfaces. They came under Hughie Yeates, the Loco Painters' Foreman. Des's father Fred was a semi-skilled 'factoryman', so that would be his lot also and he was apprenticed to metal machining:

> I went into R Shop starting in the 'scraggery' then on to drilling machines in T Shop – Brass Finishers, with chargeman Harry Higgins and foreman Hyde. My last move was into the A Machine Shop, where I stayed. A group of Russians were shown round during the war: they got a good reception presumably because of recent victories against the Germans. Some of our chaps gave them the Communist salute. On another occasion as visitors passed down the aisle a 0-1" micrometer was stolen from my machine while it was unattended.

The machine section of A Shop occupied the north-east part of the building, it covered about two and a half acres. A Shop as a whole was the largest workshop in the Works by far, covering 11¼ acres. There were 250 machine tools and about 500 operators and staff in the 'AM'. So that heavy work could be set up, the largest machines were within range of 4½-ton walking cranes. As well as being a hot place to work in summer, A Shop could also be very cold at times. With the huge locomotive doors open in winter, Des and others would stand at their machines with their coats on.

Des was automatically kept on when he finished his time in 1947 because of the shortage of skilled men and they were working the Saturday morning as well. He was put on Churchill universal grinders; there were two of these and they could be used for plain and cylindrical grinding while other types did one or the other. Bert Stratford used a Churchill quadrant or radius grinder, which would grind the surfaces of curved parts such as locomotive radius or expansion links, either 27 or 84-inch radii. The work was fixed to an arm with the fulcrum above and swung slowly past a fixed wheel like a pendulum. Assuming grinding wheels were dressed and balanced properly and not too much was ground off at one time, very fine finishes could be achieved on steel faces. Locomotive piston rods were ground using plain grinders, motion bars using surface grinders and holes could be accurately ground on vertical grinding machines. Work in hand arrived from other shops or from the stores and the Chargehand, Charlie Bowen, dealt with the paperwork.

Des said:

> Workmates my section were: Fred Winchcombe, Bill Holloway, Gordon Walters, Ray Shipley, Bill Gunter, Bill Lambourn, Albert Smith and Norman Davis. Fred played cricket for Wiltshire and Bill Holloway was the Amalgamated Engineering Union steward. Most of the tradesmen were AEU rather than NUR. One chap was always

late going off in the evening, he would get outside then go back to check that his machine was switched off and see that everything was as it should be. This ritual was performed two or three times before he finally went home. Ted Dafter was chargeman shapers, Bert Plaister was maintenance chargeman and Stan Clark was the inspector. Charlie Bailey, Harold Glass and Charlie Richards were on the new work fitting section of the rod gang, Harold sang in the Christ Church choir. Other work done on the fitting sections here were assembling valve gear and machine tool maintenance, the latter involving electricians as well as fitters.

The 'AM' rod gang received connecting and coupling rods from the Steam Hammer Shop. The big and small ends of the rods were to be bored and slotted before fitting the bushes, which were then also bored to high finish. The blades or shafts were rough then finished, machined by a plano-milling machine. Fitters then filed down sharp edges, tapped oil holes and fitted restrictors. Ken Farncombe was a fitter brought over from the 'carriage side' in wartime to work on the 'rod gang': 'I would go to the erecting section and measure the crank pin diameters with a micrometer and give the measurements to the men turning the bushes. The crank pins on 'new builds' were of

Grinding machines in the AM Shop. The upper picture shows a connecting rod bore being machined on a double spindle vertical grinder manufactured by Churchill Machine Tool Co. Ltd. The distance between the heads could be adjusted with a vernier scale for accuracy. The lower picture shows a small Churchill plain grinder, used for finishing piston valve spindles and rods among other things. (GWR)

course a standard size and therefore so were the bushes for the rods.' Frank Raven was 'AM' foreman and Sid Nash was chief foreman – machine shops.

'W' and 'R' were the other machine workshops on the loco side, although most workshops had some machine tools. Locomotive frames and cylinder blocks or castings had various machining operations carried out on large machines in W Shop. R Shop is remembered for the 'scraggery' and its nut facing lathes made by Etchells & Sons Ltd. So to its automatic machine tools, particularly combination turret lathes because this was often apprentices' first experience of machine work. Heavier work was also done in R Shop on milling, boring and slotting machines; they had planning machines with tables of 9 and 11-foot lengths too. The operators would have to put on gloves and pull all the swarf from the bottom of the machine and put it into bins. The labourers would sweep what went onto the floor and take it all away. No repairs were supposed to be done by the machinists; the chargehand would call the maintenance gang and get the paperwork ready for them. The idea was that as little time as possible was lost so the piecework was not disrupted.

Terry Couling was the last person taken on as a locomotive painter. From 1956, Works painters would have to work on both locomotives and rolling stock. They didn't consider Terry tall or strong enough for heavy manual work so he was offered tinsmithing or Drawing Office because he was good at art. He told them he wanted to work with locomotives so then they offered him painting. The 'take it or leave it' attitude to vacancies of the once-dominant employer was obviously changing by 1955. Terry travelled in from Stratton Park Halt by workmen's train, then later got himself a bike. Mr Couling senior, Wilfred (Clanny) Couling, was in the Rolling Mills; he got his nickname because he came from Clanfield in Oxfordshire. Grandfather was a 'wagon basher' in the wagon building and repair shop and his uncle was in the Wood Yard and later moved to somewhere in the Stores Department. Terry had an older brother, Anthony, in the Tool Room and another brother, Mick, in the loco side Blacksmiths' Shop. You weren't allowed to smoke in the Tool Room so Terry and Anthony would both walk down to the Con Yard and have a cigarette in one of the withdrawn engine cabs. Watchmen were instructed to stop staff wandering around there but you could usually stay one step ahead of them.

Even engine painters had to work in the 'scraggery' and Terry did 9 months facing and chamfering nuts on a simple lathe before starting his apprenticeship. Apart from not going to night school, he did what all those learning a trade 'inside' did: picked it up as he went along. Another engine painter, Denys 'Charlie' Ruggles, served his time from 1939 and he spent a period in the Works Fire Station to start with. Here he was painting items such as fire buckets before moving over to the less exacting parts of locomotives. Later, as a skilled man, Denys would go over to the Fire Station whenever they needed a painter.

Some locomotives in for 'light' or 'running' repairs were not repainted; if the general condition of the paint was thought sufficiently good to last until the next Works' visit, it was cleaned down and one coat of varnish applied. Terry said:

The loco painters had a cabin in the middle of A Shop: the cleaners used one end and we used the other. Our chargeman would be issued with a list of engines nearing completion on the Monday morning and allocate us accordingly. We would collect the paint and exterior varnish from the main stores in B Shed, on a sacktruck. We didn't strip the old

The AM Shop 'Social and Educational Union' football team, 1929/30. They were runners-up in Swindon and District league division 2 that year. The only players identified are Albert Smith, a machine shop grinder and a Boys Brigade officer in his spare time (top left), Tommy Stanton (top right) and Bill Harber (middle far right). Sitting far left is Herbert Brine, far right is George Barrett and holding the ball is 'Darkie' Richards. (*D. Griffiths*)

The naming ceremony of the last new steam loco outshopped from Swindon, or anywhere else in the country, in March 1960. The name was chosen from suggestions invited through the staff magazine. The very first locomotive on the company's books was *North Star* so it made sense to name the last *Evening Star*. This was the last of a batch of class 9 2-10-0 heavy freight engines. In a rare break with tradition, it was given embellishments reserved for express engines. A copper-capped chimney and green and black, fully

lined livery were added, as well as two nameplates using GW-style lettering.

I have heard it said that BR wanted Swindon to stop building steam locomotives by 1956 because Crewe could build them quicker and cheaper. That's why Swindon had so much diesel work put their way. The unions resisted and they got the last steam engines built here. This would temporarily safeguard the traditional steam trades such as foundrymen and smiths and offset the sagging morale. (*Ken Ellis*)

paint off unless previous layers were coming away, then we chiseled it off. Care being
taken not to score the metal underneath. It took about one gallon of black and a half
gallon of green to cover the bigger engines, excluding the tender of course. The D800
diesels took more and six blokes were assigned to one of those; as the painters liked to
sing it could be quite a racket around one of these. The single coat of varnish took less
time to apply as we missed some bits that couldn't be seen. I think the foreman was Ernie
Hewlett in the early days. Freddie Porter, Bert Leighfield and Harry Welsh were painters
and Art Cannon was our chargehand, he always gave Harry the lining on the Kings for
some reason. I marked off the numbers of engines I worked on in an Ian Allan ABC
book. So for instance, I know I worked on all the King class engines over time.

All steel parts had been coated to stop surface rust and a gang of cleaners degreased
the surfaces prior to us starting. Two of us were allocated to a steam locomotive: a
tradesman and me. The apprentice would complete two engines a week; if there was no
lining to do, two and a half engines. The tenders were done in B Shed where they had
their own painters. We started by filling holes and indentations with yellow stopping.
The boiler was painted first so as to stay clear of the fitters who were still 'finishing
off'. We had ladders that hooked over handrail for this stage. On unlined tank engines
we also painted the brass including safety valve covers. As we didn't roughen the brass
first the paint came off quite quickly in service. The inside motion and undersides
were done last, these were difficult to get too and fiddly, especially the pipework at the
back end; the standard classes were even worse. We had already painted the underside
of the boiler before it was lowered into the frames; the wheels too were painted by
us before assembly. The cab roof and footplating were painted by labourers and like
everywhere else they just got one coat of paint. The buffer beam alone might require
two coats of red to cover it. The driver's side could be more difficult if there was a
reversing rod, mechanical lubricator and/or a vacuum pump etc, so on the next bay
you would alternate with your mate. We used long bristled brushes for the lining out
of the passenger engines: this was where the skill came in. A compass was used for the
corners and for the long lengths: a chalk line, otherwise the lining was done freehand.
The varnish would get rid of any chalk marks. Did I work on the last steam locomotive
built at Swindon? It's possible, until the green was put on, which I did not do, no one
knew which of the last 9F's would become the famous *Evening Star*. When I finished
my apprenticeship in December 1960 I was a 'cat (category) 2' tradesman.

Shortly after Mr Churchward took office, a new standard design for nameplates was
introduced which lasted until the end of steam. It consisting of a steel plate arc framed
in tubular brass beading with (by 1930) hollow brass letters; being largely handmade,
they were not cheap to produce. In BR days, the bead was altered so that only half
the amount of brass was needed. In 1930 there were well over 400 named passenger
locomotives on the GWR, each with a two nameplates. This number would increase
still further because of a policy of naming new mixed traffic types in the 1930s. After
being removed from the incoming engines, nameplates were stored in wooden racks
on the shop floor. They would be taken upstairs in pairs to be repainted and lined
in a room behind the A Shop toilets. In Terry Couling's time it was Freddie Hinton
who painted them: 'He did about 10 or 15 nameplates a week. The labourer would

completely strip all the old paint off and buff the brasswork. Sometimes us loco painters would work on nameplates if Fred or his mate was away.'

Alf Tutt from Purton worked in N Shop, where certain types of bolts, nuts and rivets were produced. He would heat metal bar produced in the Rolling Mills to white hot and feed it into a split-die hot-forging machine. This ingenious machine made blank nuts and bolts with a minimum of waste. Semi-automatic nut frazing machines were also used here and in R Shop. The fumes from the oil-fired furnaces and the heat made the Bolt Shop an unpleasant place to work but Alf got used to it. Apart from his war service, part of which he spent as a prisoner, he spent all his working life in the N (or Bolt) Shop. 'Despite being bent over due to the years in that position at his machine and a hard life, Alf lived to a very good age,' said Stan Leach.

In the mid-1950s, the General Manager of the Western Region arranged for more of the principal passenger train services to be named. The rakes of coaches were to be turned out in chocolate and cream, the old Great Western colours. Swindon was to cast new headboards which were to be more decorative than the earlier ones made at Doncaster. Tom Stanton in the Drawing Office carried out the research on the coat of arms and heraldic devices that would surmount the new boards. The final designs were passed on to the Pattern Shop. An extract from the *Swindon Railway News* described the next stage of production: 'After studying the drawings the pattern maker [Viv Rogers] marks out a full size lay-out of the job on a drawing board. In doing this he has to increase all dimensions quoted to allow for shrinkage which occurs when molten metal cools within its sand mould.' 'Jack' Fleetwood remembers Viv as a very good pattern maker. When, as in this case, only a few castings were to be made of each pattern, soft wood was used. Patterns, such as for brake blocks or axleboxes, which were used many times were made of metal.

The new patterns were then passed to the Brass Foundry, where the moulder's skill would be in packing the pattern into green sand and withdrawing it to leave a

The 6-ton Bretts steam-powered drop hammer in the centre of the Stamping Shop. This was the largest of five here in the 1940s. It had been used extensively in the manufacture of armour plating during the war. The ground shook when the hammer block, weighing several tons, was dropped onto the white-hot steel bloom. Even though the Stamp Shop was in the middle of the Locomotive Works, people living near Redcliffe Street corner knew when the 'big hammer' was working. (*Ray Eggleton collection*)

perfect impression. To be able to do this the mould was made in two halves of an iron moulding box, requiring four men to lift them apart. With the pattern removed, the two halves were slotted back together and molten aluminium at 750 degrees celsius was poured through the channel previously let into the mould, care being taken to skim back the dross while pouring. Thirty minutes later, the casting could be knocked out. There were to be at least two of each of the fourteen new types of headboards. The (piecework) price to the moulder was 23s each if he completed one every three hours. Jack was a 'sand rat' in the foundry at that time and told me:

> Some trials were done using hard resin but a man from the General Manager's Office at Paddington said he didn't like them. So they were to be of LM6 aluminium, this specification gave them some flexibility and was less brittle than the Doncaster ones [In service, the Enginemen handling them were not always very careful and although they stood up well to vibration on the locomotives they could, and did occasionally break if dropped]. Strangely enough breathing in the molten aluminium fumes would cure a headache, even a hangover.

Ian Sawyer went onto bench fitting in AM Shop in 1952. He started with built-up bar frames of pony trucks, the two pivotal wheels at the front of some locomotive types. Jack Singer was the chargeman here:

> Old Jack was one of the old school, he left me to read the drawings and do any jobs he didn't like. Later I moved over to Bill Clark's gang on the 'marking off' table.

The 1.30 p.m. train from Paddington to Penzance became The Royal Duchy in 1955, a title that required royal consent. The train is seen here at Exeter in 1957 with a Swindon headboard. (*Ken Ellis*)

I marked off rough castings with a white chalk which was produced from spent carbide from oxy-acetylene machines. Only for the more accurate work did we use engineer's marking blue. We had to establish whether a casting had distorted which would change the positioning of subsequent machining. If it had it might be possible for the angle iron smiths to heat it and straighten it. I hadn't been there long when Bill wanted to make me up to 'leading hand' but the head foreman said no, it was too soon. We did all the 9F locomotive pony trucks and another 15 for Crewe Works; the GWR types seemed old fashioned in comparison. When the Britannia Pacific crashed at Milton near Didcot we stripped its bogie frame down. People from Paddington and the Railway Inspectorate all came to have a look at it. Other engine parts we had 'on the table' at various times were frame stretchers, axleboxes and hornblocks. AM Shop foremen in the 1950s were Messrs Johns, Scaplehorn, Gundry, Fricker and head foreman Mr Fortune. Of the four inspectors we had at any one time, I remember two: a man named Clark and another by the name of Jefferies.

Doug Maisie and Roy Brett were maintenance fitters in the 'AM' but most came over from G Shop when required. Roy also looked after the stationary locomotive test plant.

After the war, a lot of rules that had been strictly enforced for years were starting to be disregarded. You were not, for instance, supposed to wander away from where you worked, even in the dinner break. Jack Fleetwood remembered being questioned as to his business outside his workshop when he was an apprentice: 'It was the Carriage and Wagon Manager, Mr Evans, who stopped me; what was he doing over our side anyway?' said Jack indignantly. Jim Lowe said wandering about became more acceptable after a firm from Bristol was given the contract to supply and wash overalls: 'They would be delivered to the workshops on Friday afternoon and the cost was deducted from the paybill. You might well have to visit other shops to find your laundered overalls. Even so if you went over to the 'carriage side' via the General Stores subway you were likely to be questioned by a rather enthusiastic watchman,' said Jim. Bob Grainger said he wouldn't have been questioned at length if he had gone to the 'carriage side' in overalls; this was as late as 1960. Inevitably, old habits died hard and some staff continued to exercise their authority.

Diesel Rail Car Work

In preparation for the overhaul and repair of diesel engines, part of B (tender) Shop was partitioned off in 1956. It was planned that a good deal of such repair work would eventually be undertaken 'outstation' as facilities were put in place at selected depots. Initially, though, all major work was to be done at Swindon in what would be known as BD Shop. Local and regional diesel training schools were set up for CME staff from mechanical foremen to works managers. They were sent on courses being run at the Derby BR Training College; other mechanical engineers and engine drivers received instruction at Swindon, in premises set up in the railway estate. As well as contractors' manuals, Swindon Works produced their own technical literature and various workshops were gradually transformed.

The Rolling Mills consisted of a 10-inch and a 14-inch mill, seen here, each driven by a steam engine. A third mill had a set of 24-inch blooming rolls. Rolled sections of steel or iron heated to more than 1,000 degrees centigrade were squeezed through the rolls until reduced to the desired cross section. This photograph dates from around 1960. (*R. Eggleton collection*)

Ernie Wiggins is photographed examining a British Timken roller bearing on a D800 wheelset yet to have its tyres fitted. On the back of this snapshot is written: 'AW Shop 1958'. Ernie, a former engine erector who lived in Cobden Road, carried out the Ultrasonic Flaw Detection tests on axles in both wheel shops. He was a big man and a doorman at the Locarno Ballroom in those days. (*Derek Wiggins*)

The Great Western had been using AEC-built single rail cars since 1934 and they had proved successful for certain types of light passenger and parcels services. Twenty years later, the Modernisation Plan required that the country's railway works produce various types of diesel locomotives to replace steam. In 1956, Swindon outshopped its first InterCity diesel multiple units (pictured). Initially these were two sets of three-car trains designed here and built in the Carriage Works for 'long distance express passenger services.' They consisted of power vehicles and trailer cars; the power car had a diesel engine and transmission on each of its two bogies. A feature of these three-car multiple units was that they could be coupled together and driven from the leading vehicle's driving cab. In 1958 Swindon Works were building batches of three-car 'Cross Country' DMUs, designed for 'fast passenger services with more frequent stops'. After that came another batch of InterCity sets, with modifications. In 1960 they built the Trans-Pennine six-car DMUs and used Leyland Albion 230hp engines for the steeply graded route across the Pennines.

Somewhat unfairly, the Swindon DMUs (they didn't build single rail cars) have become one of the least memorable forms of motive power built during the Works' long history. This is perhaps partly because the engines and power transmission components were bought in and partly because most of them were sent to work on other regions of British Railways.

BD Shop staff would overhaul rail car power transmission components: engines and fuel equipment, four speed gearboxes and final drive/reversing units. They arrived by rail from the depots in special flat-top Enpart wagons. Internal transport then brought these components in and out of the workshop using Conveyancer fork (lift) trucks. As more diesel locomotive work was taken on, so the BD Shop expanded and the steam loco tender area was reduced.

Denis Raven was one of the first fitters to work on the new section. Denis, whose father was a foreman in the AM Shop, had been in G Shop working on plant maintenance. His work would now involve stripping and replacing worn or defective parts of six-cylinder horizontal engines made by AEC and later Leyland. Replacement parts were produced in R Shop under chief foreman Stan Godwin; he oversaw all the diesel repair work on the loco side. Denis was sent on courses where the component parts were made. This would involve a couple of weeks in the workshops of AEC at Southall or Bosch in Coventry, where they made fuel pumps. He learned the arrangement and principle of 4-stroke oil engines and 6-cylinder fuel injection pumps. On the train home each evening, he would rewrite his shorthand notes made throughout the day. In the late 1950s Denis was sent on courses so that he could work on Maybach, MAN and Paxman engines too.

> I loved the work especially when I moved to fuel injection pumps and injectors but the oil did make your hands sore. The factory doctor gave me various fluids to get the oil off my skin and he kept his eye on me. Another potential hazard was testing injectors: if the high pressure spray hit you it could cause serious damage to skin or eyes. I soon became chargeman then inspector and in about 1960 I became junior foreman in BD Shop. Peter Spackman 'followed me' which meant he got the posts I vacated. I remember the Locomotive Works Manager bringing three men from Paddington [senior WR managers] round one day. They came and spoke to me and I suggested an alternative way of calibrating fuel pumps from rail cars. I found out later that the Loco Works Manager was very pleased because my suggestion contributed to the decision to keep the contract for repairing the pumps when they were considering giving it to the makers: CAV of Acton.

Building the D800 Class (See also chapter 8)

In 1957 construction began on the first new main line diesel hydraulic locomotive in the A Erecting Shop. Freddie Dew was put in charge of the first D800 gang. They laid the foundation for the underframe: two steel tubes 6½ inches in diameter which ran throughout the length, onto which was welded a honeycomb of steel plate cross-stays designed to support the mainframe floor. As the D800 underframe progressed to the side frame stanchions, the underframe gang moved to the next pit and started again (Not long after this, Freddie went back to standard steam building). Tony Illesley's gang took over on the first loco and fitted the bodywork and bulkheads and Pete Brettel's gang, which became known as the Maybach gang, the mountings, engines and British-made steam generator for train heating (Pete Brettel's experience of working on steam turbine engines in the Merchant Navy was put to good use when the Works started maintaining the gas turbine

'Steam' and 'diesel' being built alongside each other in A Shop. This was the first half of 1957 and the steam locomotive being built was a Standard class 4 4-6-0 for the London Midland Region. In the foreground can be seen the initial frame members: two steel tubes 6½ inches in diameter which ran from end to end of the new 2,200-horsepower diesel. Onto these were fitted a honeycomb of steel plate cross-stays 5/32 inches in thickness which would support the lightweight superstructure. The framework was then welded and x-rayed for cracks, cleaned and painted with primer. (*Author's collection*)

locomotives, 18000 and 18100). Another gang was formed to assemble the final drives and bogies while another dealt with the assembly and testing of transmission equipment in the AM Shop; all came under section foreman Dennis Cole. Later, the respective gangs would be responsible for the overhaul of what they were now assembling.

A lot of the electricians were recruited from the London area for the diesel building programmes; few if any had worked for the railways before. Bert Ball was one of the chargeman-electricians and George Gale and Brian Menzies became their first foremen. As well as the D800s, electricians were needed for building batches of 0-6-0 diesel shunters (with mechanical transmissions) at the same time. Prior to the coming of these diesel classes, A Shop required just one electrician and his mate – they would wire up the Automatic Train Control equipment. Howard Smith, whose father was the Works chief fire officer, was one who did the ATC work on steam.

The first three engines, D800 – D802, were prototypes; they were hand built without jigs, gauges and specialised tool equipment and relied on arrangement drawings that were subject to alterations as building progressed. The A2 bay pit roads between the new work section where BR standard steam engines were still being built and Lewington's gang were the ones used for these, the first of the class. As they took shape, a production line was being prepared. Rayer's light repairs steam gang would now only occupy the section at the back of the shop (see diagram). The construction then moved forward, from where the finished products could later be either towed outside through the AW Shop or pulled onto the traversing table by rope and capstan.

The contracts to supply components from German companies included providing service engineers in the initial period of production. Swindon fitter-erectors and electricians would learn to assemble and test the twin Maybach engines and other transmission components as well as their associated heating and cooling systems, etc. All had to be fitted into smaller bodyshells than they were designed for. Engineers from Maybach and other factories in Germany worked with the diesel gangs and were found to be very capable engineers; they even spoke reasonably good English. A Mr Stark from Friedrichshafen was the senior Maybach engineer. They stayed for up to twelve months, initially being put up at the Great Western Hotel opposite the station. Alan said:

> The Swindon men were a little uneasy with the visitors at first; the war still being fresh in everyone's minds. Generally though we all got on well together and our German guest was invited to sit with us during the breaks. However we noticed that our labourer Les was no longer joining us. The chargeman found out that Les had been a POW in Germany so he asked Richard, our German engineer who would have been too young to fight in the war, to have a word with him. Richard was a very likeable young man and soon they became good friends. The visitors couldn't understand why we were so heavy handed and kept shearing bolts and rounding off nuts. It was because we were used to much heavier mechanical work.

Jim Lowe told me: 'Two of the Germans had the first name Otto so one became known as 'young Otto'; he decided to stay on after his contract finished and went on to work with the Maybach and MAN engine repair gangs. Sometime later, 'young Otto' became a running inspector on the Western Region.'

It was learned, almost by accident, that alterations would have to be made to each of the four 100-ton cranes when lifting the new locomotives, including the North British-made D600s (at 117 tons, the latter would only ever be lifted without bogies). Although the cab of the crane was to one side of the lift, there was a natural tendency for the suspended load to swing as it travelled horizontally along the bay. With steam locomotives there were no problems: with even the largest types, the buffer beam was below the crane driver's cabin. The full profile combined with the extra length of the diesels, however, provided no clearance. It was solved by lifting the cabins up about two feet. Various Works tradesmen carried out the alterations and not the crane makers, Ransome & Rapier. No doubt it was done during a bank holiday weekend or during the annual shutdown in July.

Sometime in 1958, Pete Brettel moved from the Maybach gang to supervise the final work required for the first new locomotive. Just before apprentice Alan Lambourn finished his time, he went onto this D800 'finishing off' gang in its early days:

> This soon became known as 'the place to be' because men on this work were promoted quicker than elsewhere. Another reason was that the 'finishing off' included putting right any problems that occurred during trials. Therefore several men of this gang were riding about on the new engines a lot of the time, something everyone considered most agreeable.

Some of the diesel 'finishing' jobs done by the erectors were: connecting the final pipework and train heating boilers, filling the oil systems, filling the radiators with water and fitting the detachable roof panels.

Outside, the first jobs included fuelling and watering prior to 'functioning', starting the engines, checking for leaks and watching temperature and pressure readings. An inspector would now check the 'functioning' of the locomotive's working systems. Pete Brettel was appointed to this post while Jack Blackmore became chargeman of the Maybach gang in his place. Alan said:

Men of the 'finishing off' gang also took each new loco out on the three stages of its trial period. First was a light engine test to Badminton and back during which we could get very wet tightening leaks in the water cooling systems. For the next three days, if nothing major needed doing, it would pull ten empty coaches down the line to Badminton and back. The last period of the trials was spent working trains diagrammed for Swindon Shed locomotives. Usually the 10.47 to Paddington was the turn chosen for this, returning on the afternoon Plymouth parcels which left from the Paddington parcels platform and changed engines and crews at Swindon. They always tried to start this stage of the trials on Monday morning and work through to Saturday with the same engine. Back at the shed after each London trip we (the 'finishing off' gang) would attend to any problems. If a major component had to come out and we needed a crane, the loco went back to A Shop. On more than one occasion we replaced an engine and didn't knock off until late at night. I still had to be in the next morning at 6.00 a.m. to switch on the locomotive's pre-heaters; like everyone else, I didn't want to turn down the overtime.

It was my job to record the readings for: engine revs, oil temperature, cooling water levels and temperature and transmission temperature: this I would do every fifteen minutes. The chief A Shop foreman Mr Simpkins would invite senior office staff onto these trips so it often got crowded. Some instruments I needed to see were duplicated in the engine compartment behind the cab but not all. On one occasion I gave up and returned to the Works with a half empty record sheet. My section foreman Mr Cole queried this and told me I had his permission to elbow the chief out of the way next time it happened, so I did. After that they were a bit more considerate.

Some early photographs show trains hauled by diesel hydraulics being rescued by a steam locomotive but this was not Alan's experience: 'Even with a single engine failure, which was uncommon, we could usually limp home on the other.' Tom Stevenson from Ferndale Road was one of the first, if not the first to drive D800. A few months earlier he was also the driver when D600 was delivered from the manufacturers in Scotland to Swindon.

As the first D800s were going into traffic, the D600s started arriving at the Works with their less reliable and non-standard MAN engines. They were slightly longer than the D800s and weren't allowed onto the A Shop traverser. Therefore, they were shunted into the Erecting Shop through the south-west door and worked on there, something they also did with the gas turbine locomotives. The NBL (D600) gang included men who had worked on the early Swindon-built diesel electric shunters. Roy (Spud) Taylor was their chargeman; when he became inspector, Ken Morgan took over.

Alan said:

Diesel work was considered superior to steam probably because no one had yet got used to it; certainly the motor mechanics that were starting to come in gave the impression that they thought they were better than the old steam fitters. They were more militant too. The pride in the job wasn't the same anymore, although it was complex we were just assembling parts made outside, whereas the steam locomotive was designed and built at Swindon from scratch.

Bob Grainger summed up diesel erecting by saying: 'The work wasn't so heavy but was less accessible.'

The British Transport Commission report of 1955 said that the pay of the lower grades on the railways had fallen behind comparable work outside. The following year some of the younger men in the machine shop started leaving to work in the new car body plant, Pressed Steel. Des said, 'I could see the writing on the wall,' which led to the general pessimism felt among his kind 'inside'.

> Ex-colleagues kept telling me to come to the car factory as they were crying out for skilled men, but I was happy where I was despite the prospects. I was nervous about giving up the job I had done since school even for an extra £5 a week and overtime. When I found out I would be operating the same sort of machines I was used to, I did go, in 1958. Although I was working with a lot of my old mates, it seemed it was now every man for himself. Within a very short time we were all out on strike.

Men leaving the Works could find that high standards were a disadvantage. Colin Bown said: 'Two sheet metal men were taken on as inspectors at Pressed Steel and they were constantly being told not to reject such a high proportion of work. Both men returned to the Works in time.' While some men were leaving, others, like firemen off the footplate, were arriving. Fed up with the unsocial hours, a number came into the workshops; another attraction for them was the piecework money.

D818 *Glory* and D819 *Goliath* being built in A Shop on 17 March 1960. (R. Grainger)

CHAPTER 8

The Drawing Office and D800

The Drawing Office was the place where ideas became tangible. There was a universal respect for the draughtsman, whose job it was to interpret those ideas or show that they were unworkable. Orders for new work (anything that could not be classed as planned maintenance) came into the office having been approved by the Chief Mechanical Engineer. At the Board meeting of October 1920, it was agreed that he could authorise and carry out works not exceeding £100, increasing to £250 in 1944. For anything above that figure, contracts were proposed before the relevant management committee at Paddington with a recommendation from the CME. With the General Manager's approval, authorisation was then sought from the Board. Work involving the Drawing Office was either classed as design or development; the latter was usually submitted via the Works Managers or from the Running Department Superintendents. Some work was also undertaken at Swindon for the (Civil) Engineers and Signal Departments.

The appropriate section leader allocated work to the individual, who might need to arrange to visit the foreman or chargeman on site. He would make sketches, take measurements and where possible look at existing drawings. Sometimes the 'chief' (draughtsman) would allocate special jobs to someone he considered especially capable. The initial plan and any preliminary sketches were drawn using a pencil and cartridge paper. The size of the drawings varied, depending largely on what scale the draughtsman chose to use. Very small components would be drawn larger than actual size and large plans or general arrangements were 'laid out', scaled down. Component parts shown in section were indicated by various cross hatching. Before the war, drawings had any subsequent alterations coloured in to highlight them. Rolling stock general arrangements were normally 1½ inches to 1 foot. Until the use of copying machines and the dyeline process of reproduction were adopted in the 1950s, traced copies were printed in the print room. In the drawing stores, paper-backed linen copies were wound around a wooden pole with a brass numberplate on the end for use in the shops. Rolled drawings could be laid out flat using paperweights in each corner. Colour washing to produce blueprints was also done in the print room, care being needed to achieve an even tone. As well as engineering drawings, the draughtsman would produce illustrated booklets to be kept for reference. Two in the possession of the author are: *Notes on Valve Setting as Applied to Steam Cranes* and *Travelling Crane Diagrams*. The Works had been binding their own books since Mr Angle, a clerk, set up a section in the 1930s; before that, they 'sent this work out'.

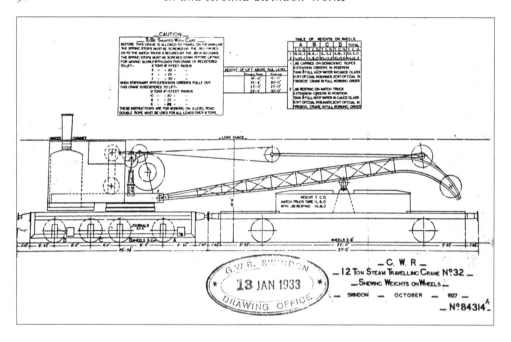

_ C. W. R _
_ 12 Ton Steam Travelling Crane Nº 32 _
_ Shewing Weights on Wheels _
_ SWINDON _ OCTOBER _ 1927 _
_ Nº 84314 _

G.W.R. SWINDON
13 JAN 1933
DRAWING OFFICE

Beryl Hunt was accepted into the DO as a lady tracer in 1955. She had written to the chief draughtsman while she worked temporarily in the Mechanics' Institute library:

He came over personally to ask me to come and have an interview. Because I had stayed on at grammar school until I was 18, I did not have to take the entrance examination or start as an office girl. Mrs A. Maureen Downey was the first tracer in the Works; she came over from the Drawing Office at Marine Mountings in 1951. Mrs Downey was in charge of training four girls and we were her second 'brood' so to speak. We were: Pat Williams, Patsy Truman, Christine Fleming and me – Beryl Hunt, all based in the Loco DO. There were three rows of desks as you looked down the office; our section was in the centre nearest the entrance. Above on the wall, to inspire us, was the drawing board of Isambard Kingdom Brunel [Nearby some wag had hung a sign saying 'All hope abandon, ye who enter here']. We were all younger than our years but Pat was particularly shy and always took everything seriously. Her guinea pig had a litter the same day that Billy Smart's Circus came to town. She was called to the telephone because Billy Smart had heard the news and enquired 'could they act.' Pat explained they were not yet trained which started everybody laughing and gave the game away. [It is not difficult to understand why management had long resisted men and women working together]

It was our job to make ink copies of drawings on tracing linen ready for copying. We 'pounced' the linen with French chalk to cover the greasy surface and used ruling pens that were adjustable, for lines of different thickness. In those days women were not allowed in the workshops so any technical knowledge was picked up from the drawings. It took a long time to become competent in tracing and letterwork. We also coloured 'blue prints' for use as office copies and 'photo prints'. The latter were printed onto photographic paper and when necessary, taken to board meetings at Paddington. One of the first tracers, Ann Haig, a tall model of a girl, was reprimanded for taking too long on a tracing. Ann drew herself up to her full height of 5 feet 10 inches and said to the senior draughtsman, Mr Harland, 'Do you require quality or quantity because I can do either.' Poor Mr Harland (a rather short man) walked away embarrassed. The story went into the annals of the DO. In the late 1950s the Works' Study people recommended the tracing pool be split up and I went to the survey section. Soon after, we moved to an office built above B Shed and accessed by way of an overhead walkway and the print room; previously this had been the experimental section.

Sometimes foremen on the shop floor would recommend their brightest staff to the Drawing Office. All draughtsmen had to have some training and experience of working on the shop floor. In recent years, some former staff have even developed asbestosis, normally associated with exposure due to working where asbestos was used. Young men straight from university did a tour of the shops like craft apprentices, only theirs was condensed into two years. They may well need to liaise with the person doing the work so a good knowledge of production and its potential problems was required. In a lecture to the GWR Swindon Engineering Society in 1929, the speaker said: 'At Swindon they were rather proud that the Works [shop floor] worked exceedingly well with the Drawing Office.'

Just as shop floor experience was required to be a draughtsman, so time in the Drawing Office was essential for engineers applying for senior positions with the Works Manager's staff or the Divisional Superintendent's staff. For example, Mr Dymond, who had worked on both locomotive and carriage design sections, was

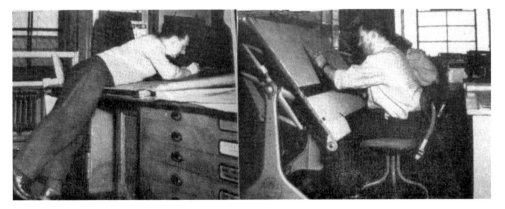

The old working position of the draughtsman was bent over the drawing. The new drawing boards shown on the right were not appreciated by everyone at first: some men adjusted the angle and continued as before. The swivel chairs, too, took some getting used to. Beryl Stanley said Eric Hill, seen here on the right, of the plant and machinery section, was quite musical and could get a tune out of the counterbalance cords either side of the board. All office males were expected to wear a tie but jackets could be removed while working as they restricted the outstretched arms. However, if you were called in to see the boss you were expected to be 'properly dressed'. (*BRW magazine*)

appointed Assistant to the Divisional Superintendent — Cardiff Valleys, a senior position in a division of low status. Mr Coltan, head of the carriage design section of the office, moved to become Assistant to the C&W Works Manager — Swindon in 1939. The reshuffle caused by Mr Stanier's departure to the LMS was exceptional; to fill the void, the brilliant young chief draughtsman Mr Hawksworth was moved right up to Assistant to the CME.

For a few years after the war, there was little new design work and consequently a surplus of draughtsmen. Some staff were seconded or moved permanently as a result and a number took up principal posts when the new Motive Power Department was formed. Appointments at this level were often reported in the local evening paper. The surviving rough books of Alan Peck of the DO buildings section show he was drawing plans of workshops, offices and buildings in 1948. This was for the purpose of calculating the requirements of electric lighting, the cubic area for heating or for plumbing installations or alterations. He spent some time redrawing the internal plan of St Mark's Church and working out 'improved illumination' because the contractor (GEC) had been supplied with plans of two different scales. This was only discovered when Mr Peck queried the cost submitted. Mr Hawksworth, by then the CME and a member of the church choir, bore the cost of the work himself. Mr Peck was sent to Newport as temporary Assistant to the Motive Power Superintendent in early 1951. By October of the following year, his books show he was back in the Works (No. 4 Office, Motive Power Department), recording the weights of standard locos and tenders; these were 78000, 78001, 46503 and three Western Region Britannias. This he did by totalling the weights on each wheel as recorded in the Weigh House. Such was the diversity of work for the draughtsman on secondments.

The L-shaped combined Drawing Office covered an area of 11,100 square feet; it was designed to be open plan, which added to the good natural side and overhead lighting. A case study document dated October 1957 gives the numbers of technical staff (as opposed the managerial, secretarial and clerical) as forty-two for both the Locomotive and Carriage and Wagon offices and another fifty-two for the General, Mechanical and Electrical office. The sections within each office were 1) General: stationary boilers, buildings, surveying, pumps, cranes, machinery and electrical; 2) Carriage and Wagon: running gear, bogies and special loads; and 3) Locomotive, which until the early 'fifties' was: boilers, frames, experimental and valve gear and motion. Sometime in the 1930s or 1940s, a centre section of desks was added, into which newcomers would be placed, only moving out to the window desks if and when seniority allowed. Allied to the Drawing Office at the eastern end was the Estimating Office immediately above the CME's office; here, the work was costed from the drawings. Until Mr Churchward took office, most of these sections were in different places. He had another floor added to the main office building, most of which became a combined Drawing Office.

Normal starting time was changed from 9 a.m. to 8.30 a.m. in the mid-1950s, which did away with the Saturday morning shift. Each sub-office had a registrar who signed in the staff as they arrived. They would draw a red line in the register under the last person in before the bell went. Sam Trollope and Fred Spindler worked in the loco office as clerks/registrars. As well as timekeeping, they collected and

6955 *Lydcott Hall* on a controlled road test for partially fitted brakes in March 1958. The photographer was Ken Ellis, a technical assistant travelling in the Dynamometer Car behind the locomotive. He told me that they had stopped between Hullavington and Little Somerford because the fireman had 'dropped a plug'. He had let the water level get too low in the boiler and the heat of the steam had melted a lead plug in the firebox crown. Driver Bob Jefferies from Swindon Shed is seen climbing back into the cab now that the steam had cleared a bit. The wooden screen fitted to the engine provided three technical assistants with a place to observe recording equipment at the front end. They could communicate with the Dynamometer Car via a telephone although, because of the noise, it was probably a one-sided conversation.

returned the drawings to the store and got prints made. Sam would also go out as a labourer with the track testing car, still known by the old name of whitewash car. In the Administration Office, Gordon Thorpe and secretary Gwen Ives looked after the clerical side of the Loco DO; Gordon was a football league referee in his spare time.

Management knew that Swindon would be getting its share of new work following the announcement of the Modernisation Plan in January 1955, and that the Drawing Office would now have to increase its staff. As well as their ongoing commitments, new design work would include diesel shunters, diesel multiple units and new main line diesels, all to be built at Swindon. Notices were posted in the Loco Works for time-served men to train as draughtsmen. Reg Willcocks applied and joined the salaried staff there in October 1956. He was a boilermaker who had moved to the 'L2' Shop and become a chargeman plater at just 27 years of age. There Reg had worked on the first track relaying machines, which had been designed in the Swindon DO. To accommodate a larger workforce, a 1,600 square foot room above the junction station became a temporary office for training new draughtsmen. Newcomers had traditionally started off in the general sections but now it was locomotive draughtsmen that were required. Reg and Graham Norris, who had started on the same day, found themselves on one of the only sections still dealing with steam engines. Reg said:

> Ron Webb and John Ireland were among those I remember here, together with Ken Dadge, the section leader. There was a carriage and wagon section of about eight people in this 'overflow' office too, making twenty in all. We were given only minor jobs at first, my first task of any substance was to work out and draw an auto brake system for Doncaster built engines based on our own Automatic Train Control.

George Connell came up into the loco DO from the workshops the following year. His training was usual for such a position; he had been apprenticed to fitting, turning and loco erecting and had gained his Ordinary National Certificate at the College. Reg was qualified in engineering to City and Guilds standard and was now being encouraged to go back to night school and study for the ONC, which he did. George stayed in the station office for the first six months, drawing small modifications to locomotives so they might be investigated for viability. The ideas had originated from the staff suggestion scheme. He would go and find the right type of locomotive in the factory and make rough sketches with dimensions of the parts involved: 'I remember I worked on cab controls at first, they were submitted together with my report to the suggestions committee via my section head,' said George.

In 1957 new gradings were introduced, so that some draughtsmen became known as technical assistants. Previously, only the Research and Development staff were

The relaxed appearance of these technical assistants emphasizes the difference in conditions for them and for the footplate men. (*Ken Ellis*)

known as TAs. After their six-month probationary period, Reg and George were made professional and technical grade 'A'. The tracers too became P&T 'A's and all were now expected to work unsupervised. An old tradition that was slowly changing, no doubt due to all the outside influence after nationalisation, was promotion. Draughtsmen and other salaried staff had traditionally moved up the seniority scale only after years of service. Many of the older staff resented the new P&T grading structure, which made the juniors equivalent to the old grades more quickly. A P&T 'A' would now be judged on his or her ability rather than his time in post when promotion was being considered, something the old regime had resisted and been constantly criticised for.

The Chief Draughtsman, Mr Scholes, had a personal secretary while his assistant had a registrar and two lady tracers allocated to him. Under the new gradings, Mr Scholes became Chief Technical Assistant. Several ex-staff I have spoken to agreed that Mr Scholes was rather refined, a gentleman in keeping with his position, commanding respect without ever raising his voice. The 'Chief' had started in the DO in 1925, becoming assistant Chief Draughtsman in 1945, and took overall charge from 1953. Both he and the previous 'Chief', Mr Mattingly, had spent all their working lives in the office after their apprenticeships. Wally Harland was the senior draughtsman in the loco office and he now took the title of Chief Draughtsman. Like many others, he had come up from one of the small companies (the Taff Vale Railway) when they were absorbed by the GWR in the early 1920s. Mr Harland would not succeed Mr Scholes as they were both near to retirement in the late 1950s. In the locomotive DO at that time, Arthur Sly and Roland Lowe were next in line of seniority. In the carriage and wagon office, Jim Innes had been in charge since 1950 and Jim Rideout and George Palphramand were heads of sections. Mr Hutchins and Mr Wallington were the senior men in the general office. Lloyd Roberts had been section leader on cranes and previously docks sections for 31 years until he retired in 1960, probably a record. Mr Palphramand took charge of Sudbrooke Pumping Station in the late 1950s.

Young graduates usually went straight into junior management after nationalisation in 1948. Having completed their degrees, they would have to spend time on the shop floor and in the DO initially, however, to gain experience. In the late 1950s there were seven Batchelor of Science graduates in the Works learning electrical or mechanical engineering. Many of the senior staff in the office had successfully completed the Institute of Mechanical (or Locomotive) Engineers examinations and became associate members of one of those professional bodies. Capable and ambitious staff presented papers to one of the Institutes on a subject within their area of expertise. Membership and participation in the Swindon Engineering Society was also readily undertaken by aspiring draughtsmen, while some taught evening classes at the College. The Engineering Society was affiliated to the railway and attended by some of the department's most senior staff as well as the presenter's contemporaries. This platform gave him a chance to improve his standing among them. Jack Dymond (in the Swindon DO until 1936) for instance was remembered as much for the papers he presented as he was for his impressive professional qualifications and achievements. He had been in charge of the rebuilding of the stationary locomotive test plant in the 1930s, and the gas turbine locomotive experiments later.

Virtually all technical staff (draughtsmen) worked at 6-foot-wide drawing boards resting at an angle of 10 degrees on benches 3 feet high. The benches contained plan-chests with 4-inch and 5-inch-deep drawers, all of which were considered old fashioned by the late 1950s. A tee-square slid up and down the board from the left, this giving a horizontal datum from which a steel set square could be used for the verticals. 'You had to provide your own compasses, set squares and slide rule; pencils and rough books they supplied,' said Reg. Pencil extenders too were provided, so pencils could not be exchanged until they were no more than an inch long. In the temporary office George and Reg had new Admel drawing boards, which were designed to be used in a more upright position, taking up less room than the old equipment. When they moved over to the main office, this equipment went with them. An external investigation made in 1955–6 found that 'an excessive amount of non-productive routine work of a semi clerical nature was being done by senior technicians which diverted them away from their specialist work.' They also criticised the unnecessary amount of detail given on drawings, which then required they be produced to a larger scale. The Drawing Office and other offices were refurbished as a result of these investigations, and by Works study officers later in the 1950s. That's when the old desks/filing cabinets and boards were replaced.

Manfred Spindler from Osbourne Street was German and had been a prisoner of war in Swindon. At the war's end, his parents advised him to apply to stay in Britain as his home was now in the Russian Zone. Manfred's application was accepted but it was not until later that he was allowed to go into factory work. So in 1951 he went into the

Great emphasis was placed on the exterior shape and decoration of the new D800 mainline diesels, scope for which was mainly confined to the two ends. It was claimed to have caused more argument and divergence of opinion than any other element of the design. The Design Research Unit in London was engaged and, in co-operation with the Swindon Drawing Office, came up with the finished shape. A half inch to one foot model was made and rejected before the British Transport Commission accepted the styling of a second model. They wanted a simple outline and therefore no effort was made to over-dramatise the locomotive with streamline decorations and irrelevant front end shaping. (*BRW*)

Works and was sent to No. 8 Shop (new carriage painting) office, where a Mr Prosser was the senior clerk. After two years, some of which was spent in the Correspondence Office, a senior officer from the Motive Power Department rang Manfred and asked if he would go and work for them. He said yes and at first he was dealing with free passes for staff throughout the WR; then he realised why he had been headhunted. Like all railways at that time, the 'Western' were interested in replacing steam locomotives with some form of diesel power. They were impressed by the power/weight ratios being claimed of new German locomotives. The (Technical) Assistant to the Motive Power Superintendent, Humphrey White, and a colleague were to be sent to Germany to investigate further. They were to write a report for Mr Grand, the General Manager, and would need an interpreter. Manfred says the trip was as early as 1953, when he and the two engineers went to the German Federal Railway's central offices and the Krauss-Maffei Locomotive Works in Munich. After that, the three went on to the factories where engines and transmissions were being produced. 'Translating technical detail was rather daunting for me as I had no engineering background at all. We all got the same allowance for the four day trip. My senior colleagues were more used to spending than I was and were soon borrowing from me.'

In 1954 the chief draughtsman asked Manfred to come and work in the DO and again he said yes. No doubt 'the chief' had in mind the language problems that existed with the Swiss engineers over the gas turbine locomotive after the war. Although drawings started to arrive from Germany in the spring of 1956, Manfred says he was translating German technical data from the time he arrived two years earlier.

The bulkhead panel at the rear of the cab of a newly completed Swindon D800 locomotive. (*BRW*)

For this he worked in an office in Park House, the old medical examination centre. The draughtsman who was assigned to the work concerned took it to Manfred and between them they would interpret the detail; the draughtsman had already converted the metric measurements. With the war still fresh in everyone's mind, Manfred experienced some prejudice. However, in the Drawing Office they took to the likeable newcomer without exception but they did insist on rechristening him Fred. Ray Smith of the electrical section had also been a POW in Germany, but there was no bad feeling between them; in fact, they got on very well. For all his valuable work, Fred was never promoted beyond a grade 4 clerk, something he feels was down to his nationality.

A new main line diesel was on the drawing board by late 1956; now most of the loco office was devoted to diesel work of one sort or another. Key workshop personnel were by now being sent to Germany to learn about new production methods. The K Shop welders' foreman, Roy Taylor, and AE Shop fitters' foreman, Jim Tuck, accompanied the Loco Works Manager in 1956. The new locomotive type was to be known as the D800 and the class would later be named after British warships. At the same time, the British Transport Commission pursued another project whereby hydraulic diesels could be designed and built in Britain using German components. The result was the D600s, built at the North British Works in Glasgow. They were always going to be a compromise but it was hoped they would lead to the development of a successful British design. Work on the Swindon version was split up into: 1) body and underframes; 2) bogies and brakes; 3) engines, cooling and preheating equipment; 4) transmissions, axle drives and carden shafts; and 5) electrical and carriage warming equipment.

The D800 was to be a modified version of the German diesel hydraulic locomotive, the V200. The main difference was a reduction in the size due to the restrictions of British Railways' load gauge. Mr Scholes said in his paper to the Institute of Locomotive Engineers that 'had the load gauges been similar a V-200 type could have been purchased immediately and put into service' for evaluation purposes. The underframe and body had to be redesigned, incorporating the existing engines, transmission units and bogies but with different wheel diameters. Reg said that even the senior staff in the office admitted they were no better able to cope with the new type of work. Two things caused particular problems for the designers used to working on the mechanics of steam power. One was the stressed skin body shell that had to withstand the loading forces when being lifted; the other was the electrical engineering detail required to assemble components arriving from the manufacturers.

Reg worked on the mountings for transmission and cooler units of the D800s and those of the D1000 class in 1960. George worked on diesel engines with section head Peter Kembrey in early 1958. Mr Kembrey had a degree and taught HNC students at the College some evenings. George remembered Les Slade, John Godfrey, Edgar Snook, Frank Bassett, Ron Webb, 'Nobbie' Clark, Derek Norris and Ray Smith as all working in the locomotive office at that time. Another section leader here, Donald Gimlett, would sometimes use a Polariscope, an instrument designed and built at Swindon to give accurate results from photoelastic stress analysis of steel. Other sections of up to six men included Jack Preedy's 'diesel investigations' and Sid Robinson's 'modifications'. Newcomers like Reg and George would spend time on all the locomotive sections before being permanently placed. In the C&W section, the

The Loco Drawing Office cricket team sometime in the 1950s, either at Wills sports ground or the BRW sports ground in Shrivenham Road. Sometimes practice matches were played on Ferndale Rec. An annual cricket and football match was held between the loco and the carriage sides of the office. In the all-line 'Kelynack Cup', the Loco DO had faced the Stores in the final on more than one occasion, said Fred Spindler. From left to right, standing: Brian Stevens, Vaughn Williams, Fred Skinner, Phil Smith, Graham Norris, Norman Wells, unknown, an unknown umpire from the carriage DO, Alan Moore. Seated: Manfred Spindler, Tony Mills, Roy Hazell, Reg Willcocks, George Kirkham. (*Manfred Spindler*)

most exacting work in the 1950s was probably the design of the InterCity and Cross Country multiple diesel cars. In conjunction with this, refuelling pumps at certain depots had to be designed by the General DO; Terry French made the drawings and compiled a parts list based on sketches and measurements he had taken on site.

Some of the new diesel work was held up because of demarcation disputes on the shop floor. Boilersmiths and coppersmiths, for instance, argued about whose job it was to machine plate of a certain thickness and this held up the work of the draughtsman. George got some unwanted overtime due to such delays. Bob Grainger told me that some work was held up because parts made outside were, at first, held by the workshop stores. He said some issuers guarded diesel parts like their own and junior erectors would have to convince them the foreman had sent them for it. Overtime was now regularly being worked in the DO and the draughtsman could, to some extent, choose whether to stay on in the evening or put in a few hours on Saturday. Design work connected with steam locomotives was rare after the mid-1950s. However, when George returned to Ken Dadge's section, he did spend a few weeks drawing a complete smokebox arrangement for the Standard class 4. Some of the Swindon-built engines were to receive a double blastpipe and chimney to improve their draughting. George still has a copy of the drawing which shows it was checked as complete in October 1958, although most of the work was done several months before.

After the D800s first entered service, the Loco DO was kept busy investigating teething troubles. In the first half of 1959 nearly 50 per cent of defects reported from the first five were due to electrical apparatus and wiring faults. By the autumn, with twelve in service, it was expected that a new engine would leave the Works every three weeks. It was also predicted that this rate should increase with time, implying that production problems were still causing delays.

The new designs for double-access doors and four-character indicator panels on the D800 noses were drawn by George Connell. This, an early modification, would replace the lateral disc indicators to accommodate the new system of train reporting numbers to be introduced at the end of the decade. Around this time (1959), George was also given the job of calculating the buckling strength of the various body sections of the new D1000 class. With that done, he then had to work out whether the body shell would support the weight of the locomotive: 'There was as yet no formula worked out that I could use, it was all trial and error.'

Sam Ell ran the Research and Development section with his assistant 'Chick' Ockwell, later Herbert Titchener; they had about a dozen staff. This team is best remembered for collecting and analysing the data from steam locomotive testing. This was done on the stationary test plant with the aid of a long, mainly home-made instrument panel. The official interpretation was that they were analysing 'draught arrangements, maximum evaporative capacity and establishing relationship between the coal rate, steam rate and power at the cylinders and drawbar.' The tests could not be completed without running the locomotive under normal conditions, known as controlled road tests. With both methods, the engine was connected to instruments in the Dynamometer Car.

Alan Fairbanks, John Smith, Maurice Herd, Ron Lucas, Bob Hancock, Doug Stagg, Ken Ellis and Ernie Nutty (the Senior Technical Assistant) were in the R&D office in the late 1950s. Most of them had progressed quickly to become Professional and Technical grade 'B' staff while still quite young. In the past, a person would have to be in post for a set period of time and a P&T 'B', or equivalent of, would be at least 40 years of age. With these senior posts came first class concessionary rail travel too. The R&D section had split from the 'experimental section' in the late 1940s and moved out to occupy the floor above the telephone exchange sometime after it was completed in 1952. After nationalisation, Mr Ell became 'Technical Assistant to the Chief Mechanical Engineer', although by now 'Chief' was officially dropped from the title. George Connell worked here later for a time and remembers Mr Ell spending a lot of time developing an emergency automatic brake valve. It would provide a graduated brake application for the D800s and avoid 'bunching' while hauling unfitted goods trains. Another problem these new lightweight locomotives had in slowing such trains was that their small wheel mass reduced heat dissipation and the brake blocks and tyres became very hot. Several options were considered, including fitting double brake blocks at each hanger, something that was to be incorporated in the 'larger locomotive now under construction': the D1000 class. The problem was solved by running a few braked vehicles in unfitted trains until the latter became obsolete. A new mathematical procedure to determine economical timing of trains was being tried in the office with a view to extending it throughout British Railways. In connection with this, Ken Ellis was working out accelerated timings for 'Class C' freights in 1957. Using gradient profiles and working timetables, he mapped out paths for the future diesel hauled trains.

Fifty years on, it is only possible to obtain first-hand recollections from staff who were young at the time. For them at least, the social side of the Drawing Office seemed particularly well organised and supported. Beryl Stanley (née Hunt) summed it up by saying that it was a wonderful life:

Pat Williams and I joined the Railway Debating Society at Paddington and the Swindon Engineering Society. The latter also organised factory visits, both local and further afield, in the summer. It was on a visit to the Crown Derby Works that I met my future husband, Don Stanley from the Tool Room. Sometimes in September we got concessionary rail travel to the continent. In 1957 we went to the SNCB railway workshops in Brussels, rebuilt after the last war.

Four of us: Pat, Patsy, Christine and myself, all loco side tracers, stuck together, we went dancing on Thursdays and Saturdays. In winter it was to the Majestic ballroom at Milton Road baths but in summer they took the floor up for swimming, then we went the Regal ballroom in the Mechanics' Institute. There was always someone in the office going to the pictures or arranging to play tennis and inviting us to join them. I can't speak for the men but none of us girls had any romantic expectations when invited out like this. The Staff Association organised all sorts of games: we liked to play putting in the summer and skittles in the winter. An office walk to a nearby village and an outing to the seaside were arranged every year too. On the first Friday in January we were allowed to leave work early and go to London to see a show. We had an office newspaper called 'Bloggs Weekly' for which I was the token

Beryl Hunt was presented with an illuminated address and a set of cutlery by the combined Drawing Office upon the occasion of her marriage. With her here are fellow tracers. From left to right: Andrea Hewlett (Carriage and Wagon office), Pat Williams, Beryl Hunt, Christine Fleming, Maureen Downey, Alison Ridgeway. Alison's father became the Locomotive Works Manager at about this time (1960). This photograph was taken by Roy Nash of the DO survey section. (*Beryl Stanley*)

F. W. Hawksworth was unique among the senior staff for two reasons: he spent all his working life at Swindon and rose from a lowly apprentice in the Locomotive Works to become head of the Chief Mechanical Engineer's Department, employing 37,000 staff.

Swindon locomotive design work was all but complete before Mr Hawksworth took over at the top, his best work having been done in the Churchward and Collett periods. However, F. W. H. is best remembered for the developments during the turbulent years of 1941–9, his term of office. (*Author's collection*) lady reporter. It was full of humorous and interesting snippets about life in the office. Christmas Eve was a special time and anyone who could play an instrument made up an orchestra. One year they got a piano up four flights of stairs to the office, and we all sang carols.

The men's annual outing had started in the 1920s and was well attended each June. Beryl remembers that the ladies' outing was in May during her time. Some of the outing committee were allowed time off to go to the destinations in advance and make the bookings. Nearly everyone went, from the chief down; in 1955 the men went to Bognor via Hogs Back and Hindhead and in 1958 they went to the Isle of Wight. By this time, several staff had motor cars and they held an annual car rally/treasure hunt. Fred Spindler said that on one occasion, he and his navigator, Dick Eatwell, got lost and ended up on the runway at Kemble airfield. It was around this time that Fred won the Works chess tournament for the first time, in the Mechanics', beating off stiff competition, especially from other DO staff.

Many in the office were of course naturally artistic. Manfred said Phil Nethercot and others would produce humorous sketches and present them as part of an illuminated address when someone retired. Beryl said that George Connell was another one particularly good at penmanship: 'I received a lovely address upon getting married in 1960, everyone signed it and contributed towards a gift.' Sometimes a person was found out for a misdemeanour or else some other incident worthy of gossip. Then someone known for their cartoon ability was called upon to record the event in a humorous sketch. The *Swindon Railway News* referred to the handiwork as an 'illuminated crime sheet'. This type of mockery and high spiritedness was traditional and even encouraged from above, but there was a limit. Reg remembers one of the female tracers who was a good dancer 'showing off' outside the chief's office one day. Mr Scholes called her in and she came out in tears.

CHAPTER 9

Accidents

As well as preparing staff to deal with victims once accidents had occurred, the GWR worked hard to promote awareness of potentially hazardous situations. 'The Safety Movement' was started in 1913 and promoted through the staff magazine. Free pocket tokens were issued to employees on application: they were embossed with slogans which the company hoped would catch on, such as 'Look before you leap' and 'Is it safe?' It was the GWR that first coined the phrase 'Safety first' in this country. The movement was, in their own words: 'A definite attack upon the causes of personal injuries sustained by employees in their work, and a campaign designed to sharpen the appreciation of risks and to cultivate forethought and caution.' The company handbook also instructed staff to educate contractors on safety matters before they started any work for them. Accidents which kept a man off work or worse did decrease in the Swindon workshops but when they did occur, they were the most effective reminder to be careful. It was said that if a wood machinist in the Sawmills retired with all his fingers, he was very lucky. By the 1930s the company knew it was no longer enough just to lecture the men and issue booklets. An all-line competition was organised and awards given for teams with the best safety records. The Freedom from Accident Competition began in 1926 and by 1931 the number of accidents throughout the company had fallen by 56 per cent.

Two men suffered fatal injuries in 'the factory' in 1933 according to the local newspaper, the *Evening Advertiser*. They were Gordon Kendrick, who was crushed in the X (points and crossings) Shop, and William Hobbs, who died instantly when an emery wheel burst in A Machine Shop. A third man, Frank Cox, fell through the roof of 13 (wagon frame building) Shop; he survived, perhaps because his fall was broken by an internal roof. Another accident towards the end of that year but unconnected to any Works activity was the death of Swindon's best known and perhaps most capable design engineer, Mr Churchward. Tragically, he was knocked down by a train while crossing the tracks to visit the Works well after he had retired. The inquest concluded that failing eyesight and hearing, together with his preoccupation with the condition of a section of track, were to blame for this accident.

A three monthly 'statement of accidents' in the CME Department was issued to each dressing station in the Works. Unfortunately, this source of information relating to 1933 is not available to me, which would provide a better picture of accidents that year. For the first three months of 1927, however, a surviving statement shows that one person was killed and 168 were injured throughout Swindon Works. These figures showed only injuries requiring an absence from duty of more than three days under the terms

A Works pilot engine about to tow a tender from B Shed, where it has been overhauled, to the reception shed, where it will be reunited with a locomotive. Jim Lowe thinks that the shunter on the ground is the man who had the accident on the crossing outside A Shop. (*Author's collection*)

of the Factory and Workshop Acts. Without official figures year by year, it is difficult to say whether 1933 was a typical year for such incidents at the Works. Did the reduced industrial activity due to the Depression bring down the accident rate per man hours worked? It is conceivable that with fewer men, all working harder, there was more carelessness, but that was not always the cause. Herbert Sillett made an application for compensation after being discharged along with 820 men in August 1932. His argument was that with injuries to both eyes received in the course of his work 'inside', his chances of finding paid work 'outside' were very small. While employed as a rivet 'holder up' in 1924, Herbert suffered a penetrating eye injury. He subsequently lost the eye and received compensation, presumably after the court found his employer negligent. While using a pneumatic riveter in 1931, a fragment of steel shot into his other eye; this time the sight was saved, but Herbert said his ability to judge distances was now a severe handicap. His claim was, this time, turned down, perhaps because he had returned to work, proving he was to some extent still up to the task.

Des Griffiths told me of two incidents that happened in the AM Shop:

I remember Jack Titcombe machining motion bars, four at a time on a Butler planing machine, when a piece of hot swarf (metal shaving) shot up into his eye. He subsequently lost the eye and badly burnt his fingers getting the swarf out. This happened around 1946 or 1947; goggles were available then but wearing them for this type of work was not compulsory. 'Cocker' Howell was a well known character on the loco side and he had a glass eye. My father-in-law told me this was due to an accident at work. First Aid men took 'Cocker' out on a stretcher to the main line and flagged down an up express [more likely the signalman at Rodbourne Lane signal box was telephoned by an official and told to stop the train] and he was taken to the Royal Westminster Ophthalmic Hospital in London. This was, I estimate to be about 1936 or 1937.

I was testing a small turbine engine with compressed air when a locating nut undid itself and caused the spindle to fracture. The wheel flew off and hit Bert Hazel, a surface grinder, cutting his hand badly enough for the first aider to send him to the Medical Fund Outpatients department. The chargeman believed it was an accident so Mr Raven the foreman wrote to the Works' Manager recommending no further action be taken, and it was not. My father was on 'factory transport' and had a nasty accident sometime in the mid-1930s. He was kneeling down on the back of a two-ton flatbed lorry as there was no room in the cab. They were travelling along through the main tunnel entrance when he got a sudden and severe pain in his leg. To try and relieve it, he straightened up and was struck by a girder in the roof and thrown off the lorry. Although he recovered and returned to work, he gradually began to mix his words and get easily confused. He had to retire before his time, almost certainly due to the accident.

Jim Lowe said Gordon Clack was the best first-aider in AE Shop; he worked on Lewington's finishing off gang. Fred Drinkwater in the Weigh House was another and his medical skills helped bring the Directors Challenge Shield to Swindon for the first time, in 1947. Fred was also one of the people on the scene following Mr Churchward's fatal accident, which has already been mentioned. Herbert Webb, a lengthman, was cleaning points near the B Shop crossing in January 1943. His mate had just gone to collect a wheelbarrow and no one saw the fatal accident. Herbert was struck by a locomotive running tender first, having come off the turntable. Mr K. J. Cook attended the inquest on behalf of the company. There, it was established that the engine driver had taken the correct precautions of sounding the whistle and having a pilotman walk alongside. It was therefore decided that Herbert Webb must have stepped backwards into the path of the engine immediately before it passed him.

There were at least two further fatalities in or near A Shop that were talked about for many years after the war. Both happened sometime before my informants arrived in the 1950s. One man was climbing onto the footplate of an engine being overhauled, and grabbed the reversing lever to pull himself up. He had expected it to be fixed tight but it gave way and he fell backwards. A platform with safety rails pushed up against the back of the cab came into use as a result of that. Another poor fellow had his legs crushed by a moving wagon between A Shop and the Weigh House. 'A shunter was running alongside and uncoupling wagons being loose shunted into the yard beyond. He slipped on the steel plates which had been laid for heavy internal transport vehicles using the crossing there,' said Jim.

Two more shunters were involved in accidents in 1960 and both had a happier outcome. Charles McCord and Brian Webb both suffered life threatening injuries and underwent immediate surgery with blood transfusions, and both made a full recovery. Brian was fitted with an artificial leg and returned to work as a watchman at the tunnel entrance. Their stories were used for publicity to encourage staff to attend blood donation sessions held twice a year in the Works. Stan Leach on the 'carriage side' remembered:

Around 2½ cwt of coke was required to melt one ton of iron, although some of the furnaces in the Iron Foundry were oil-fired by the 1940s. The Iron Foundry had an overhead crane and swivelling jibs in the 'heavy bay'. Elsewhere, large amounts of molten iron and large cores had to be carried manually from the furnace to the mould. With this hot, heavy and unstable metal being moved and poured into moulds, the Iron and Brass Foundries could be dangerous places. If the various methods of allowing the dispersal of gases, particularly in sand moulding, were not carefully worked out, then explosions were possible. Jack Fleetwood said: 'You never forget the details of serious accidents, even 60 and 70 years on. The most spectacular was when a 12 ton casting for one side of a large drop stamping machine, which was about the largest single work we normally undertook, exploded and molten iron shot through the high foundry roof and set it alight.'

Another hazard of molten metal was that it spluttered whenever it came into contact with something cooler than itself. Small balls of metal would burn a man's skin if he was not protected. Jack said: 'Most missed and were trodden in to the earth of the floor and forgotten, it made us complacent. I remember a 'ladle runner' was guiding his ladle backwards after filling it and stepped onto one of these 'iron shots' which burnt through his shoe. The pain caused him to let go of the handle which held the ladle upright and molten metal poured across the ground where he fell. A similar accident happened when I was an apprentice in the Brass Foundry: one of the four lads carrying a ladle in a frame caught his overalls on a stack of rough ingots. Thinking he could free himself without stopping, he said nothing and the ladle with 5½ cwt of molten brass tipped towards him. In both accidents the casualties got badly burned but eventually recovered and returned to work.' Later in the 1940s, perhaps due to such incidents, ladles with shock absorbers and wheels were introduced for smaller repetition castings. These 'prams' were much more stable and could be moved about by one or two people, usually labourers. (*GWR*)

Sometime after the war a fella was killed near the Acetylene House next to the Frame Shop. He was climbing down a manhole to see what was stopping waste water mixed with acetylene gas from draining away. This man, I think he was Polish, had a lighted cigarette in his mouth; there was an explosion which blew him back out and he was killed instantly.

Ian Sawyer remembers a man being hit by a four-wheeled boiler trolley outside the P1 Shop. It had been run out of the shop and he crouched down to stop it with a chock block, which was normal, except that it was moving much faster than usual. The trolley slewed towards him when it hit the block, and ran over the top of it, pinning him down by his shoulder. All three first aiders from AM Shop attended, said Ian, 'Billy Bown, Tom Smith and myself.'

Artificial limbs were made and fitted in a workshop on site. The staff magazine said in 1940 that there was an average of ninety cases dealt with each year. Although most of these were 'renovations and renewals', the majority of men affected must have been injured since the company had made conscious efforts to reduce accidents. There was no real alternative to common sense.

For railwaymen and women convalescing after accidents at work or outside, there was a rehabilitation workshop in the Carriage Works. It opened in 1953 after a scheme was studied at Vauxhall Motors. Dr Watkins, the Swindon Railway Medical Officer, prescribed the treatment and Micky Austin, the foreman, saw that it was carried out. Providing follow up treatment and physiotherapy got staff back to work that much quicker. Machine tools had been modified by Mr Austin, who had worked in the 'carriage side', to make them productive as well as therapeutic. Aubrey Wykeham-Martin broke his leg in 1958 when a wagon door fell open on him. He later attended the rehabilitation workshop and operated a drill that was powered by himself walking slowly on a treadmill. Aubrey recovered sufficiently to return to the A Shop stripping gang on lighter work; his speciality was burning through nuts that had seized and perhaps been rounded off, underneath locomotives and tenders. At this time, the Works ambulance was being called out about five times a week, although it also covered railway areas beyond the Works.

A derailment outside the Loco Works due to the severe weather of the winter of 1962/3. A lightweight 03 class 0-6-0 diesel shunter built here in the late 1950s has run off the track on compacted snow. The photographer, Bob Grainger, said: 'Word soon got round the shops nearby when something like this happened. Some of these people had just come out to have a look and give needless advice; I think the Brass Shop foreman is there somewhere. I was taking a chance as a young apprentice with a constant desire to get a good photograph. Staff taking photographs was forbidden or perhaps by this date, at least frowned upon, and you had to be careful.'

January and February 1940 and 1947 were the worst winters in living memory in Swindon until 1962/3. However, most winters were severe enough to cause disruption to internal transport movements and freeze points, water pipes and tanks.

CHAPTER 10

The GWR Estate and Hospital

There were 300 terraced cottages in the GWR estate, sometimes called 'the company houses'. They had been built over a twenty-year period for the first workers of Swindon's Railway Works. By 1930, of course, the workforce and those who served them were spread across a number of housing developments in the town and beyond. The eight streets in the estate were laid out in a regular grid pattern. Typical of workers' homes of the period, they were built of local stone with Welsh slate roofs, but were said to be larger than colliery and similar houses being built in the north. The Medical Officer for Health said in 1936: 'The houses are of excellent construction, kept in good repair and the tenants are selected. For these reasons it is protected from ever becoming a slum, a fate which otherwise might threaten it, for the spacing is poor and the houses, owing to the fewness of rooms, liable to overcrowding.'

The roads in and out of the estate had white gates, which were closed on one day of the year. This was done by the GWR to assert their right as owners. 'The long bar that was usually locked open had little spikes across the top to stop us kids balancing along them,' said Colin Bown. Colin's family lived at No. 46 Bathampton Street, about half way down; Church Place was at one end and Emlyn Square at the other. In the 1930s, the houses were little changed from the original design; they all had cast iron guttering and down pipes, lead plumbing, sash windows and a solid (unglazed) front door. There was an outside lavatory with high level cistern in the small back yard. The front garden had to be kept nice or the 'rent man' warned you about it. Around the garden was a low wall and railings with a fleur-de-lys decoration and a cast iron gate. Some people, mainly retired men, would lean on the front gate and have a word or two with passers-by. The ironwork was taken away during the war; then anyone that didn't already have one grew a privet hedge.

Most of the homes had one large bedroom occupying the whole of the upper storey, although by the 1930s some had been partitioned off. A lean-to kitchen extension had also been added by the 1930s and the cooking range moved into here from the living room. The coal-fired copper was also moved to the kitchen to provide hot water for washing. Gaslight sconces on the downstairs walls provided lighting and there were fireplaces in all rooms. The furniture and effects were mainly what had been handed down from previous generations.

Gas was provided by the company's own Gas Works and it was the same price as outside. They were not allowed to undercut the Swindon United Gas Company, which supplied the rest of the town. Recipients of the company's gas had the advantage of

Houses in Bathampton Street: in the background is the 1872 water tank in the Fire Station yard, Bristol Street. (*Bert Harber*)

Marie Jacobs cycling through 'the estate'. Marie was a Jewish evacuee from Bow in east London: she arrived as a nine-year-old in 1940 and stayed with the Harbers until 1945. Colin Bown said a lot of evacuees were sent to Swindon and the schools struggled to cope. (*Bert Harber*)

a higher pressure supply in the evenings and at weekends because the Works was not drawing on it so much, whereas the town's gas was reduced at the time they most needed it because of greater demand. The railway provided gas for their houses and street lighting until about 1950. Between 1939 and 1944, the streets were blacked out. 'Puddy' Moore and a chap called Kemble were the lamplighters in the 1930s and they dealt with the factory gas lighting too; both were based in the GW Gas Works. The two of them would start their rounds at sunrise as the lights were not to be left on any longer than necessary. 'Puddy' was the Gas Works' 'bookies runner' as well.

Colin told me:

Monday was always washing day and most of it had to be hung out the front as the back yard was so small. When I was not at school I had to put the washing through the mangle in the back yard. All the men in these houses worked on the railway somewhere; can't remember who was on one side of us before the war, later it was watchman Jimmy Mutton, the other side was Archie Menham who was a Carriage Fitter, he made the door locks and catches. Not all the men worked 'inside', there were footplate men, guards and shed workers, all of whom worked shifts. You could hear their hobnail boots on the brick paths and back alleys at all hours. In the years before the war, maintenance was carried out on the company's cottages by 'factory men'. If you needed any work doing you told the rent collector and he passed it on: water and gas plumbers, carpenters and 'brickies', etc from D Shop would then be sent out as required. They had a workshop/store in London Street for estate maintenance: it was next to Knee's the newsagents, which was on the corner with Emlyn Square. External painting was done every seven years; all houses had dark green doors (the same shade as was used on locomotives), white windows and black guttering.

The company did not provide for the chimneys to be swept and I think some people deliberately let theirs catch fire rather than pay a sweep. The lintel between the living room and the lean-to was a length of old broad gauge rail. Someone had the slates on their lean-to kitchen replaced with thick glass panes and this started a trend, they charged an extra tanner a week on the rent for that. Every so often our back yards would have to be limewashed or what we called whitewashed. The company would send a message to your place of work via an office boy. A bucket, brush, ladder and the lime was collected from the limehouse in Taunton Street. The hospital porter would come and issue it out three days a week. The annual cost to the company for lime and brushes for its employees was about £30. You mixed up the powder with water and took care not to get any on your skin as it would burn. Limewash was a cheap but effective type of white paint which was brushed onto the masonry to brighten it and keep moss away. A road sweeper was employed by the GWR until the 1930s, to keep the streets clean. He kept his handcart and brooms in a shed behind Higgins's house in Exeter Street. All over the town a layer of black dust would cover windows and sills: it was fine sand from the Foundry. Being so near the Works, 'the estate' was particularly badly affected and you could hear it crunching under your feet in places.

In my first book, *Working for Swindon Works*, there is a photograph of a street trader in the GWR estate. Colin told me:

Children celebrating the Queen's Coronation in Bathampton Street in 1953. Bert Harber's niece is 'Queen' and Bert is following the procession on the left. 'Ike' Hayes, who worked down the Running Shed, is the tall man in the background and behind him the Bowns chat to passers by outside their house. (*Swindon Museum and Art Gallery*)

That's old 'Lemmo' Sheppard, his real name was Lemuel. His newsagent shop was up Bridge Street until about 1938 then he moved down Faringdon Road, past the Medical Fund Baths. 'Lemmo' is talking to my parents [Bill and Winnie Bown] and our cat Pretty is there on the right look. This would have been a Sunday as dad's got his bowler on which he wore to the Bakers Arms of a Sunday dinnertime. There were three pubs in the estate and the different trades kept to certain ones. In those days only the Cricketers had a spirits license; old Mrs White the landlady always managed to block applications from the other pubs in the area. The Baker's had no cellar so during the war the cool room where they stored the barrels was used as an air raid shelter. A couple of families and us were invited to go there if the hooter went to warn of approaching enemy aircraft. We went there and dad would report to the Works Fire Station.

Partly submerged and enlarged 'Anderson' type shelters were erected down the road in The Park as part of the local air raid precautions.

Bert Harber's memories of the estate in the 1930s are very similar to Colin's, seventy years or so later. Both their fathers were retained firemen and Bert too joined the brigade, in 1939. Some of the following comes from notes Bert has made over the years. He was born at the family home, 3 Taunton Street; this was one of the larger houses in the south-west corner of the estate.

My father William Harber had come down from the north and mother was born on the estate, in Chester Street. They moved to the house in Taunton St sometime during the Great War. Father became a chargeman fitter in the AM Shop, he spent 54 years in The Works. My three brothers also served their time 'inside' but unlike me they did not spend their whole working life there.

Colin and Bert's recollections about access to the estate vary; Bert said:

> The estate was private so all but one gate was locked to road traffic: the duty fire officer had a key of course. On Good Friday a rope was put across the main entrance into the estate as well and tradesmen's and other vehicles required permission to pass from the attendant watchman. Due to conditions in 1939–40, the army and fire brigade requested the gates around the estate be removed, which they were.

What traffic there was in those days was mainly horse and carts, with the occasional motor lorry and steam wagon. A Corona pop lorry came round once a week; two brothers, Les and Vic Badnell, ran it. Bamford's then started a rival pop round; they used a horse and cart, as did the rag and bone man. Other roundsmen were Archie Withers from Oriel Street (the muffin man), Walter Godwin (the bread man) and a man selling watercress on Sundays, but few of them used road transport. Mr Cuss, who lived in Church Place, had a motor car and apart from possibly Mr Sealy, he was the only owner on the estate. Bert's terrace was just behind Park House; the backs ran alongside Faringdon Road. This became one of the only parts of the railway estate to be demolished, in more recent times. Park House was the medical examination centre for CME staff seeking employment or promotion; it was also the residence of the company's Chief Medical Officer.

> At the other end of the row was the limehouse next to Mr and Mrs Bridges at No. 1: James Bridges was a platelayer on the permanent way. The lime was free to householders and could be collected at very limited times. My immediate neighbours in Taunton Street were Jack Allen at No.2, he was chargeman fitter – outstation; the other side of us was Ernest Tombs, a boilermaker, at No. 4 and at No. 5 was Mr Hook, a GWR Plumber. Further down was Percy Moulden at No. 13, he was full time [Works] fire brigade, his son Norman was killed when *Ark Royal* was sunk in 1941.

Part of the railway estate looking west down Bathampton Street towards The Park. From this angle, taken from the top of the Mechanics', the Locomotive Works can be seen at the top right. (*Swindon Central Library – local studies collection*)

I remember our house had three, what would now be considered small bedrooms, two downstairs rooms and a kitchen extension. The kitchen was the heart of the house as 95 per cent of the household activities took place there. It was where food was prepared and we had our meals on the large kitchen table. It was also where the ironing, homework, letter writing and model making, etc took place. There was a range for the cooking which was lit most days, even in the summer, to heat kettles of hot water. A porcelain sink and cold tap were against the outside wall and in the corner stood the copper into which anything combustible was despatched to heat water for wash day and bath day. For a small sum the residents could use the washing baths at the Medical Fund building in Milton Road. There was a gaslight in the kitchen and on the chimney breast in the front parlour. Our house got electricity about 1933–4; each street got up a petition and if more than ten households would convert, they laid all the pipes and connected those that wanted it. Also, in the 1930s, modern tiled fireplaces and new grates would be put in for an extra tanner a week on the rent. On wash day we used a galvanised tub because the sink in the kitchen was too shallow; it hung up in the yard with the bath. Washing and mangling was hard work and everything would get black specks on it when pegged up outside. In the back yard there was a coal bunker and an outside toilet which was unlit and uninviting. Colin's mother had a couple of budgerigars in an aviary out the back; a few families kept chickens. All the houses shared common back alleys, usually called 'backs's or 'backs'. In the warm weather the women would take chairs out there and sit together, knitting or sewing. Nobody locked their doors when they went out, day or night; strangers and anyone that looked suspicious were very noticeable. My brother Jack got stopped one day by a policeman as he was going to the station. He was carrying his tool bag as he was an outstation fitter and was asked to account for it.

I can still name dozens of families that lived in the streets around us in those days. The Chief Mechanical Engineer, Mr Collett, lived at 5 Church Place just around the corner. He retired in 1941 and moved away shortly after. The only other manager who subsequently lived in this comparatively modest house was S. A. S. Smith, in the early 1950s. Mr Sealy the fire captain lived next door to Collett at No. 6 (throughout the period). We didn't know much about what went on the other side of Emlyn Square. The boys that side went to Sanford Street and the girls to College Street schools; on our side they usually went to Westcott Place (school) even though there was a choice. The school year started in August; I was not quite four when I first started. When we were not at school we would be off out somewhere or playing games in the street despite the large park at the end of the road. Football and cricket and for the girls skipping and hopscotch were popular, marbles and whip and top were also played, each had its season. The Works hooter was our clock, you could hear it anywhere so we knew exactly when dad would be home for dinner and tea and made sure we got back then too. On the anniversary of the Armistice the hooter sounded at 11 a.m. to mark the start of the two minutes' silence and everybody stopped what they were doing including the men working 'inside'.

When dad was manning the Fire Station callboard on a weekend we would take his meal in to him. If there was nothing happening we were allowed to look round the

Mr and Mrs W. Bown outside their house in Bathampton Street, suitably decorated with bunting for the Coronation in 1953. (*C. Bown*)

station. The 1912 Dennis engine was the showpiece, it was said to have been the first motor fire engine in Wiltshire. I rode on it on my first call when I joined the brigade [this vehicle went into the old Wesleyan Chapel building in Faringdon Road when it was converted to a railway museum in 1962]. Some houses had front doors facing in towards each other under a common porch. On winter evenings when it was dark and later during the blackout, we would tie the two door knockers together with some stout cord. We would then knock the doors and watch from behind the hedge as they tried to open them (Colin also remembers this and similar pranks). Along with most other children, my brothers and I went to Sunday school: we attended St Mark's while some went to the Wesleyan Chapel.

The estate was described by Bert as self-contained; in Emlyn Square there was Knee's the newsagents, Beasant's the grocers, a sweet shop and a pillar box. There were three public houses in the square as well but the nearest workmen's clubs were outside in Milton Road, or the 'Monkey Club' in Rodbourne Road. Several 'outdoor beer houses', what we now call off-licences, existed in the streets adjoining the estate. In London Street there was the GWR savings bank; a Mr Cripps was the senior clerk here in the 1930s. Next door was the GWR Locomotive & Carriage Sick Fund Society; nearby was a nurses' hostel, mutual improvement classes for enginemen and the headquarters of the Swindon Engineering Society. The GWR orchestra too had their headquarters in Emlyn Square. After the war, and possibly before, the Retired Workmen's Benevolent Association met on the estate. The Medical Fund hospital building stood in front of the Mechanics' Institute and the Great Western Park was situated at the western end of the estate. The latter was exchanged for some Borough Council land in 1925 but

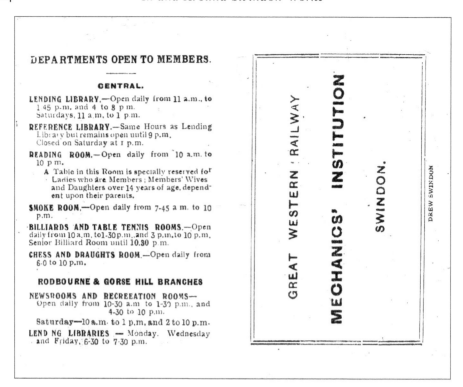

DEPARTMENTS OPEN TO MEMBERS.

CENTRAL.

LENDING LIBRARY.—Open daily from 11 a.m., to 1 45 p.m. and 4 to 8 p m. Saturdays, 11 a.m, to 1 p m.

REFERENCE LIBRARY.—Same Hours as Lending Library but remains open until 9 p.m. Closed on Saturday at 1 p.m.

READING ROOM.—Open daily from 10 a.m. to 10 p m.
A Table in this Room is specially reserved for Ladies who are Members ; Members' Wives and Daughters over 14 years of age, dependent upon their parents.

SMOKE ROOM.—Open daily from 7-45 a m. to 10 p.m.

BILLIARDS AND TABLE TENNIS ROOMS.—Open daily from 10 a.m, to1-30 p.m., and 3 p.m.to 10 p.m. Senior Billiard Room until 10.30 p m.

CHESS AND DRAUGHTS ROOM.—Open daily from 6-0 to 10 p.m.

RODBOURNE & GORSE HILL BRANCHES

NEWSROOMS AND RECREEATION ROOMS— Open daily from 10-30 a.m to 1-30 p.m., and 4-30 to 10 p.m.

Saturday—10 a.m. to 1 p,m, and 2 to 10 p.m.

LENDING LIBRARIES — Monday. Wednesday and Friday, 6-30 to 7-30 p.m.

GREAT WESTERN RAILWAY MECHANICS' INSTITUTION SWINDON.

DREW SWINDON

Swindonians continued to use its former title. The old cricket pavilion still stood in the Park in the early 1930s, derelict by then, and a Drill Hall stood in the top far corner which the army used for territorial training. The Labour Party and sometimes the Tories held meetings there and the GWR Gymnastic Society also had use of the hall. Nearby was the large parish church of St Mark's for the railway community, with the Vicarage next to it.

Bert's notes state:

> I left school and went to work at J. Compton, Sons and Webb the clothing manufacturers in Sheppard Street. Six months later in June 1937 I went into the Works, still not yet 15 years old. My apprenticeship would start when I reached 16, until then I was an office boy in the GWR Gas Works. In September of the following year I moved to E Shop to learn the trade of electrical maintenance. After I got married in 1944 I continued to live at home for a while then moved to Bristol Street alongside the Works, until 1953.

Both Mr Bown and Mr Harber senior were still living in their houses on the estate until at least 1966, when the council started taking them over for refurbishment.

The Mechanics' Institute was in the centre of the railway estate in Emlyn Square. It catered for the social and educational needs of the railway workers and in 1930 there were nearly 15,000 members. The subscription was a shilling a quarter for the lowest paid and for retired workers, and up to half a crown for the higher earners. People not employed by the GWR could also join but their rates were higher and payable in advance.

The President of the Institute was C. B. Collett, the Treasurer was Mr Kelynack and the Secretary was Mr G. R. Davis. The day-to-day running was the job of the thirty-one council members and the trustees. The MI received some concessions, financial and otherwise, from the directors and management of the company. Above the doors, just inside the main entrance, was a nameplate from an old 'dean single' locomotive. There was a large reading room supplied with current newspapers and magazines and 'a fine dance hall', a smoke room and rooms for billiards and draughts/chess. Also on the ground floor was a lending and reference library which included a juvenile department. The library operated an 'open access system' from the early 1930s, allowing users to 'go directly to the shelves and select their own books'. Des Griffiths said that his school, Sanford Street, had an arrangement whereby pupils could use the Mechanics' library. No doubt other local senior schools were included as well until a public library opened in the town in 1943.

The MI library and presumably other parts of the building were apparently not short of staff. Ernie Ruggles left school in the summer of 1943 and got prior notice of a vacancy coming up as a library assistant. Gordon Clack was leaving to take up an apprenticeship in the Works so Ernie applied and got the job. Pete Heavens and Frank Gearon were also assistants in the library at the time, while Stan Jarman was librarian. The chief librarian and secretary of the MI was Mr Phillips, who had his own office. Dorothy Palmer was Mr Phillips's secretary; she lived in Aldbourne and would cycle in after the weekend if the weather was reasonable. Ernie said:

The Mechanics Institute after the rebuilding, in 1932. (*BRW magazine*)

Later when I went into the stores to work I found out that Mr Phillips's brother worked as a materials inspector. My job was to issue and receive books, put away the returned books and keep them stacked in the correct places. Members were issued with four tickets but could borrow only one book free; any more incurred a small charge. The borrowing period was two weeks. I remember we got a bit carried away with the news of the invasion of Europe in June 1944: that morning Frank and I started throwing books over the shelves at each other. Normally I was very careful with the books so I suppose it was the excitement of the war news. It was Mr Jarman's job to send out notices if books were overdue and when they did come back he checked for stains or damage; he was responsible for collecting the fines. He left while I was there and was replaced by a Mrs Wright. I would have liked to have stayed on in the library but 'assistants' were only temporary staff, for up to two years. So my father had arranged for me to go into the Works General Stores and I went 'inside' in March of 1945.

Beryl Hunt worked in the library for a short time in the mid-1950s, she said: 'On Wednesdays or Saturdays I worked a late shift on my own. At 8 p.m. when the last person had left I had to turn the lights off at the far end and walk back through. As it was such an old building it felt very eerie.'

On the first floor of the Mechanics' Institute was a spacious hall for concerts, shows, dances and public meetings. The upstairs hall, the boiler room and the theatre stage had suffered considerable damage due to the fire of 1930. When it reopened nearly two years later, the hall had been enlarged and modernised and was renamed The Playhouse. The GWR Amateur Theatrical Society put on dramatic and operatic performances in the Mechanics' annually. The production for 1932 was *The New Moon*. It had been moved to the Empire Theatre for its one-week run while the Mechanics' was rebuilt. Presumably their *Princess Charming* the year before was also put on at the Empire. A smaller hall downstairs catered for gatherings such as the AEU No. 2 branch meetings, hobby groups, lectures and exhibitions, and after the war the Staff Association indoor activities were, in the main, held here. The building was renovated in 1959 to improve the facilities.

There were facilities for members, on a smaller scale, at branch Reading Rooms in Bath Road, Rodbourne Road and Gorse Hill. Membership also covered the Athletic and Sports Club Branch at Shrivenham Road. There were various inter-shop and office leagues for most popular games. In later days the so called 'all-line' competitions (against other departments across the Western Region) took place here if the Swindon team were competing at home. Away fixtures allowed travel concessions and, in the later stages of competition, paid leave.

Following 'Trip' holiday in July, it was not long until the next big event, the children's fete, which was held in the Park. Like 'Trip', the organisation of the fete was the responsibility of the Mechanics' Institute committee. Locals watched with anticipation the huge vehicles and steam traction engines moving in and out of The Park and the equipment being erected. During the weekend, all the large vehicles were parked up in the streets bordering the Park. The event was really a huge fairground with lots of rides, swings, and stalls selling sweets and novelties. The children's fete took place on the second Saturday in August every year until 1939. Families would arrive early in the afternoon and a cannon was fired at 1.30 to announce the start. The admission was 3*d* and for children included a bag containing half a pound of fruit cake and a ticket for a free ride on the roundabout. Large urns filled with tea were brought in from the Works and it was given free of charge if you brought a mug with you. A big stage show was put on; the Great Western Silver Band would be playing, showmen were trying to attract people in to their sideshows, acrobats performed and for the highlight of the afternoon 'The Great Blondini' did a highwire act. He then dived off a 40-foot tower into a pool which had burning oil on the surface. In the evening, when the light faded a bit, the trees were lit up and a large balloon was released, signalling the start of a grand firework display. Alas, the children's fete did not resume after the war.

Other events that were looked forward to in the railway town of the 1930s were the labour fete, the Co-op carnival and a carnival in aid of the Victoria Hospital. The latter formed up in the side streets of the railway estate ready for the procession through the town. A garden party/fete took place every year in the grounds of St Mark's Vicarage. The old friend of St Mark's, the poet and writer John Betjeman would often open the fete with a speech. Between the wars a day out at the seaside was laid on for the children of the poor. The Swindon newspaper the *Evening Advertiser* paid for the special train to take them and some supervising adults to Weymouth; in 1930 it was reported that more than a thousand were looking forward to it. Youngsters from the district whose fathers had fallen in the Great War or were unemployed were sought and offered the free day out. There was some stigma attached to the outing and for this reason some mothers refused to let their children go.

Dorothy Grimes lived at 28 Taunton Street; her father Bill got employment 'inside' as a labourer after the First World War:

Don't know what he did exactly, he worked over by R (Fitting and Machine) Shop. They called it 'Grimes's Corner', it was very physical work and he developed a heart condition. I remember Lem Sheppard would stand outside the tunnel entrance as the workers poured out, selling the *Evening Advertiser*, dad called it 'the penny liar'. I was born at my grandparents Little's house in Oxford Street on the estate. Frederick Little had walked from Chippenham to get employment at the New Swindon Works years before. He became a horsebox trimmer; two of his brothers also worked on the 'carriage repair side'.

Mr Hewer came round the estate with a horse and cart selling hardware on Fridays: he had a shop in Manchester Road. You could get paraffin, soap, candles, min cream wood polish and mansion floor polish for lino from him. Mr Moulding the coalman also came round with a horse and cart, he delivered company coal. I got told off by my mother and sent to my room for asking him why he had such a big nose, my brother Frank dared me so I did. Some men would shovel up the horse dung for their roses. Scrap wood for getting the fire going in the morning was also available from the Great Western. Once a fortnight you exchanged a ticket at the wood wharf in the fire station yard; delivery to your door by handcart cost you extra. Like the coal, the money for wood tickets was deducted through the paybill. Our house only had one bedroom which was partitioned off so we moved to 17 Oxford Street which had three bedrooms.

The public houses on the estate were always busy. Dorothy's father helped out at his regular, the Glue Pot, renamed because of the smell of glue in there from carriage carpenters and others who worked with it 'inside'. It was usual for carriage and loco men to socialise separately and this was more noticeable in the pubs. Mr Durrant says in his book *Swindon Apprentice*: 'The Glue Pot was untypically allied to the carriage side.' Dorothy said:

In the wartime blackout the landlord Charlie Thomas would strike a match and check the till; if he thought he had taken enough over the bar he would want to shut up early. Father would talk him into staying open by running the place for the last hour or so. Charlie died during the war and in his will he had stipulated that Bill Grimes should be offered the tenancy, this was done and he accepted. At the same time Devenish's brewery bought the premises from the 'Western'. We moved again, into rooms above the Glue Pot at 5 Emlyn Square. All the family helped run the place as it was such hard work, Works fireman Jessie Collett too. There was usually a queue at opening time.

This is not to imply that all railwaymen were in the pub when not working. Bert Harber was typical of many young men of those times; when he was old enough to drink, he was saving to get married. March was the most popular time for railwaymen's weddings because they got a tax rebate from the start of the financial year eleven months earlier.

Dorothy went on to say:

There was sawdust on the floor and spittoons into which grandfather and others would spit tobacco and not miss. Mother said she was not having any of that and she didn't. We washed the floor every day and disinfected it with Zoflora every Wednesday and Saturday evening after closing. The opening hours were 11 a.m. to 2 p.m. and 6 p.m. to 10 p.m.; Sunday opening was an hour later dinnertime and evening. I pulled my first pint for Stan White, there was so much head on it he took off his tie and tied it round the middle of the mug. A coke 'tortoise' heater stood in the middle of the bar room with a big pipe coming out the back. It went up and across the full length of the bar and kept us nice and warm in winter. An old tradition was putting a red hot poker in the beer and sprinkling in some ginger powder which we gave out. Mother insisted ladies go into the back room in case of any bad language in the bar. The only exception was when Mr Ottaway, a clerk in the Works, bought his wife in of a dinnertime when it was quiet.

There was full employment with overtime in 'the factory' by the middle of the war. Beer was a shilling a pint and was not on ration and we sometimes ran out before the drayman called on Thursdays. He would drop off 13 hogshead barrels a week: they contained 52 gallons of ale each. Of the other public houses: Mrs White ran The Cricketers with her mother and Jim Bishop ran The Bakers, and a chap named Golby took over there in the 1950s.

Bert Harber said Jimmy's place (The Bakers) was 'rough as blazes' before the war. Bill had given up working 'inside' and taken on the Glue Pot because of ill health but further health problems forced him to give that up as well, in about 1951. 'It then became a scrumpy house and got a bit of a reputation,' said Dorothy.

Medical Fund Hospital

In 1930 a conference was held at Paddington with representatives of the Medical Fund Society and the GWR company. They discussed a proposal to build a new four-storey hospital to replace the existing one on the same site in the railway estate. The directors declined the request for a loan of £45,000 due to the worsening economic conditions and the idea was shelved. The existing building would have to serve the railway community for many years to come and continue to be subsidised by the company.

In 1931 there were 753 patients admitted to the Great Western Hospital; of these 711 had 'major operations', thirty of which resulted in death. Gastric and duodenal ulcers were common, especially among the men, and this was thought at the time to be due to poor oral hygiene. A perforated ulcer was life-threatening, even with immediate surgical intervention. A very respectable figure of 1 per cent was given for appendicitis mortality at the hospital during this period. Malignant disease was the reason for many major operations among Swindon's railway families; the word cancer was avoided whenever possible. The hospital authority prided itself on the regular blood transfusions given during surgery, thanks to a thriving donation programme among the community.

By increasing the number of hospital beds from thirty-six to forty-one and increasing the routine operating sessions from two to three afternoons each week, the waiting list of sixty was brought down to ten that year (1931). There were 2,112 minor operations for things like tonsils and adenoids, piles injections, lancing boils and stitching cuts. Most of these cases would be given a general anaesthetic and sent home the same day. By far the biggest ailment needing surgical treatment was varicose ulcers and veins.

With honest business sense, the annual report for the year says of varicose vein patients: 'Attention is drawn not only to the suffering but of work efficiency of sufferers.' The average cost of running the hospital the previous year was 1s 7½d per patient days spent in the hospital, which worked out at £14,115. The directors of the GWR authorised an annual donation of £50 and the company also bore the cost of gas, electric, coal, cleaning, repairs and decoration for the hospital and all Medical Fund Society premises.

Kathleen Hemming told me of her time in the hospital as a child having her tonsils and adenoids removed. This was in 1922 and no doubt her experience was typical of the whole period between the wars:

I went in early in the morning and had to change into a gown and be put on a trolley. You were wheeled into a big room with a huge lamp on the ceiling. The nursing sister was getting all the instruments laid out ready and a doctor held a mask smelling of ether, over my face. The next thing I knew I was in another room recovering on a

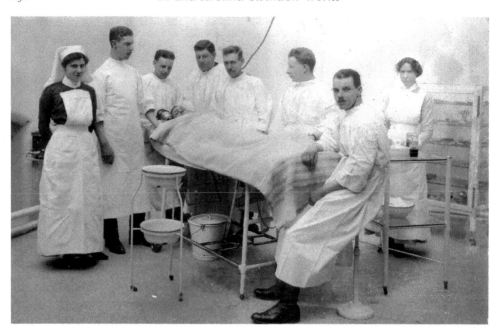

On the back of this postcard view of the operating room is written: 'The G.W.R. Hospital Nursing Staff, Faringdon Street, Swindon, Wilts. An Appendix case' and no doubt some enthusiastic young medical trainees. The writer also records the matron as Miss Ira Hutton and the nursing sister as Miss Mabel Woolford. The names of successive matrons from 1918 onwards are given in the annual reports but these names are not among them. A Miss Wood was matron from 1923 until 1947 but of course there were others to stand in or 'act up' on occasions. There is little shown to date this rare view more precisely than sometime between the wars, perhaps even earlier. (*Author's collection*)

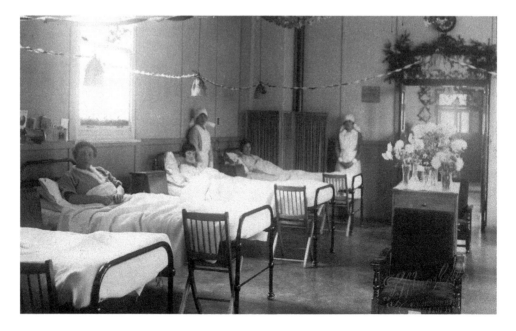

A scene at Christmas time in the female ward, dated 1927. (*Swindon Central Library – local studies collection*)

mattress on the floor; I remember I felt very sick. Mother came to collect me after a few hours.

A hefty 6,840 casualties were recorded in 1931; I wonder what proportion were industrial injuries from inside the Works. X-Ray examinations were limited to minimise the exposure of radiation to the radiographer. The average number of MFS paying members during 1931 was 14,827 (plus 2,680 retired and widowed members), a figure that was lower than normal because of a depleted workforce due to the economic depression. Another consequence of the times was a reduction in the fees received from the Wiltshire Health Insurance Committee, which in turn led to cuts in Society staff wages and salaries. Both were fully restored by 1935 but the Medical Fund hospital continued to have problems. The Superintendent Medical Officer's report for 1936 made the following observations: 1) 'Too many patients are still being sent to other hospitals due to lack of accommodation'; 2) on the position of the hospital: 'It is situated in a very low lying and noisy part of the town and does not afford that restful atmosphere necessary to recuperation of patients.' Throughout the 1930s, a large sign hung on a redundant tram line post outside saying: 'QUIET PLEASE – HOSPITAL'. The nurses' accommodation, too, said the SMO: 'Left a lot to be desired.'

In the last full year of its independence, 1947, the MFS had 42,656 members. The annual membership figures now included dependants who were eligible but did not include those still to be demobilised. Nurses were in short supply in 1947 because of ongoing commitments abroad. The total expenditure for that year exceeded income by £10,018 according to the annual report. The previous year they had shown a profit of £315. The committee decided against increasing the subscription and to fall back on reserves until the takeover by the National Health Service the following July. This, the original Great Western Hospital, closed in 1960.

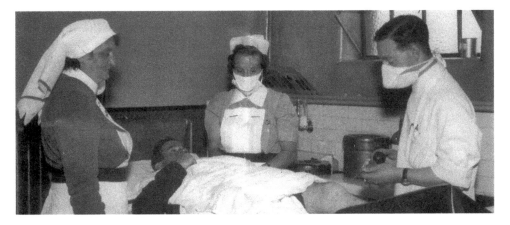

A patient about to undergo a minor procedure in the small operating theatre of the Surgical Outpatients Department. This photo was taken after the war and may be after the introduction of 'free health care' on the NHS. (*Author's collection*)

CHAPTER 11

The Works' Fire Brigade and the On-Call Arrangements

It had been decided quite early on that the Works could not rely entirely on the town fire service and sometime before 1900 they set up their own brigade. It covered not only the Works but also the GWR Estate, the Junction Station, the Transfer Goods Depot and all the yards in between. If a fire was discovered, the Works Fire Station was called on 2098 and the location given. Alternatively, the exchange was called and the operator would take details and pass them on: there were two different ways of contacting the Works operator in the 1930s, depending on whether the caller was using the old or new pattern phone. The full-time firemen acted as 'watchroom attendants' round the clock, supplemented by part-timers at weekends. During the working day, part-timers could be summoned from their place of work via the telephone exchange; in later days they carried bleepers. Out of hours they were on-call seven days then seven days off. If needed, the fireman in the station would call the men on-call that week, the 'A' list, starting with the chief or his assistant. Men could be called individually or as a group by pressing buttons on the call board. A loud bell would go off in the appropriate houses in the railway estate; a total of sixteen houses were connected to the station. Each had a wooden stud wall known as 'the partition' between the two bedrooms and the bell was fixed to it. Six rings was the code for a fire. The men then had to get to the station and change into their uniforms, leather boots and brass helmets. The latter changed sometime before the war to rubber boots and black resin helmets, the ornate brass ones being kept for competitions only.

If additional men were required, there was a 'B list' and for major incidents even a 'C list' of retained firemen. The call boy might have to cycle out to other districts of the town to knock up men on the 'C' list out of hours. Eight men were called at a time and during the war an extra team of part-timers was recruited. After the war they struggled to keep pre-war numbers and the rule that 'A' and 'B' men must live in 'the estate' was dropped. The 6s 6d call out money had become less of an incentive, so it was doubled. Ian Sawyer was a part-time fireman in the 1950s and he still has a list of personnel from the station. It shows there were three regulars, nine who worked in the station workshop and another nineteen part timers. A surviving document shows that for the year 1958 there were seventy-one fire calls.

Detailed maps showing the layout of the whole area and all the water supplies, including the fire points, were kept in the Fire Station. They showed that each backway behind the company houses had two hydrants and the streets mostly had firepits, sometimes called ground hydrants. These had a cast iron cover which was

This 1912 Dennis fire pump, No. 10, was superseded in 1942 but retained until 1956. Ian Sawyer remembers the 1942 engine being used to pump out a flooded service tunnel: 'It was working continuously for three days: I think that's what finally finished it off,' he said. (*GWR*)

lifted off to reveal a well with a mains valve. This was turned on with a long-handled 'T' spanner and water flooded the well. Hoses with weighted ends were placed in the water and drew it up when the pump was started. Two motorised fire engines were available at anytime; the 1942 engine could pump about 450 gallons a minute.

Cyril Moulden, Eric Carter and Bill Grace among others worked in a workshop next to the Station, checking and repairing fire equipment. In BR days, 5,000 extinguishers a year were reconditioned and all the hoses were checked annually. Some of this was unskilled and some skilled work, but all the men were part-time firemen. Other part-timer firemen in the 1950s included Jimmy Little ('L2' Shop), 'Budgie' Pretlove (C&W Stores), Ron Adams (T Shop), and 'Charlie' Bowering (Brass Foundry Foreman). When on-call firemen were in the Cricketers or the Glue Pot public houses, the kids would have to stay at home in case a 'shout went out'. Bert Harber's father was also a part-time fireman, 'Bert' said: 'As kids we soon got used to the night alarm bell ringing and by the morning we couldn't say whether it had gone off or not. Even during the day we could not remember whether it had gone five minutes later.' The bell was tested every day at 1 p.m., just one ring, and a fire drill was carried out once a month. Full-timers employed over the years included Percy Moulden, Jessie Collett, Frank Baker, Sid Smith, Horace Jones, Les New and chief Ray Sealy. They worked either 6 a.m. to 2 p.m., 2 p.m. to 10 p.m. or 10 p.m. to 6 a.m. Colin Bown earned a couple of extra shillings on top of his apprentice wages by cycling round all the fire engine routes in the factory and seeing that they were kept clear.

Colin was born in Bathampton Street in the railway estate; two nights later, his father was out fighting a serious fire nearby. Late on Christmas Eve it was discovered that the Mechanics' Institute in Emlyn Square was ablaze. It started in or near the

The Swindon fire fighting competition team in 1953. After the war they were regular winners of the five-man trailer pump inter-regional shield and the Westinghouse cup. Right to left: Sid Smith, Bert Harber, Art O'Farrell, Jimmy Little, Jessie Collett, Ron Adams, Charlie Bowering and Ray Sealy (the chief officer). (*Ian Sawyer collection*)

stage of the theatre on the first floor. Later it was said the fire was due to a faulty electrical fuse. Sawdust, no doubt from the Carriage Works, had been packed under the stage to dampen the noise during the performances. This accelerated the spread of the blaze and the weather hampered efforts to bring it under control. Bill Bown told his son years later: 'It was terrible weather that Christmas of 1930, people in nearby homes brought out hot water to try to thaw the firepit covers and hoses before we could use them.' It was 7 a.m. the next morning when the firemen from the Works and the town brigades finally left the scene. The fire bell rang twenty-four times that night in Bert Harber's house as more and more calls for assistance went out. A brief entry in the Loco Works petty cash book shows that an outlay of 10½*d* covered milk and sugar for the firemen during that long night. No mention of the fire at the Mechanics' was made in the GW staff magazine, although they did a piece about the MI library shortly afterwards. Colin remembers his dad saying the extension and tower added after the fire incorporated new fire safety features in the design.

Colin said:

As kids we would run out and watch the fire engine turn out to a fire. It was fitted with a device which worked off the exhaust and sounded like a klaxon siren. I think

it was invented by Mr C. T. Cuss who was the fire chief (or captain) in the 1920s and 30s: he was also an Assistant Works' Manager. Later when employed 'inside' I always worried I might be in the tunnel when the engine came through with the siren going. When the new Dennis engine of 1942 was first used, we thought there was something wrong with it. As it went down Bristol Street into Sheppard Street the bell seemed to work only intermittently and the engine kept cutting out. When father, who was aboard, came home later he said Tom Kench was supposed to flick a switch to activate the siren but kept turning off the ignition instead, much to the annoyance of the driver, Mr Sealy. The elevated water tank in the Fire Station yard provided the water to fight fires in 'the estate'. In wartime a look-out post was built just underneath the tank for the firewatchers, before that they had to climb up on the top of the tank. Father told me he could see the glow from the bombing of Bristol from there one night.

Because of the size of the site and the particular fire risk of some buildings, it was essential that the Works had a motorised brigade. That other large GWR centre, Paddington, also had its own brigade. The Works Fire Station was positioned near the most vulnerable buildings: the large Sawmill and the workshops that built new carriages. However, the fire engine route to get to them and other parts of the site was a roundabout one. These buildings had overhead sprinklers fitted shortly after the Paint Shop fire of 1911. Various types were used depending on the risk; they worked with a bulb containing a chemical or gas that expanded or exploded when the temperature went up. Water was released onto a deflector plate, spraying it outwards in all directions. The resulting loss of pressure in the main activated one of the alarms on the Fire Station callboard, showing where the fire was. Fire was indeed a real threat

Vehicles in the Fire Station in the 1950s. Far left is the back end of the major trailer pump; then the bonnet of the Bedford 'shooting brake' which brought on-call staff in from home; beyond that the Ford ambulance, which was soon to be replaced by a 15hp Morris model; then the '1942 Dennis'; and at the far end the Austin Champ. The Champ arrived in 1956; it had a Rolls Royce engine and finally allowed the 1912 Dennis engine to be taken out of use. Electric cables, which charged the vehicles' batteries, can be seen hanging from above. (*Ian Sawyer collection*)

here: the 'carriage side' Carpenters' Shop was gutted in the early 1930s and had to be completely rebuilt in 1934.

The Works telephone directory for 1935 shows that the Bodymakers' Shop had their own watchman. It is likely that he patrolled this and perhaps the other nearby shops as an extra fire precaution. Another serious fire started in the hair carding building and spread to the adjoining Carriage Carpenters' Shop on 22 May 1945. The Carding Shop recycled horse hair from carriage seats – a machine combed it out and washed it; official figures say 338 tons a year was being dealt with in the late 1940s. It was said that a cigarette had been discarded and lay smouldering over the weekend even though smoking was forbidden in and around these areas. The watchman's 'tell tale' clock proved he had completed his rounds, which included unlocking the Carding House door to check for fire. When he opened the door at 2 a.m. on the Monday, he said the drought ignited some horse hair. This and some of the adjoining buildings were eventually gutted and some carriages were destroyed. Colin Kibblewhite and carpenters from D Shop spent months there re- roofing and refitting the inside. The cost to put right the damage was worked out, for insurance purposes, to be £3,800; this did not include lost production and the use of an alternative site to continue the work. The new carriage Paint Shop near 'Webb's entrance' also had a major fire, in the 1950s. As well as inflammable paint, this shop used cellulose, which was sprayed on panels and fittings of carriage interiors.

Erector Jim Lowe said he often saw the men from the Fire Station around A Shop in the late 1950s. They made up the coolant and antifreeze supplied by the laboratory and it was pumped into new diesel engines by the Austin Champ. They also came round periodically, weighing all fire extinguishers to check for leakage. The copper extinguishers with their brass fittings had all been made in the Works. Jim also said that the managers would leave their motor cars in the Fire Station yard. He said that fire staff would clean them and if necessary mechanics from the Internal Transport Depot would work on them. This area had been used for managers' vehicles since before the war and it is possible this unofficial arrangement was nothing new.

The Fire Station call board was also used to summon breakdown crews and maintenance men out of normal working hours. In this case, the man in the Fire Station would contact the call-boy. A young Colin Bown was rostered to cycle round and knock up staff on-call, several bicycles being kept in the station for this purpose. Colin said:

Mr Philpott the G Shop maintenance foreman who lived in Dean Street told his men to call him as well if they were required. We were always told to rap the knocker several times but he always seemed to have the front door open before you finished knocking. As a senior first-aider my dad [Bill Bown] would be called if a medical emergency occurred in his part of the Works. After hours he also took his turn on-call with the motor ambulance and a driver. Most of the firemen were ambulance trained and went out on medical emergencies too. The bell code put out for them by the Fire Station was two rings, a pause then two rings. I found out by accident years later that the ambulance had a timber frame: I welded a steel plate to the chassis and it caught alight. Others close by yelled at me as I hadn't noticed the flames, then

The Platelayers' Shop women's fire fighting team. Left to right: Doreen Guy from Birch Street, Rachael Scarrott from Tilleys Lane, Nora Wilkins from Wootton Bassett, 'Dot' Grimes from Oxford Street. This photograph was taken at a studio near Woolworths one Saturday in about 1943. (*Dorothy Cook*)

ran for it leaving me to find the extinguisher before the petrol tank 'went up'. In the days before they had the Ford ambulance they took out a stretcher mounted about four feet off the ground on cane wheels called a 'litter'. For me to remember it, this appliance must have been in use well into the 1930s.

If an accident or subsidence damaged the track somewhere on the system, it needed immediate attention. The permanent way and civil engineers' people in the affected division would repair the main line but they might have to ring the Works at Swindon to supply points and crossing trackwork. A damaged road at a running shed stopping locomotives coming in or out was one thing the CME Department had to deal with immediately. X Shop made right or left hand 'turnouts' and 'crossovers' from blank rail: they machined it, shaped it and fixed it to tieplates and sleepers as complete assemblies. An incoming call would be received, stating a code for the type required. The man in the Fire Station would call the X Shop foreman, who would go and open up the shop, then get the staff on-call in. Once the section of track was made up, the transport driver would be called. This type of emergency was usually only carried out during the war years because of bomb damage. Depots too would sometimes need wheels or axleboxes due to loco or carriage breakdown. These could usually wait until they could be sent by rail.

The station register shows that in the first week of December 1956 the ambulance went out on four occasions; a fitter or electrician was called out three times for the Central Boiler Station and twice for the Oxygen Plant; Manager Smith was taken to the King's Arms Hotel; and the 1912 fire engine was dispatched to the Curator of Historical Relics, Clapham.

Dorothy Grimes left school in the late 1930s and worked as a shop assistant. In the early 1940s she was told she would be needed for war work:

> They offered me a start at either Vickers Armstrong [Phillips & Powis Ltd until 1941] or the 'Western', I chose the latter because it was nearer home. I went into the Works Fire Station on £3 a week replacing a Freddie Aplin who went into the army. The station dealt with all hoses, whether fire or otherwise. I was assembling new or repaired flexible train hoses and locomotive coal watering pipes which were 5 feet 6 inches and 6 feet 6 inches in length. The ribbed steam heating and vacuum pipes were cut to length, connections fitted and clips tightened. We rolled the diamond pattern on the brass ferrule collars using a 'honking' [knurling] machine. The Platelayers' Shop looked after the water supplies around the Works including those with which fires would be fought so they had close links with us in the Fire Station. Several men in the Platelayers' Shop were part-time firemen and Ray Sealy the fire chief oversaw the work there, as foreman. About five girls worked in our shop; all our administration was done from the PL–Platelayers' Shop and we had PL check numbers as well. The work caused blisters on my hands and I asked the women's welfare officer if she could get me moved. I wanted to be a machine operator in E Shop because they were on piecework, but I was turned down. Reg Redwood, Sid Pugh, Doreen Guy, Jean Thorn and Rachael Scarrott were on my section; the chargeman was Sid Eburne. Vera Edwards whose family ran the funfair business, worked with me, she was allowed to work part time. Two other girls worked on fire extinguishers in Bert Speck's section.
>
> The Fire Station and the PL Shop formed several fire fighting teams which was to teach us to deal with air raids, should they come.

Swindon was always the host for the trailer pump competitions held in the Bristol division and judging was done by Wilts Fire Service officials. An all-line competition was held annually from 1942; two years later, it included all four British railway companies. 'The various fire drills were judged on speed and we had a ten second penalty when our team was made up of full time firemen,' said Bert Harber. The men's teams were either three or five-man; the two women teams only did extinguisher drills and did not have to pull large pumps and equipment about. Women in the Fire Station teams were Nora Wilkins, a clerk in the Fire Station/Platelayers' Shop, Doreen, Rachael and Dorothy. Mr Sealy's daughter-in-law Rose stepped in when Dorothy went down with appendicitis. Rose Sealy worked as a tractor driver in the 'Western'. Dorothy continued 'inside' because of the labour shortages after the war until she married at St Mark's Church in 1947. She then wrote and 'got a release' from the railway factory in December that year. The newlyweds lived with Dorothy's parents in Emlyn Square for about a year until they got their own place, not an uncommon situation in those days.

CHAPTER 12

Wartime Work

Air raid precautions were being put into effect in the Works during the period immediately before and after war was declared in 1939. Much of the Works was built on land higher than the town and an extensive network of pedestrian and service tunnels ran between the two and beneath the railway which divided the site into three. Those working near to a suitable tunnel used it as a shelter; for others, blast-proof shelters were built. The blackout precautions caused problems because as well as all the windows, a lot of roofing was glass so as to make the most of the natural light. A black paint was used for the workshops, and not just those that had a night shift, so everyone now worked under dimmed lighting. Blacking out the workshops commenced shortly after the outbreak of war. Later, some of the paint was removed in favour of blinds which could be opened during the hours of daylight. At depots, locomotives that had side windows had them plated over. Tarpaulin sheets, too, were fitted between tender and cab roofs to stop glare from the fire after dark. The materials were prepared and sent out from Swindon Works.

'Dean Goods' 0-6-0 tender engines were to be made ready for the War Department to send overseas. Nine of the class that had been recently withdrawn were also included in the plan. The work included removing the automatic train control apparatus and replacing the vacuum brakes with Westinghouse air brakes. Fifteen were dealt with at Eastleigh and eventually more than ninety at Swindon. The same class had been chosen to be sent to France in the First World War and some of the same engines were to go again. It had also been planned to build a large batch of the modified 28xx class 2-8-0s to send to the Continent, but with the fall of France in 1940 the order was reduced and none were sent. This Churchward design modified by Collett was the company's principal heavy freight locomotive. They were built in batches until 1942, by which time the government's War Department decided that a standard 2-8-0 freight type based on the LMS 8F would be built by all the largest locomotive factories, including Swindon. Although locomotives did not generally stray from one company's territory to another, this was not their first experience of these LMS engines. Twenty-five had been loaned to the GWR earlier in the war and they had converted others to burn oil for use overseas.

Before the war began, the Carriage Works started preparing certain rolling stock for the anticipated conditions ahead. For air raids 'Siphon G' milk vans and 'brake third' coaches were converted and made up into casualty evacuation trains. The idea was that if local medical services became overwhelmed, the trains could move casualties to

A Sunday morning or weekday evening parade of the GWR Home Guard company in 1940. The location is between two of the carriage body shops, probably No. 7 and 8, south of the main line; if so, the Carriage Painting Shop, soon to be converted for war production, can be seen in the background. Mr S. A. Dyer, a member of the CME's personal staff, commanded the GWR company throughout its four-and-a-half-year existence. As lieutenant colonel, he led 'the factory' men who signed up as Local Defence Volunteers in May 1940 following an appeal by the Secretary of State to the nation. In 1943, on account of its growing strength and importance, the GWR company broke away from the 5th battalion to form the 13th Wilts battalion, with its headquarters at 3 Emlyn Square and hutments in Church Place.

A lot of the elderly recruits who grew up in Victorian times had a strict Christian upbringing. Some objected to Home Guard methods designed to defend their homeland and men who refused to train were called to account. In 1943, the local evening paper reported the hearing of a GWR Swindon man who objected to learning how to kill or take part at all on Sundays. He said that 'quiet on a Sunday was necessary to building up of the Christian character' but failed to gain exemption.

According to the official history, the GWR Home Guard's primary objective was: 'The defence of the railway works against attack. Its operational role was somewhat limited, but as the perimeter of The Works, Station and yards was, to a large extent the north and west perimeter of the town, it was possible without difficulty to incorporate it into the general town scheme. The new battalion expanded rapidly, but never lost its identity as the GWR Battalion, and when a drumhead service was held on the County Ground it was possible to put five full companies on parade.' It goes on to say that at the time of standing down in late 1944 those five companies comprised 50 officers, 932 other ranks and approximately 1,300 weapons of all kinds. (*GWR*)

hospitals elsewhere. The Railway Executive, the government's controlling committee for British railways in wartime, required the GW to convert six train sets for casualty use. Eighteen LMS coaches also arrived at the Works to be turned into ambulance trains for use at home and overseas; the US Army took possession of these at a small ceremony outside the Works in 1943. Three fire-fighting trains were made ready, again by converting ordinary stock. As part of the anti-gas measures, other passenger coaches were converted to mobile decontamination units; they were painted yellow and fitted with steel shutters. There was a real fear that the Germans would use gas against Britain but this did not happen. Swindon men working 'outstation' at the carriage depots blacked out some windows of ordinary passenger stock. They also fitted all the carriage lamps with shades, which were made in the Carriage Works.

From 1940, blood collection centres were set up periodically in workshops and offices. At this time the demand from regional hospitals was great and so was the willingness to give. Dr Darmady from the Army Blood Transfusion Service in Bristol wrote to Mr Collett and Mr Cook. Part of his letter said: 'I am informed that the number of donors obtained [at Swindon Works], 3,443, shows a greater proportion than any so far obtained from a large works anywhere in the south-west of England.' Under Civil Defence measures, local factories including the Railway Works could be used as mortuaries if large numbers of civilians were killed by enemy action. Provisions were made for roof spotters to be positioned on top of Works buildings as part of the ARP measures. The famous Works hooter was now used to warn of enemy aircraft in the area instead of heralding the beginning and end of the shifts. Mr Millard in the Hooter House said that between 1940 and 1944 the hooter blew nearly a thousand times. Klaxon horns were installed around the site and a system of wall-mounted lights was rigged up in workshops and offices. A blue coloured bulb lit up when the hooter blew; if it changed to the red bulb alongside, it meant enemy planes had been spotted and everyone was to go to the shelters.

Representatives and prominent industrialists from the Ministry of Supply visited the Works to assess the potential for making armaments. They were, according to company publicity after the war, amazed at the range of manufacturing facilities available. One said the Tool Room was 'second only to those of the tip top aircraft firms'. At first the CME, Mr Collett, managed to resist the outside work being put his way by the Ministry of Prodution. All such additional work would have to be done by cutting back on normal wartime work activity and he believed the importance of maintaining an efficient railway should not be underestimated in times of war. There was little doubt they had a vital role as it was, but the Works' facilities were considerable and armament and ammunition work had to go somewhere. Other railway factories were taking on war work and their men were getting overtime, so the Works Committee as well as the government was leaning on Mr Collett to conform. This, together with the desperate situation unfolding in 1940, would eventually override the resistance.

Most of the war work was to be making parts or carrying out specialist operations on components for other firms. Where carriage underframes and bogies had been assembled, field gun carriage assembly lines were now laid out. Axles and brakework for the 25-pounder guns were made in the Carriage Fitting Shop and special grade cast iron brake drums were made in the Loco Works Foundry. After he retired, Mr Johnson the C&W Manager would tell a story on occasions about artillery guns that were made at Swindon during the First World War but never used. He said they were discovered and sent back to Swindon for the fitting of recoil and non-recoil mountings and used in the Second World War.

Machine tool chucks and tooling were altered on the loco side for operations necessary to convert rough forgings into fully machined shells. Shells of 9.2 calibre were produced to high standard according to government inspectors. Orders from ICI (Metals) among others required the Works to produce copper shell bands that caused the shells to spin and keep them on a true trajectory. The copper tube normally used could not be supplied so discs of half an inch thickness were heated, pressed and cold drawn, then parted on a lathe. Most of this work was done using female labour. From 1940, bombs were manufactured here too; the GWR staff magazine says of the types made:

The general trend was a progressive increase in size to keep pace with the advancing technique of aerial warfare. At first two classes of bomb were undertaken: one was

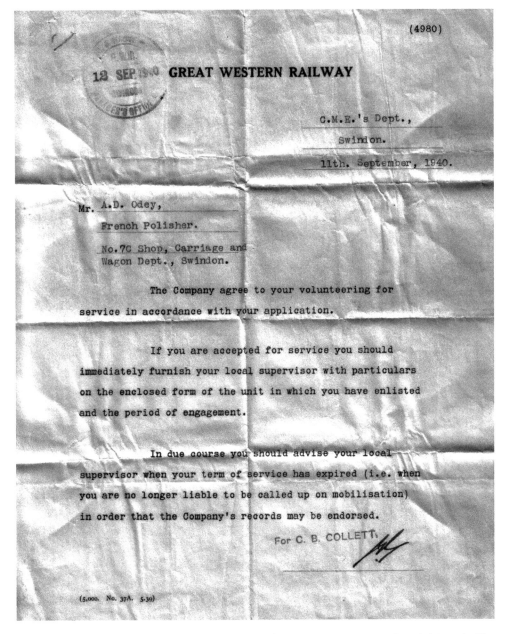

(4980)

12 SEP 1940 **GREAT WESTERN RAILWAY**

C.M.E.'s Dept.,

Swindon.

11th. September, 1940.

Mr. A.D. Odey,

French Polisher.

No.7C Shop, Carriage and
Wagon Dept., Swindon.

The Company agree to your volunteering for service in accordance with your application.

If you are accepted for service you should immediately furnish your local supervisor with particulars on the enclosed form of the unit in which you have enlisted and the period of engagement.

In due course you should advise your local supervisor when your term of service has expired (i.e. when you are no longer liable to be called up on mobilisation) in order that the Company's records may be endorsed.

For C. B. COLLETT,

(5,000. No. 37A. 5-39)

French polisher Albert Odey wrote and volunteered to 'go to war' in 1940: here is his reply. The men in the Works would soon find themselves in a reserved occupation. However, the country needed more and more men and women for war service, so the Ministry of Labour had to amend the schedule of reserved occupations. They increased the age of 'call up' by one year from the beginning of 1942; the minimum age was lowered to 17½ soon after.

Roy Bown had become a skilled blacksmith during the early part of the war and like many young men 'inside' he wanted to go and fight for his country. Many of his workmates had joined up but now he found himself in a 'reserved occupation'. Roy's father had been a pilot officer in the last war and no doubt his stories impressed the youngster greatly. Mr Bown senior wrote to the Air Ministry on his son's behalf; this did the trick and Roy joined the RAF as air crew. Later, when they found out about his occupation in Civvy Street, he was grounded and had his blacksmith's skills put to good use on maintenance work. This did not please Roy but, with so many bomber aircraft being shot down, it may well have saved his life. (*Mrs B. Wynn*) a 3 inch trench mortar bomb, forged from steel bar and machined in the Carriage Fitting Shop, very largely by women workers: of these 60,000 were high explosive and 11,000 were smoke pattern bombs: the other was a 250-pound high explosive bomb for aircraft, of which 33,000 were manufactured. Each line of production for the larger bombs comprised of: five lathes, two other machines, a varnishing oven and assembly benches. Suitable machines were selected from various depots and works and brought to Swindon for tooling and fitting up. One plant was erected in the Points and Crossings' Shop.

The Boiler Shop had no backlog of work at the start of the war and the Ministry of Supply were quick to take advantage of this. They negotiated a large contract of plating for Daimler light-wheeled tanks or armoured cars. Jigs were produced to drill the steel plates; they were then heated and quenched in oil to make them tough enough to resist bullets. The tricky part was to avoid distortion because once hardened they could not then be corrected. The contract stipulated they be tested on site using a rifle range and this was set up near the V Boiler Shop. One of the last jobs undertaken for the Ministry was for 5,600 shackles for the Merchant Navy in October 1944. By now, a lot of munitions were being supplied by specialist firms here and in America and production plant in 'the factory' had started to be taken out.

At the start of the war, the total workforce was already lower than it had been since the height of the Depression – somewhere around 11,000. Of the large number of discharges announced the previous year, many were rescinded or the men taken back.

An emergency canteen built in the Carriage Works in 1941, presumably in 17 (road vehicle) Shop. Its purpose was: 'To provide the company's staff with snacks and hot and cold drinks at popular prices where feeding arrangements have been temporarily disorganised' due to the air raids. The canteen trailer was designed by the company's Road Transport Department at Slough. It had all the facilities of a modern kitchen and serving area and could be put on a train and quickly taken to where it was needed. (*GWR Magazine*)

Eventually, young females were brought in to work day shifts and replace the men being called up. As with munitions work, 'the factory' was slow to take (or receive) women workers, although in this case the fault probably lay more with the Ministry of Labour than with the Works. Initially brought in for repetitive munitions work, some females were soon moved to railway work proper: a fair indication that they were gaining the trust of their overseers. They were tried on overhead cranes, steam hammers and various work in the two Boiler Shops. The latter included cutting the flue tubes to length and expanding them onto tubeplates and removing and replacing boiler stays. Much of the boilermakers' work required the use of specialist heavy machinery. Later, women were put on night shifts as well. It was soon recognised that women rivet hotters complained the most; not only was this hot work, but noisy and dirty too.

Two sisters from Percy Street went 'inside' in 1941: Elma Howard went into the Boiler Shop and Phyllis Howard into the Smiths' Shop as a steam hammer driver. A third sister, Violet, worked out on the permanent way, cleaning then oiling the points with the Engineering Department (Elma is the female seen in the photographs on pages 27 and 30 of *Working at Swindon Works*). With this integration, there was bound to be some lasting relationships formed. The staff magazine reported that L. Collard and Miss Durbridge, both of the Iron Foundry, were married in 1943. Another was Reg Arthurs, a Coremaker also in the Foundry; he married a crane driver named Violet. Those who opposed women in the Works would point out that as soon as they became useful, many left to be married.

Jack Fleetwood said that the women made good overhead crane drivers but one needed to get her confidence, so they put her on nights where it was quieter. She told Jack she once moved a locomotive boiler in V Shop and clipped another, sending a row of upended boiler shells over like skittles. Facilities to accommodate women were provided and later expanded between 1941 and early 1943. Cloakrooms, lavatories and mess rooms were installed in the following shops: boilermakers; boiler repairs;

A partially erected three-ton electric crane, seen here at one of the company's south Wales ports. These ports were considered safer from attack than those on the east coast and consequently their sea-borne traffic increased. Thirty-four additional cranes were required here and normally Stothard and Pitt of Bath would take on the contract, but like everyone else they were working flat out already. Swindon was responsible for the mechanical work at the docks so they undertook to build all the cranes using drawings supplied by the designers. The cranes stood on travelling gantries and with the jib in position they were 94 feet high. The part-built structures could just stand under the lofty roof of the Boiler (AV) Shop. (*GWR*)

points and crossings; brass finishers; steam hammers; oil works; coppersmiths and tinsmiths; and all three foundries. After the war a lot of women in the workshops were kept on, due mainly to the slow process of getting men demobilised. They had initially been treated with suspicion and sometimes hostility but: 'When the men did get back from the war it was the unions and not their male colleagues who wanted them out,' said Alan Lambourn.

The Works' holiday trains were cancelled at the 'last minute' in 1940 and until further notice. The Borough Council then had the job of getting people to spend their summer holidays within the town. The GWR magazine said at the start of the first 'holidays at home' season in 1942: 'Swindon has become the playground of Wiltshire.' The Council arranged an impressive programme with orchestras, brass bands, open air shows, variety concerts, an eisteddfod, music festivals and sport. Swindon's famous Edwards' Fair spent six weeks in the Park in 1942 and returned again the following year. Fred Drinkwater, a chargeman in the Weigh House, was the town mayor in 1944. He wrote a forward for the 'holidays at home' programme that year:

> My Council are again providing attractions and entertainment with a view to encouraging the people of Swindon to spend their holiday at home. The restrictions on travel are well known, particularly in a railway centre such as Swindon, and it is hoped that the public will readily respond by avoiding unnecessary travel and thus release rolling stock for essential war purposes.

By the middle of the war, the Swindon workshops were building up to 4,500 new wagons a year and repairing another 20,000. The availability of wagons had been a headache for the authorities from the start and they were now all classed as 'common user'. This eased the problem by allowing wagons to be reused after arrival, regardless

A female wartime worker pressing super-heater copper joints in 1942. (*GWR*)

Locomotive frames for new LMS-designed 8Fs at various stages of assembly in A Shop, 1943. A hydraulic riveter hangs from an electric crane and beyond that a gun mounting is being built. (*GWR*)

of who owned them, instead of being returned, perhaps empty, to the company of origin. The company's road vehicles too were similarly pooled for collection and delivery services. Swindon was required to speed up the turnaround time of goods wagon repairs and they introduced a 'green card' system. Three roads alongside the huge 21 (Wagon Builders) Shop would be used for light repairs to bodywork and flooring; each road held thirty wagons. Inside, the five long roads could hold twenty-five open or covered vehicles and heavier repairs would be carried out here. On the south side of the building, a further nine roads would be used for complete overhaul with facilities for lifting and re-roofing wagons. Restrictions had already been implemented regarding the repainting and lettering, which continued. This was done for two reasons: 1) some pigments in paints were scarce; and 2) many painters had been called up or transferred to other work. Now, also, priority would be given to vehicles needing light repairs. Up to 500 wagons of all kinds were soon being 'turned around' each week under the green card system. 'Patching up' rolling stock and locomotives would leave the company with an increasing amount of stock that would eventually need heavy repairs or withdrawal but in the short term it served its purpose.

Mr Bishop had been chief foreman of the polishing, coach finishing and bodymaking shops since they were amalgamated in 1934. Mr Barrat, who lived in Broad Street, took over from him in early 1941. He was then in charge of seven areas, including three sections of polishers, a small stores and a sawmill. There were junior foremen but Mr Barrat oversaw the whole of the building and internal furnishing of carriage bodies and their subsequent repairs. In wartime these workshops took on more and more carriage work connected with the extraordinary fitting out for total war. New vehicle building was suspended from 1942 and Mr Barrat's men were converting coaches to form ambulance trains for use at home and overseas. They produced mobile fire-fighting vehicles and US Army HQ personnel vehicles as well as rebuilding carriages damaged by enemy action. In 7 Shop, the finishers built wooden models and superstructures for the Admiralty. Upon Mr Barrat's retirement after 46 years' service, it was stated that he had 518 men and women in his charge. This was in January 1945, when numbers were depleted due to men being away on war service.

Work indirectly connected to the 'national emergency' included ongoing machine tool renewal and the conversion of gas lighting to electric. Later, 'the factory' was busy converting electrical equipment from DC to AC. Much of the electrical work was sub-contracted but the expected benefits were hampered because of the limited supply of electricity from the corporation power station. Some ambulance trains sent overseas had been captured by the enemy and in the autumn of 1944 had been recaptured; 15 Shop were required to build nine pairs of bogies and 16 Shop twenty-seven pairs of wheels and axles, to be sent out for them. A different kind of wartime job at this time was to be done in 19 Shop according to the new work orders. They were to prepare a condemned goods brake van for use as accommodation for Italian POWs at Exeter Goods Depot. The cost of this was estimated to be £17.

Colin Kibblewhite provided a detailed and valuable account of the work done by D Shop carpenters during the war. When Colin was thirteen, his parents bought him a set of secondhand carpenter's tools for Christmas; he was keen on carpentry and it was hoped it would prepare him for such work 'inside'. Mr Kibblewhite senior was a boilermaker in 'the factory' and 'outstation' and he was told his son could choose from machining or moulding, on the loco side. A week prior to him starting, however, the Loco Works Manager, Mr K. J. Cook, queried the type of tools he could provide on his application form:

He noticed they were wood working tools, in which case I was to learn carpentry and joinery. This was 1938 and I would work in B Shop for the 15 months before my 16th birthday and the start of my training. On my first day though, I was directed to the Tube House where blank boiler flue tubes were machined. I was to be a 'tube expander's mate' for three weeks, helping Fred Smith and another fella whose name I can't recall. Using hydraulic machines we stretched one end of the tube so it would fit into the steel tubeplate at the front of a locomotive boiler: the other end which fitted into the copper backplate, was reduced. After that I did go to B Shop, still called by its original name of B Shed by the men. I worked with a gang of three boilermakers as 'rivet boy' on small engine and tender tanks. Harry Harris and senior man Sid Eatwell were riveters; Walter Ford was the 'holder up' and I heated the rivets on a

During late 1943 and the early part of 1944, it was well known that the country was 'on the eve of major military operations' – what we now know was the invasion of mainland Europe. This appeal was issued to every GWR man and women in March 1944, reminding them of the hazards of 'careless talk'. Details of their day-to-day work, especially the movement of government goods traffic, might be useful to the enemy, it warned. This particular copy was issued to Peter Oland of A Shop stores. (*Author's collection*)

GREAT WESTERN RAILWAY.

Circular No. 3658

G.1/I.D.234

GENERAL MANAGER'S OFFICE,

PADDINGTON STATION, LONDON, W.2.

10th March, 1944.

SECURITY

It is common knowledge that we are on the eve of major military operations and, as with previous campaigns, the element of surprise will be of vital importance in these new operations

In the past the staff have fully co-operated in keeping secret the movements of military personnel, equipment and stores, and other Government traffics, not only to and from the ports but between other places in the country. There was no suggestion of careless talk by railwaymen in connection with the considerable movements of troops and munitions for the North African and Italian Campaigns and the advantages of surprise were secured.

The major movements which may be expected in the near future call for the greatest care on the part of each one of us to avoid passing on to anybody any information which may come to our notice. In sending this reminder, I am confident that each of you will be constantly on your guard against any action which might give the slightest assistance to the enemy.

DON'T discuss Government traffic movements, except where necessary in the course of your work.

DON'T discuss the types of traffic you may have seen or heard of.

DON'T, where telephoning is necessary, refer to traffic movements or enemy action in a manner which, if overheard, would give any information to enemy agents.

DON'T answer enquiries on the telephone on matters of this kind or take instructions unless you are satisfied of the identity of the caller and his authority to make enquiries.

DON'T pass on any information in your possession about enemy action, except where necessary in the course of your duties.

DON'T underestimate the value to enemy agents of any information which may be in your possession.

DON'T encourage others to talk to, or question you, on such matters

LT COL J. MILNE,

General Manager.

A copy of this circular to be handed to each member of the staff.

2583—3-44.

---

small forge. Another job I remember was helping Freddie Cockhead fit stiffening plates or patches to the horn ways of locomotive main frames. Cracks sometimes appeared from the corners where the axleboxes were held, after being in service for a time and seemed to be a weakness peculiar to GW engines. We fitted the horseshoe-shaped plates around the gaps with cold rivets or threaded studs.

In December 1939 I started my apprenticeship in D Shop after signing my indentures witnessed by Mr Gee, the Works Manager's Secretary. D Shop was near the Running Sheds and home to one lot of Works carpenters; the bricklayers too came under D Shop, they were known as D2 and had a building nearby. The CME Department carpentry work excluding carriage building was divided between D Shop or 12 Shop. The types of work allocated to each were changed just before the war: 12 Shop would manufacture and repair furniture, platform trolleys and wooden fixtures, etc throughout the company and D Shop would look after all the Works and mechanical outstation carpentry. Fred Gooding was our foreman and Bill Harper was the Bricklayers' (referred to as masons by the company) foreman. Jim Hayward had recently taken over from Joe Boots as head foreman. Other apprentices in our shop were Arnold Woolford, Bill Maynard, a lad by the name of Swatton and Arthur Halliday. D Shop carpenters were divided into five gangs; I was put on Bill Ayres' gang who normally refurbished the offices in the CME building. Bert Selwood was my mate for a short while, until he retired; he used to tell me about his time during the Boer War. Another gang maintained the managers'/pay office block and the shop offices under chargeman Fred Keen. This work was among the many types of non-essential maintenance that was put on hold so that internal and external war work could be done. One gang did carry on as normal but with fewer men: they worked with the loco erectors fitting the wooden floors on locomotive footplates. They also fitted elm boards into tenders in B Shop, onto which sat the tank before it was bolted to the frame.

When I first arrived some carpenters were fitting roller blinds in the offices as part of a programme of air raid precautions. After the blackout work I remember we had to crate up some machine tools which had arrived from Avonmouth Docks. They had been on route from America to France but the French surrendered before they got there. I think the machinery had some water damage so the Works were asked to check them over before sending them on to factories up north [Des Griffiths said that a machine tool from a ship's cargo was collected by his father who worked on the Internal Transport. This was, he said, bedded down in the Tool Room during the war so perhaps it was one of these]. As well as Bert and his half brother Cecil, Charlie Humphries and Bill Prior were in Ayres's gang; others had been called up [Years later, Charlie Humphries was editor of the *Swindon Railway News*]. We stripped and refurbished several offices upon the retirement of Chief Mechanical Engineer Mr Collett in July of 1941, including his former office. After the decorators had repainted the window frames and walls, we assessed the furniture, fitted cupboards and panelling and repaired or replaced as necessary. My job was to remove all the brass draw pulls, handles and locks, clean them and replace after the French polishers had finished.

It is interesting to hear that this type of work was still being done when much essential maintenance was being put off.

The Works' day shift continued to end at 5.30 p.m. in the shops, with the option of a couple of hours' overtime in the evening. To encourage men to stay on, the smoking ban was lifted from the start of 1940, but only after 5.30 p.m. and only in the shops where it was safe to do so. Later it was lifted altogether after threats by the men, backed by the Federation of Railway Trade Unions. As 'the factory' took on outside work for the Ministry of War Production, everybody, including apprentices, started working 12-hour days. Where the delivery time was short or where the order was large, the work continued day and night, the night shift also being 12 hours. D Shop men did not normally work at night, even during the war. Where the Works was doing government work, tighter conditions were observed. A person who was persistently late or absent would be given a warning by his shop committee; if this didn't work, the Ministry of Labour could take him or her to court under the Essential Work Order of 1941 and this did happen, albeit rarely. On the other hand, skilled workers were needed like never before and were therefore not easily sacked. The *Evening Advertiser* reported that a machine setter 'struck his foreman across the face' in 1943. He was arrested by the Works police and received a £2 fine but was not dismissed. The EWO Act also allowed the authorities to direct skilled labour to wherever it was most needed. D Shop men Fred Keen, Burt Bryant and others were sent to make concrete pillboxes and defences somewhere down south. They would make the wooden formwork or moulds to hold concrete until it set. For some reason, Colin, still a junior apprentice, remembers having to tell them of their temporary transfer.

Most non-railway war work was of iron and steel manufacture; the limited wood work that was undertaken was mainly confined to the Carriage Finishers' Shop. New coaches were not being built from 1942 and this shop – No.7, which normally fitted out new coaches with the internal timberwork – was turned over to war production. They made the now well publicised midget submarine superstructures and the wooden mock-up of a Besa machine gun. At the time this work was secret, particularly the submarines. During late 1941 and 1942, Colin Kibblewhite was spending a lot of time making and packing wooden cases for shells, bombs and armaments; they often reused material from incoming cargoes.

A gauge or part of a gauge used on the turret rings produced in 1941 and 1942. This was a large contract undertaken for the Ministry of Production: one of the first at the Works in this war. They were turned on wheel lathes in the A Wheel Shop then went to the Tool Room for gear cutting. On another face is stamped 1.4 +.197: this is the length of the gauge in inches on the vernier scale. Presumably this was an upper limit allowed on a turned recess cut around each ring: if the gauge fits into the recess, too much has been taken off. This was found in the Works in the 1980s.

One of the largest contracts undertaken was tank turret rings for various types of armoured cars. The Wheel Shops and others involved with them worked continuously, finish turning thirty or forty a week. The photograph on page 128 of my first book, *Working at Swindon Works*, shows the turret rings on a specially adapted gear cutting machine in O Shop, watched over by apprentice Maurice Parsons. He would centre each ring and clamp it down. The arbor moved on a vertical plane and the milling cutter produced the gaps to form the teeth on the internal diameter; after each cut, the work moved round by automatic indexing until 392 teeth had been cut. Once each ring was up and running, there should be no need to do anything except make sure it didn't come loose or a milling cutter break, or both. The operation took four or five hours, depending on the size of the turret ring, and Maurice was sometimes moved to other work while each was being machined, leaving a 'dilutee' or a less experienced apprentice to watch and hit the quick stop lever if something went wrong. At the end, one of the men would slide the mild steel ring towards them and lift it down to the ground by their shoulder and roll it away. A new cutting tool was then fitted for the next.

Doreen Dominey, who had been an evacuee from London and took employment 'inside' when she left school, was often required to watch this gear 'hobber'. She did not work nights, so then Maurice had to watch the work throughout himself: 'very boring', he said. On one night shift, he arranged to meet Doreen outside and take her out after setting a turret ring up and running. Being a motorcycle dispatch rider in his spare time, he had his own transport and took her up to Uffington White Horse. I said, 'Well, someone must have been keeping their eye on things at work,' but Maurice said not. Depleted numbers of carpenters boxed up the finished turret rings and they were sent to Birmingham for assembly. Mr K. J. Cook, the Loco Works Manager at the time, said:

> The cost of gear cutting with full toolroom overheads was £2 9s 6d per ring. In order to get the production up to the tank builders' requirements of fifty sets per week, it was necessary to place sub-contracts and the lowest quotation obtained from an outside firm was £11, ultimately reduced under pressure to £9 per ring.

By 1942 the Works were making all sorts of parts to fight the war, including shells, cutting tools for use at home and for outside firms, parts for aircraft, radar equipment and gun mountings. Another job for D Shop was making long wooden tables for production lines to produce shells in 24 (finishers' repairs) Shop. Only once did Colin go 'outstation' during the war; that was to Fishguard Harbour with a gang overhauling platform bridges. These were portable wooden crossings allowing people and cargoes to cross between the quay and station platforms quickly. They could be raised and lowered for storage by a jacking mechanism.

The O Shop Tool Room needed more space because the government Machine Tool Control placed additional machinery here. They did this for balancing purposes, to get the maximum out of the plant already there. The electricians had occupied the area where the new machines were going so they were moved into part of D Shop. Because of this, the carpenters' end of the shop was extended and Colin worked on the new roof timbers.

A female working a 10-cwt steam hammer in the late 1940s; she would have been taken on during the war then chose to stay on afterwards while there was a labour shortage. Many women proved to be good workers in the shops, not least those driving steam hammers and overhead cranes. (*BRW Magazine*)

Towards the end of 1942 I spent three weeks with the 'house maintenance gang', the chargeman's name was Bert somebody or other. They did any carpentry work required on the company houses and Medical Fund buildings. I made or repaired some 2-foot diameter covers which sat on top of kitchen coppers, in their workshop on the estate. One of the gang was making backrests for hospital beds, I remember. In 1943 I was back in the Works in Jim House's gang, they normally dealt with structural timberwork such as roofs, window and door frames. With the ever growing numbers of women coming in, this gang were periodically employed on alterations to provide restrooms for them. The rest of the time they were packing goods ready for dispatch. It was at this time we built crates for new machine tools bound for America, I remember this because they had to be made watertight. [A round up of war work undertaken at Swindon was published in the GWR magazine just after the war. One part said heavy plant had been installed in the Works for forging shells, but just as it became operational it was decided to uproot it all and send it to America. This is no doubt what Colin was referring to here.]

Later in 1943 I was transferred to Keen's gang and sent to the Steam Hammer Shop with a carpenter: I think it was Harold Llewellyn. A large hammer and steel block was being bedded into reinforced concrete: we put tapered beech blocks around the base and steel wedges were driven into them. Towards the end of 1944 the overhead crane in the new Saw Mills was dismantled. We renewed the various timber packing while the fitters adjusted the track to the gauge and rebuilt it.

There were several major fires at the Works between 1939 and 1945; the only one attributable to enemy action was when one of the gas holders was hit during an air raid in July 1942. This was the last time the Works brigade requested the help of the town brigade. A fire occurred in the Oil Works over near Whitehouse Road in January 1940. No one was working there as it was a Saturday night; this, together with the building's effective black-out precautions, meant the fire wasn't noticed until flames came through the roof and oil containers started exploding. The cause was thought to have been an electrical fault. Colin remembered D Shop gangs having to replace the roof timbers on several fire-damaged buildings. One of them, due to an explosion in one of the four acetylene houses, was on Easter Sunday 1945. If Colin's recollection of the date is correct, that makes at least three serious fires around that time. Surviving authorised work orders show that D Shop men had to make good damage to cupboards, lockers and tools, etc, caused by fire in the AV Shop on 30 April. Less than a month later, a major fire gutted the Hair Carding and Carriage Carpenters' Shops, as described elsewhere. The costs of making good the fire damage was sent to head office and they claimed through insurance; the department bore the cost of disrupted production.

The war situation by the middle of 1944 had changed considerably from a year earlier. Now the company, like everyone else, was planning for the future, when peace returned. In August 1944, the huge modern Carriage Repair and Painting Shop, which had been all but given over to aircraft production in 1940/1, was to be returned to its former use. At the same time, the opportunity would be taken to update the pre-war facilities. The initial work was completed in 12 months, in conjunction with Short Bros moving out. Firstly, trackwork was put back or altered and some small buildings demolished. Walls were removed to re-establish the outer door openings. Colin's gang made and fitted the new doors, which were approximately 14 feet square, to allow carriages to once again pass in and out. The aircraft plant had been fenced off from the rest of the Works and the original toilet block was outside, beyond the fence, and continued to be used by GWR people. The temporary indoor toilets put in for the aircraft workers now went, along with the fencing and some internal walls. Offices and washing troughs were put in, steam heating and water supplies reconnected and additional electric lighting installed. The last job for D Shop men Arthur Halliday, Roy Windsor and Colin was to put up two large 'roll of honour' plaques on a single brick dividing wall: 'They were to go one either side and I said it won't hold them, but it did.'

When the old adjoining carriage washing shed was converted for roof and panel repairs in 1948, 24 Shop rebuilding was complete.

Work to remove brick shelters in R, A, J1 and V Shops was authorised in March of 1945. In May, other ARP measures were to be dismantled at the Works: first aid posts, decontamination stations and static water tanks were to go; steel shutters were to be removed from control rooms and the telephone exchange; emergency telephones were also to be taken out; glass was to be replaced and/or black out paint removed from various loco and carriage shop roofs. Twenty-four restaurant cars were reinstated in May and June of 1945; the Works stripped them out and contractors Hampton & Sons Ltd refitted them. They also added fibre glass insulation and double glazed windows and lined the roofs.

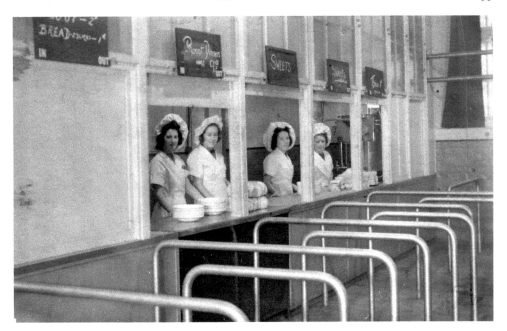

This canteen was opened in the Locomotive Works early in the war, in the basement of the Pattern Store. Female staff were employed to serve the day and night shifts and there was seating for up to 300 people. Joe Eggleton was canteen manager: he dealt with suppliers and collected groceries himself from a warehouse in Bridge Street. Until meal tickets came in, he also acted as cashier. His son Ray, known as 'Eggo', came into the Works as an apprentice coppersmith in 1942: 'Dad's Ford 8 was probably the first private car to go into The Works proper. The lorries would stand outside in Rodbourne Road and unload supplies through a door in the pattern building. He [Joe] had learnt the trade of boilermaking 'inside' and was one of the first men to weld copper fireboxes. However this is believed to have caused a permanent strain injury to his wrist and he was invalided out.'

This photo was taken in 1942 and the prices on the blackboards show that soup was 2*d*, two slices of bread 1*d*, roast dinners 9*d* and tea 1*d*. Meal tokens were available from automatic machines so as to avoid too much precious time queuing during breaks. Other refreshments and cigarettes were sold, although the whole building was 'no smoking'. This makeshift wartime canteen remained in use until 1960. (*Ray Eggleton collection*)

A lot of skilled men from the Works were retained in the army after the war, particularly with the Royal Engineers. At home their places had been filled by 'dilutees' – unskilled labour. The company had secured the 'class B' release for some trades such as wagon builders and boilersmiths, but not others. To get released from war service, you had to convince the authorities that your skills were better employed at home than overseas. Both had railways and infrastructure in desperate need of labour to get them back to some sort of normality. The Amalgamated Engineering Union district secretary, Dick Pearce, wrote to the MP for Swindon in an attempt to get men discharged and back into the Works. All efforts fell on deaf ears once their plight reached the War Office and demobilisation took 18 months or more in some cases. Some workers who had been loaned to the Short Bros aircraft factory in Blunsdon found that their prospects had been better than in the GWR. The *Evening Advertiser* reported that they were reluctant to return in August 1945.

CHAPTER 13

The Carriage and Wagon Works

Mr E. T. J. Evans had been the Carriage and Wagon Works' manager from 1922. He came from a Swindon family with working roots in the railway factory of the nineteenth century. Mr Evans lived in a large house in Bath Road and, like other senior officials, his home phone was connected direct to the Works automatic exchange. It was the Works Manager who oversaw production and repairs in the Carriage and Wagon Works and at depots around the GWR. His boss, the Chief Mechanical Engineer, was responsible for the design and modification of all equipment and facilities in the department. Mr Evans was expected, as head of department, to take part in the administration of some staff welfare and recreational activities. He chaired the general committee of the GWR Athletic Association – Swindon branch upon its formation in 1931 and was, for long periods, vice president of both the Medical Fund Society and the Retired Worksman's Association. Like his assistant, Mr Randle, who would succeed him, Mr Evans had trained and come up through the Locomotive Works. He retired in 1946, fifty years after starting his apprenticeship. The other senior staff in the department in the 1930s were, from the top: two Assistant Managers, Mr Dawson and Mr Hurle; Assistant to the C&W Works Manager, Mr Randle; Chief Clerk, Mr Ford; Storekeeper, Mr Faith. Then came heads of sections for: outstation, staff, costing, repairs, draughtsmen and special loads.

Within the Swindon Carriage and Wagon Works there were about thirty-eight main workshops; in terms of floor area, this accounted for about 48 per cent of the total. The buildings were nearly all Victorian but kept up to date with modern plant, including electric-powered machinery where required. Most of the lighting, however, remained gas until 1948. The workforce was almost completely separate from the loco side but the two did share some manufacturing facilities; the Foundry supplied both, as did the Spring Shop and the Carriage Blacksmiths' Shop. The Oil and Grease Works, the Central Laundry and the Road Vehicle Body Shop were mixed up among the carriage workshops, presumably because manufacturing facilities were developed haphazardly over many years.

The carriage stock was to be much improved under the CME, Mr Collett, from the 1920s onwards. The smooth riding qualities of various types of bogies were investigated and from the trials an improved design was introduced. Even the third class vehicles became far more comfortable and better air conditioned and all passenger vehicles started to receive overhauls at planned intervals. The speed at which the old gas-lit vehicles were replaced or converted in the 1920s and 1930s is said to be down to the efficiency of the Collett regime. The company owned more than seven thousand carriages, two thirds of which were passenger carrying vehicles,

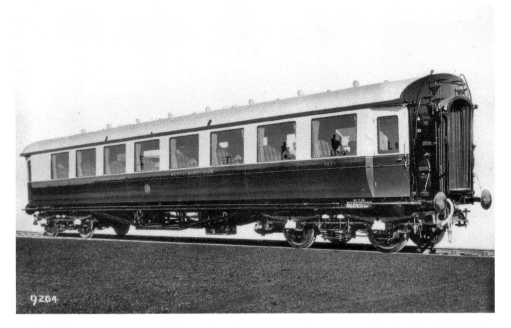

A third-class restaurant car built at Swindon as part of a new set for the Cornish Riviera Limited. Two complete sets of ten vehicles were built in the company's centenary year of 1935. Amid much publicity, they replaced the coaches built six years earlier for the same express. They were 60 feet long between the headstocks and the maximum 9 feet 7 inches wide. The recessed doors to bring the handles within the maximum loading gauge can be clearly seen at each end. As with all dining cars being built at this time, these were air-conditioned using electric fans. The company magazine said of this particular carriage: 'It was panelled in garbon mahogany and walnut, had rayon curtains, table lamps (a new idea) and oval mirrors. There was tip-up spring seating for 64 diners arranged of four on either side of a centre corridor. It had 9ft pressed steel bogies of an improved design.' These dining cars were withdrawn at the outbreak of war and returned to traffic, refurbished, in 1947. (*Author's collection*)

including dining and sleeping cars. The total stock remained fairly constant between the pre and post-war period. Bogie vehicles were being replaced at the rate of between 250 and 300 each year.

More workers were employed on repairs than on new building, and the main repair shops were of necessity the largest of the carriage and wagon buildings. Five thousand repairs were carried out at Swindon per year, more than half of which were overhauls; only the larger LNER did more. Passenger vehicles had been brought in for repairs and overhaul on a rotation, about every two years. By the mid-1930s they were brought in on a systematic basis, depending on the type of vehicle and what could be done at the carriage depots. By then main line coaching stock, except where dimensions had to be reduced owing to through working to other railways, was standardized at 60 feet long excluding the buffers and 9 feet 7 inches wide over the body, including door handles. Dining cars and kitchen cars were slightly wider as they had no opening external doors.

The directors authorised the building of eight 'super saloon cars' in 1931. They were to provide 'luxurious travelling' for liner passengers disembarking at Plymouth Millbay docks and journeying on up to Paddington. The design was based on the

Several of this type of publicity photograph were taken in the late 1930s. This one shows a Buffet Car built at Swindon in 1938, when it was becoming popular to have light refreshments while travelling by train.

Some, if not all, of the people shown in these staged pictures were employees in the Works. Photogenic office staff were asked to pose and local people still occasionally recognise themselves or their relatives long after the events were forgotten.

Pullman cars they were to replace. The first two vehicle interiors were designed and fitted out by a specialist firm to reflect tasteful high quality without being over-elaborate; Swindon would then complete most of the other six interiors. Some morale and optimism was temporarily restored in the carriage shops. The order was the talk of the town at a time when men were in fear of their jobs due to the dire economic situation nationally. They hoped the fortunes of the department had turned with such exclusive vehicles and that more might be ordered.

The Wagon Works would produce 4,500 to 5,000 new wagons every year, with another 8,000 given heavy repairs. By the late 1950s, the number of light repairs had doubled due to improved turn-around times of lower maintenance designs. Carriage and wagon development had not seen the hectic changes that locomotives had; nevertheless, manufacturing practices had to move with the times. There was a natural prejudice against such change by coach builders in particular and long-established methods were not going to be given up easily. Sophisticated machinery, for instance, was taking over from the skill of working wood by hand. This was now the age of mass-produced vehicles and extensive use was made of jigs and templates. These did away with the preparation to achieve the correct position for machining, saving both time and cost. Parts could now be produced that were very accurate and therefore interchangeable. Assembly had become less labour intensive and skillful.

Completed carriage underframe and bogies in 13A Shop yard in the 1930s. (*GWR*)

There were huge seasonal fluctuations in the number of coaches required for passenger services and this made the storage of excess stock at the quieter times a problem. In the Carriage Works the short but concentrated summer holiday period was the quietest, because all available passenger stock was pressed into traffic and where possible, the Works had sent out carriages that were 'patched up'. At other times, the situation would become reversed as excursion and holiday traffic slackened off. Preparing coaches for Christmas, Easter and other bank holidays also increased the activity in the Carriage Works to a lesser extent. The Works could not build or overhaul coaches to coincide with peak times, so they had to store them. The trouble was that sunlight and frost started a deterioration of the coachwork which, when in revenue earning service, was considered acceptable. The only answer was to keep them covered, so in the late 1930s a huge new carriage storage shed was built under the government Guaranteed Loan Arrangement. The site was some company-owned land alongside the down main lines which formed part of Westcott recreation ground. Newburn House, the former residence of the Chief Mechanical Engineer, was demolished to make way for the approach roads. The CME Department and not the Engineering Department put up the building, which would hold up to 265 coaches on ten roads. However, with the changing conditions on the eve of war, it would not now be required for that purpose and most of it was taken over temporarily by the Royal Engineers in 1940.

Mr Johnson, the Carriage and Wagon Manager from 1948 onwards, said on the subject of carriage production: 'We like to have the drawings 15 months before building starts. We have to order all the raw materials, alter our plans where materials are not available and prepare the jigs before the design can go down to the workshop.' Sufficient steel for the lot (or batch) of coaches being built was ordered from the Stores Department and arrived via the machine shop. Carriages were built in three main parts: underframes, bogies and bodies. Operations were carried out in a set sequence which was known as 'unit assembly'. The idea was that no gang was ever left waiting on another and the completed parts all came together at the same time. As the main components were erected, pipework and fittings for vacuum brake gear, suspension gear, steam heating and plumbing were also being produced, in 15 Shop. Axleboxes, drawgear, regulating gear for auto trains and trailer cars, as well as parts for diesel rail cars and slip coaches were all made there too. Virtually all the small brass and iron furniture for carriage toilets and compartments were also made in this, the principal machine and fitting shop. In the mid-1950s, a lot of the layout of 15 Shop was altered for production of parts for the new diesel building contracts.

Underframe repairs and new builds were done in 13A Shop, which was within the 15 Shop building. Rolled steel members, the solebars, headstocks and longitudinals that formed the frames, had various machining operations carried out. Axleguards were bolted (later riveted) on before they were passed to the assembly lines. Some frames were being all-welded by the late 1930s but most remained of riveted construction. It was the underframe that supported the weight of the body and its load; it also absorbed the stresses of 'buffering up' to other stock. Fabricated steel brackets were welded to the solebars for fixing the carriage body onto, which until the 1930s was held by wooden bottom-sides. Brakegear, drawgear and buffers which had passed through other workshops to be forged, pressed, welded and machined were then fitted to the frame. Before assembly by jigs, a horizontal ram was used to square up the frame by sight. The solebars and longitudinal members were given a slight upward camber using screw jacks. A wire was pulled taught between the headstocks to check when the correct deviation was reached then the tie rods were set in place; the underframe would later become level with the weight of the body. After the war, with the use of stronger angle iron members, there was no need to compensate for sag.

Adding the steel sheeting to new coach bodies in 4 Shop in the 1940s. (*GWR*)

An outside carriage
door being made
by jig and cramp
in the Bodymakers'
Shop in the 1930s.
(GWR)

The Great Western was not building any new non-bogie passenger vehicles by 1930. Their standard carriages were built onto two 7-foot single-bolster bogies until 1933. After that they used a pressed steel double-bolster suspension type which was basically unchanged until 1954. The frame of the bogie comprised of guard plates and horn block suspension brackets produced in the press and stamping shops and a side plate that was produced in the Loco Works. Before assembly in 15 Shop, the parts underwent various machining operations such as jet cutting, jig drilling, milling and grinding. A large assembly jig held the parts, which could then be riveted together. An outer frame comprising headstocks, transoms, longitudinals, fulcrum brackets and trimmers was riveted up and the two were fitted together. The three bolster pressings and brackets were riveted together and the tie plates, centre casting, rubbing blocks and slings were then added. The two assemblies were then loaded onto a hydraulic machine for the springs to be compressed and inserted and all held together by suspension bolts. Brakework was fitted prior to 'wheeling' and the fitting of axleboxes and side springs.

The Wheel Shop had turned the axle forgings and bored out the wheels; the two were then pressed together. After the war, the axles would be checked with supersonic flaw detection equipment. Steel and high duty cast iron solid wheels went for journal grinding and wheel centres had steel tyres shrunk on. The latter wheelsets would then be loaded in a wheel lathe and the tyres turned, ground and balanced prior to being passed to the bogie erectors in 15 Shop. The first two roads in the south-east corner of the shop were used for the bogies and underframes. Men of the frame and bogie gangs would push the complete underframe down the line at each operation, it being on steel-wheeled trestles. The completed frame was then lifted onto its two bogies by the overhead gantry crane and 'fitted up'. The complete assembly was then shunted over to the 'carriage body side'.

The coach body was built onto the steel underframe in 4 Shop, one of a group of workshops on the south side of the main line. The underframe was run between platforms 80 feet long made of tubular steel and 2-inch-thick decking, so the bodymakers could work above buffer level (Up until 1945, the body frame had been built complete before being attached to the underframe). The floor members were fitted and a frame of corrugated steel was laid on top; later, the floor would be coated in a red 'sanit' fireproofing compound. Felt, elm pads and floorboards were used to insulate against outside noise from rolling wheels and rail joints. Carpet and asbestos sheets were also used in sleeping cars and special saloons for additional insulation. Pads made in the trimming department were fitted into axleboxes and also helped to reduce noise. Timber was received from the Wood Machine Shop in kit form, it having been fully machined and, if necessary, shaped there. Further wood machining, if required, was undertaken in 4 Shop's own sawmill.

Part steel, part timber composite carriages were the preferred form of construction at Swindon and most other British railways. In America and on the Continent, the latest vehicles were all steel and aluminium but these were not thought so suitable for the greater variations of the English climate. Composite coaches also gave the best results in terms of reducing weight: a standard bogie corridor coach weighed 30

Groups of electricians were sent to Swindon Works in the early 1930s to learn about electric lighting being fitted in modern coaches. Here is class number 30 at the start of a two-week course in May 1931. There were sixteen men in this class, from carriage depots all across the system. The camaraderie must have been good as everyone has signed the back of this photograph and added the name of their particular depot.

Between the 1930s and the 1950s, carriage stock was altered from gas to electric. Most gas fitters who had dealt with carriage lighting were gradually retrained but some older men continued to maintain the old vehicles until they were finally phased out (yes, the carriages and the men). A belt-driven dynamo and a battery supplied the 24 volts to light each vehicle. When the coach was stationary or moving too slowly to generate sufficient power, the battery took over from the dynamo. The dynamo, being direct current, recharged the battery. The circuit was fitted with an auto switch and a resistor which maintained a constant output during the changeover. (*Author's collection*) to 31 tons. Tests showed that insulation and protection on impact were also within acceptable limits. The other considerations were maintenance costs and how much service would be gained before the coach was superseded by improved designs. With the increasing proportion of metal came the potential for welded rather than riveted seams. This would give stronger joints and allow the use of thinner body sections. However, changing workshop facilities and bringing in welding machinery would be slow due to the high costs. The Drawing Office were also still investigating the problems of contraction associated with welding, so it was restricted to use on carriage underframes before the war. By 1954, the body builders had single and multiple transformer welding sets supplied by Quasi-Arc Co. Ltd; they were used for fabricating jigged units, sub-assemblies and complete coach assemblies. For fixing studs into body frame members, and around window lights, they now used stud welding sets.

Continuous hardwood members formed the carriage bottom sides, with vertical teak pillars tenoned into them. The cant rail, a steel angle section, formed the top side and supported the ash roof timbers, known as hoopsticks. Sections of wooden body and door frames were laid out on tables with jigs and hydraulic cramps which pressed the joints together. Power tools drove in screws and iron dowels for added strength, and joints were further strengthened by steel braces. The proportion of steel used in the main body parts increased throughout the 1930s and 1940s. Steel for carriages needed to be strong, light, resistant to corrosion and inexpensive. Two main types were taking over from mild steel: low carbon, high tensile steel and stainless steel combined with aluminium alloy. The designers had to decide which combinations of materials to use and where, as none provided all the ideal qualities together. Impressive results with lightweight express trains were being achieved elsewhere and the GWR started to test aluminium alloys and lightweight high tensile steel. Less credence was now being given to the idea that weight was relative to the ability of the carriage to stay on the track when running.

With the body frame finished, the outer panels were fitted and gave additional support. Galvanised steel was used for this due to its resistance to corrosion from water and tannic acid in the oak. Another reason for the changeover from wood panels and floors in the 1920s was to minimise the fire risk. The steel panels for the carriage sides, ends and roof were made in 3 Shop. First, they were cut by guillotine, then they had holes punched in

Wagons of all descriptions were repaired in 21 Shop. Part of this shop, seen here after the war, was laid out for progressive repairs of standard open goods wagons on a 'belt system'. (GWR)

for securing to the cross members; for this, specialised machinery supplied by J. Bennie & Sons of Glasgow was used. Rolling machines and presses were also used to shape panels where necessary. In the mid-1930s, larger windows and flush sides to reduce air resistance were incorporated at this stage. Before it left the bodymakers for the steam heating and plumbing to be fitted, the outer doors were hung and transverse partitions and water cisterns fitted. Pipe Fitters from 15 Shop came and installed the: radiators, lavatory equipment, steam hot water tanks and associated lagging and insulation. Kitchen cars took up far more of the plumbers' time because of the cooking ranges, hot water urns, sinks and, later, refrigerators. More regular maintenance would be required and therefore these vehicles had a shorter period between overhauls. Sleeping cars too would be brought in more regularly to keep the motion running smooth and quiet.

In turn the finishers, trimmers and painters would then attend to the coach before it went off to be fitted with dynamos, batteries and electric train lighting. New, and later, repaired coaches were shunted through these workshops and traversing tables allowed them to change through roads if necessary. The finishers were men in white aprons who worked at benches preparing the interior woodwork in 7 Shop. They worked on such things as panels, frames for seat backs, quarter and door windows and lavatory and gangway doors, the latter having been machined and sanded in their sawmill using edging saws, 4 cutter planers and routers with jigs and templates. Some of the plywood panels were then shaped before being sent across to be painted, polished or lacquered. When the parts returned from the wood treatments, any metal fittings or glazing was incorporated. Other finishers worked in No. 4 (Body) Shop erecting the internal woodwork. Later, increasing use was made of plastics and veneers for wood coverings and a 785-ton veneer press made by J. Shaw & Co. Ltd was installed. Male and female trimmers made the moquette upholstery, canvas roofing, linoleum, carriage blinds and the flexible leather gangways between the coaches. Their colleagues in 19A Shop fitted out the coaches, and also the road motor vehicles.

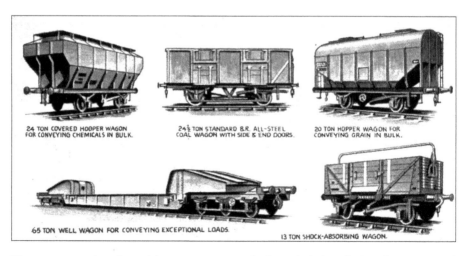

24 TON COVERED HOPPER WAGON FOR CONVEYING CHEMICALS IN BULK.

24½ TON STANDARD B.R. ALL-STEEL COAL WAGON WITH SIDE & END DOORS.

20 TON HOPPER WAGON FOR CONVEYING GRAIN IN BULK.

65 TON WELL WAGON FOR CONVEYING EXCEPTIONAL LOADS.

13 TON SHOCK-ABSORBING WAGON.

Here are examples of special-purpose wagons built at Swindon during the 1930s and 1940s; most would be vacuum-braked, unlike the majority of the company's standard wagon stock. (*GWR*)

Electricians from 5 Shop fitted the generator or dynamo and the wooden battery boxes to the underside of the vehicle to power the train lighting. They then fitted the regulator inside, which contained three resistors, and on top, the relays; this maintained the voltage required regardless of the running conditions. Lastly, they wired it and fitted the auto and distant switches. Vehicles equipped with fans, extractors, refrigerators, food warmers and fluorescent lighting were also connected up by electricians. The majority of the activity within that shop involved reconditioning and testing the train lighting equipment. The staff here did manufacture regulating and control gear and they assembled batteries but most of the electrical equipment was made by specialist firms. No. 5 Shop, part of which was occupied by a stores warehouse, had outgrown itself by the time the diesel multiple unit contracts were placed in the mid-1950s. By 1960, a new building for electrical train lighting had been proposed.

Lack of capital expenditure after the war, and then the steel shortage, affected the carriage building programme in particular. The travelling public were assured that maintenance work would be unaffected. Production of Hawksworth vehicles and,

To meet the requirements of the Central Electricity Board, the Great Western built a wagon capable of carrying a transformer weighing up to 120 tons and 24 feet in length. It was designed and built at Swindon and had an interchangeable straight or well girder to support the load. The one-off special trolley or wagon was known by the code name 'Crocodile L'. It had a twelve-wheeled articulated bogie at each end, allowing it to negotiate curves of one-and-a-half chains. Either-side and screw brakes were fitted which would hold the trolley and its load under normal conditions. Tare weight was 75 tons 19 cwt and the length between the buffers was 89 feet 6 inches. The first load carried was a 63-ton transformer being moved from Hayes (seen in this photo) to Yorkshire in 1930. The loading and unloading was supervised by men of the CME Department. 'Crocodile L' was still in use on the Western in the 1950s. (*GWR*)

later, the BR standard corridor stock was being cut back each year. By the time the Institution of Mechanical Engineers visited the Works in June 1952, they noted that the new Carriage Body Shop was full of the earlier composite coaches under repair. The only new builds were those to complete the previous year's building programme.

Diesel railcar sets and single units were first used on the GWR in 1933 for 'promoting services with limited demand'. They were built in the carriage shops for the first time between 1940 and 1942. The engines were supplied by AEC of Southall; Swindon built the underframes and bodies. The railcars were built and maintained in a similar way to ordinary carriages, with the lighting, plumbing, bodywork, windows and doors being attended to by the various trades. One major difference, however, was the access to the mechanical gear and engines. Because of the very limited clearance underneath, engineers worked mainly through trap doors in the vehicle's floor.

Building wagon underframes for the company and for private owners was done by the 'wagon bashers' of 13 Shop. Once an order was undertaken, the parts were made in the various shops or drawn from the stores. They were delivered to the assembly shops in sequence, arranged so that the operations were progressive and completed without hold ups, at the delivery date. The demand for new wagons often overstretched the facilities available and 13 Shop would then work day and night. Until the 1950s, the top corner of the shop was used to repair all the belts or straps for driving the older machine tools. Stan Leach remembers Bert Miles was one of the blokes that worked in the 'strap shop'. Artificial limbs, too, were made here, for staff who needed them due to accidents while working for the GWR.

The rectangular main frame of a wagon was made up of two solebars bolted to transoms, longitudinals and headstocks. Firstly, the steel members which would become the solebars were straightened then milled, drilled and profiles cut on one of two oxyacetylene cutting machines in 13 Shop. The fabricated frame members were placed in a jig, ensuring they were relative to each other and to the position of the motion when fitted. Axleguards, spring shoes, stops, headstock and diagonal brackets and vee hangers were then hydraulically riveted to the solebars. The main brake shaft was put into position between the vee hangers then the frame was squared up using gauges and passed under a hydraulic riveting machine to be secured. The upright stanchions were usually riveted on next, depending on the type of wagon being constructed; these would hold the wooden body. As time went on, more and more steel fabricated parts were held together using oxyacetylene then, later, electric arc and flash-butt welding. The frame was moved along the shop and lifted to receive its wheels, axleboxes and tie rods, after which the drawgear (couplings), buffers and brakework were fitted. If the wagon was to have a steel body, that was also erected here in 13 Shop.

Over at 21 Shop, the completed frames were shunted into one of four parallel roads. Each road handled certain types of vehicles, such as covered goods, specialist goods (such as fruit, ballast and salt), brake vans, sleeper wagons, iron minks, gunpowder vans, tool vans, and cattle wagons. Two further roads were used for repairs; wagons were subject to a seven-year general repair programme. For each order, a timber specification was sent to the Sawmill. When the wood arrived, it was marked off for final machining prior to assembly. The wagons moved through the workshop to emerge at the other end, completed. As with carriage body work, the lines of wagons were flanked by platforms allowing the men to work at the level of the body sides. Lines dealing with covered vehicles also had cradles suspended from above so men could work on wagon roofs. After the war, two of the roads that ran the quarter-of-a-mile length of the shop were used for a system of progressive repairs. Standard open wagons passed through and were repaired in stages to emerge at the other end no more than 12 hours later. They were then ready for painting and stencilling in the area known as '21B' Shop. Finally, the vacuum brakes were tested before the wagon went to the weighbridge and had its tare weight recorded. The company had to maintain a certain number of these small (short wheelbase) open wagons even though they were comparatively uneconomical. Larger wagons could not negotiate the curves of sidings and the small turntables and weighbridges of many private firms.

The Works blended (mixed) oil and grease to the required specification for the company's own rolling stock and machinery. This was done in two buildings and a

This is one of the first six-wheeled milk tank wagons, built in 1931 for the West Park Dairy Co., Market Lavington. The 18 foot by 6 foot diameter tanks held 3,000 gallons of milk. They were insulated and glass-lined (for hygienic reasons) and were manufactured by Enamelled Metal Products Ltd of London NW 1. The Works fitted them onto steel underframes and secured the tank in a cradle. To permit these vehicles to be coupled to coaching stock in fast passenger trains, vacuum and either-side brakes, screw couplings and a through steam pipe were fitted. They were given the same axleboxes and bearings as passenger coaches and the wheels had to be balanced to avoid wobble at high speed. Trailer tanks with pneumatic tyres were also used at this time for transporting milk over routes where part of the journey was by road. Again, the Works built special wagons to carry them.

Milk traffic was very important to the Great Western and they provided the best means to convey it. Complete milk trains usually comprised twelve or more tank wagons and a passenger brake van carrying churns at the rear. These trains were as heavy as a main line passenger train and covered the long distances from West Wales or Cornwall to London. They also had to be worked to fast timings to keep the milk fresh. Therefore, four-cylinder locomotives were used if available; otherwise mixed traffic 4-6-0s double headed would be used. The tanks only had a limited life but were, for other purposes, perfectly serviceable and the railway would sometimes buy them to use as water-carrying vehicles. (*GWR*)

An alternative to milk tanks was loading 17-gallon churns into these insulated vans. They were known by the telegraphic code 'Syphon J', and were built in the Works in 1930. All GWR goods vehicle types were given code names. This particular 50-foot vehicle only worked between Carmarthen and Paddington. (*Author's collection*)

laboratory at the eastern end of the site. Various types of oil arrived in drums from their contractors and were held in vast storage tanks beneath the floor. The shortage of oil products during the war caused a real problem in the department and circulars were sent asking users to be careful with supplies. Axlebox lubrication for Great Western wagons had changed from grease to mainly oil by the 1930s because of the increased speeds of vacuum-fitted trains. However, most wagons used on the GWR were privately owned and they were still using mainly grease which was also supplied by the Works at Swindon. The consistency of grease depended on the amount of lime soap used and the viscosity of the mineral oil. Although there were certain advantages of grease, including cost, it was not such an efficient lubricator and the company knew it cost them more in locomotive fuel to move trains with grease axleboxes. Locomotive oil was mineral oil (95 per cent) and rape oil. Annual figures from the company in the early 1930s were: engine oil issued, 590,000 gallons; cylinder oil, 225,000 gallons; grease issued for wagons, 380 tons; and carriage and wagon oil, 230,000 gallons. The reason so much less oil was used for carriages and wagons was because all the lubrication could be enclosed in axleboxes.

Axle oil from carriages and wagons in particular, but also machine tool coolant, was purified, re-blended and reused. The caustic solution that had been used for cleaning the parts of dismantled underframes was also returned to the Oil and Grease Works so that the components could be separated and used again. Jim Lowe remembers that the used solution from the A Shop bosh tanks was pumped into an old ROD tender; presumably this vehicle also collected it from the 'carriage side'. He said that after separation, the sludge was tipped down the bank at the bottom of Redcliffe Street. Although only 4 per cent of oil issued for carriages and wagons was reclaimed, it represented a significant saving in cost. Since 1926, specialist equipment had been used to spin the solution; the oil, water and solids would separate according to their specific gravities.

CHAPTER 14

C&W Tradesmen and Women

Gordon Nash arrived at the Works in his best clothes on his first day. He was to report to the registrar in the Staff Office of the Carriage and Wagon Works. According to the copy of his record card which he still has, this was 25 March 1935. Typically, Gordon had been working as a shop boy since leaving school at fourteen the year before. He was expecting to be an office boy 'inside' but instead was sent to 15 Shop to be a 'rivet hotter'. He was put with a gang on carriage underframes with chargeman Billy Bunce:

> I got eight shillings a week plus an extra four shillings war wage. Tom Hart was the riveter I served; a fella named Baughn was the 'holder up', he used to pickle snails and sell them at work saying: 'They're only poisonous if you picks em off the ivy.' Tom Ketch used the hydraulic riveter so he didn't need a 'holder up', just a boy to heat the rivets: a lad named Scutts did this I think.

They were based in the Frame Shop but the carriage frames and bogies were too big to be assembled there, so they worked nearby in the huge 15 (fitting and machine) Shop. One gang would rivet one frame while the other 'bolted up' another set; then they would swop over. Jessie Farr was the foreman in this area, which was known as 13A Shop.

> I was not entitled to learn a trade as my father Harold no longer worked 'inside'. He had been a machinist in the Stamping Shop until he was sacked about three years before. This was at the height of the Depression when a lot of men were put on short time or dismissed. Everyone was saying it was the company trying to maintain the dividend for the shareholders. My uncle Ted Cook was also sacked at this time, he said it was because they were installing hydraulic riveters in the Boiler Shop where he worked and they needed less labour. He was not long out of his apprenticeship so may have gone anyway as was company policy. Our family moved away for work and returned in 1935 as father heard the Works was 'taking on' again.

Stan Leach went into 'the factory' in June 1935; he was to be apprenticed to carriage bodymaking in a couple of months' time. Stan reported to Mr Richens the registrar and was told about safety procedures and that he would need to buy his own tools and overalls. The Carriage Works' principal machine shop was one of the few areas in 'the factory' certified to allow 'boys' under sixteen, to work there:

The earlier and later methods of 'finishing off' three link 'Instanter' couplings in 14 Shop are shown here; the links were made from grade 'A' iron bar - 1½ inches in diameter. Orders for batches of these were always coming in. Each sawn section was bent in a machine and hooked together before closing the links by hammer welding. They went to be normalised (heat treated), then to be tested in the Test House. In the early 1930s lots of men were engaged on coupling work; the inspector then was Fred Garratt. By 1940 the links were joined by a butt welding machine. The output for one machine was about 400 per week – more than double that of one blacksmith previously. (*GWR*)

Another boy Pete Hale started with me and we were put on single and double spindle drills in the north-west corner of 15 Shop. Some of the older lads would pick on us and throw things at us; it was intimidating at first. I remember vividly the clattering of the overhead countershafting driving the vertical and horizontal lathes. The speed of the individual machines could be altered by moving the belt onto different sized wheels which acted as simple gears. With a bit of practise the speed could be changed or the belt reattached with a pole so as not to stop the line.

Men would go up and down ladders seeing to the belts and pulley wheels or to oil the shafting. Black oil would sometimes drip on your head. I drilled holes in batches of carriage fittings using jigs: I can't remember what they were used for now, if I ever knew. Much of the production work was done using jigs and templates, many of which were made by the 'jig and gauge gang'. Another gang in 15 Shop made patterns for C&W castings. My chargeman was a Mr Griffiths: I remember we were told he had collapsed one dinner time near the Sheppard Street entrance: he never recovered. The assistant chargeman of our gang was Mr [Bill] Kemp, he was known for being the best skittler down at Haydon Street [Workingman's] Club. My foreman in 15 Shop was Mr White who lived in Evelyn Street: Ashley Walker was another foreman at that time; a Mr Watts was the senior shop clerk and Sammy Owen was the chief fitters' foreman: he was nice to me in those early days. We never spoke of anyone in authority using their Christian names then. Mr Owen had taken over as chief foreman from Mr Dening when he retired in 1931.

14 Shop was the Blacksmiths' Shop proper: on one side it was joined to the Wagon Frame Shop and on the other, the huge Fitting and Machine Shop. I regularly went through 14 Shop in the 1930s when running errands or to meet my father at the end

of the day. Mr H Griffiths was smiths' foreman at that time: he had lost an eye in an injury at the anvil. When he retired, Alfie Godwin took over and later, in the 1950s, his son Charlie was foreman there.

According to the company there were 200 men employed in 14 Shop – Smithy in the early 1930s; of those, seventy-six were skilled blacksmiths. There was a gas welding section, two 'hot saws' (red and white hot metal was much easier to cut through) and nine steam hammers. A lot of work done here was for brake systems, drawgear and fittings for goods containers.

The forge ran down either side of the long workshop with fireplaces and hearths at equal distances along its length. Air was delivered to the fires from a fan set into the wall and driven by an induction motor. Advancements in industrial welding and pressed steel components were to reduce the work of the blacksmith considerably. In 1944, two smiths' hearths were replaced by a specially designed flash butt welding machine and electric lighting was installed to go with it. Now, half the labour got through the same amount of work. Ken Farncombe lived in Morris Street in the 1930s. This was in Even Swindon, an estate built north-west of the Works just after 1900 to accommodate the expanding railway factory workforce and their families. Ken's father Fred was a journeyman in 15 Shop 'carriage and wagon', so Ken would be offered a similar training. At his medical in Park House, the Works' Medical Officer, Mr Bennett, measured Ken's height and made it half an inch under the minimum five feet for apprentices: 'He asked if I was still growing so I said yes.'

The C&W Blacksmiths' Shop in 1945. Before the war there were no tea breaks for shop staff and many work-weary men took risks to get a drop of tea or a cigarette. Some smiths were allowed to take a break for refreshment however, because the piecework time allowed for the furnaces to cool before de-clinkering. No doubt utilising the time in this way was proposed and accepted by the Joint Works' Committee. (*Author's collection*)

Until he reached the age to start his apprenticeship, 16 years, Ken was, as was usual, taken on as an office boy: this was 1937. He went into the Staff Office, where Mr Richens was in charge and about to retire:

There were about eight people in the office including three typists: Miss Crawford, Miss Pipf and Miss Goode. Mr Scotford was one of the clerks here and he dealt with the records of the watchmen's rounds; Mr Powell was another clerk and a Mr Dadge arrived while I was there. Mr Rawlings took over as registration officer during this period too, (later still others remember a Mr Smith as the registrar). One of my jobs was to stamp the notices of C&W Works men discharged during that awful period when so many were 'let go'. I spent what seemed like days stamping the manager's name, E. T. J. Evans, on the cards and sending them on to him for signing. Some of the men 'let go' seemed to me quite senior. I remember running home to tell my parents that even old Herbert Midwinter was going; 'Bert' was a riveter who had been apprenticed with my father, he worked in 13 and 15 Shops and was respected by all who knew him.

Gordon Nash moved from 15 Shop to No. 2 Sawmill in March 1936 to become wood machinists' boy. Here they did the initial machining of timber, as already described. Gordon was allocated to Jack Panting's gang. Besides Jack the chargeman, there was Bert Clark and three 'boys' including Gordon. Jack's daughter Ethel was secretary to one of the Works Managers; Bert came from Blunsdon, and later he became a prisoner of war. When he reached 16 years, Gordon was allowed to operate machinery unattended. Guards' flag sticks, trenails (rawlplugs), axlebox shields, handles for hand tools and later ferrules for track chairs were among the things turned out here:

I moved around the workshop and operated most types of machinery in time. We did miles of matchboards for coaches on a tenoning machine and also a lot of sanding work using the two drum sanders which could handle work up to 3 feet 6 inches wide. I remember we machined elm coffin lids for a local undertaker because no one else had a large enough sanding machine. The elm was delivered 'wet' [not fully seasoned] and would clog the sandpaper quickly. Another memorable job was hand turning a large wooden roller for the Boiler Shop. They had a machine that shaped the inner copper firebox and it needed a new 12-foot elm bending roll.

Some of the machinery was still driven by belt and countershafting, either in the roof or under the floor. There was a cellar for the latter which enabled maintenance to be carried out. Some men tried to take advantage of this concealed area and make tea. The foreman Ben Waterhouse knew what was going on and would hang around if in that frame of mind. Arthur Day was junior foreman, who eventually [about 1956] took overall charge; his junior foreman was then Dicky Dickens. One gang cleared away all the shavings and sawdust and they kept their long broom boxes in the cellar. On Saturday morning the last hour was for clearing up and on one occasion some men used the time to hold a kangaroo court. After passing sentence they put the guilty man in a broom box and somehow left him there when the hooter went. The watchman doing his hourly rounds heard his calls later in the afternoon.

A saw doctor working on a machine sharpening and setting a circular saw. This work was carried out in an area adjacent to No. 2 Shop. Up until the 1930s, such work would have been done laboriously by hand. With machinery to do the work, all the company's saws and cutters could be maintained at the Works. (*GWR*)

By 1946, the cellars were no longer required for countershafting as all remaining machinery had been electrified. Cyclone extractor fans were installed under the floor and the rest was filled in. The fans sucked all the sawdust away through pipes to a cyclone loft in the roof, where it was taken by conveyor to a furnace. The heat generated provided warmth for workshops and warm water for the company's swimming baths. Some other carriage shops had smaller cyclone systems, but with less sawdust it was not economical to burn it.

We did some war work during the early part of the war. Jack Panting's gang made some dummy fixed ammunition shells. A government inspector came down to oversee the setting up and initial production of pontoon roadways for use during a seaborne invasion. They were made of lengths of deal on a double-ended tenoning machine. We made thousands of them, which were to be strapped together to form a flexible floating roadway. Before I was 'called up' into the navy in February 1942, I was one of the operators on the 'Loch Ness Monster' machine, so-called because when loaded, it resembled the beast's perceived long form. This specially made machine tool could complete a number of operations on the longest constructional timbers upon which coach bodies were to be built. Before the introduction of the 'monster' in the mid-1930s, the bottomsides and cant rails were marked off by hand. The long, heavy sections of white mahogany then had to be craned to various machines to be sawn, tenoned, mortised, bored, recessed and grooved etc.

I returned to the Works in 1947, by which time they had started doing a night shift to spread their use of electric power. As a high power user, the Sawmill had to participate in 'load shedding' to offset the demand from the town's electricity station at peak times; this lasted about three years. I agreed to collect the union dues for the NUR steward in our shop, Jack Panting, while he was away. On Mondays I took the money to the weekly union meeting and as I would voice my opinion on certain topical issues, I soon found myself as the new shop steward. At one of the first meetings, I objected to a Communist member's proposal to send money to Russian railway workers. One day during a bad winter in the late 1940s, nobody in the suburbs could get to work on time, including me. I normally cycled in from Pinehurst but I had to walk and lost time. The workmen's trains were also late but those people were paid. I suppose the company had to admit that the staff could not be blamed for their trains being late.

The men in the Sawmills learned 'on the job', there being no formal training at that time. Labourers on 32s a week exclusive of piecework earnings could apply for a job in the adjacent saw doctors' workshop, where they would be classed as semi-skilled and paid 40s. They would sharpen, tension and set saws and cutters with no previous experience. Wood machinists who operated the lathes, shapers and spindle moulding machines in the Sawmills were not recognised as skilled tradesmen. They could, however, be paid skilled men's rates in time, which were 38–46s a week in the 1940s,

Here bodymakers are working on a carriage side and fitting a partition panel sometime after 1944. Written on the mount underneath this photo is: 'The coach of the riveting dispute – iron cant rail. 4 Shop Swindon.' Although official photograph details are often unknown, the GWR did not take random pictures. Therefore it is unlikely that this, the scene of a dispute, was coincidental.

Whenever production methods changed, there was a potential for differences over which trade did what and the price for the job (piecework rate). By the time this picture was taken such disputes were usually resolved quickly by the shop or works committees. The need for photographic evidence suggests that this matter was not settled locally. The next step in the 'machinery of negotiation' for railway shopmen was for delegates of the Works' Committee to meet with the General Manager at Paddington. (*Swindon Museum and Art Gallery collection*) depending on whether they were grade 1, 2 or 3. Gordon played a big part in getting these grades recognised in the mid-1950s, but some of the older men were not happy with this. They pointed out that when the Works cut back on numbers, they had been retained to work as labourers, and they said this would no longer happen.

Some men who deserved promotion were overlooked because someone else was in favour with the foreman. They may have gone out of their way to strike up a friendship with the gaffer in the Workingmen's Club or his place of worship. Gordon thought men known to be in St Mark's congregation got on better in the shops too. Jim Lowe said there were quite a few Salvation Army men 'inside' and a greater proportion of them seem to become chargeman, then inspector, then foremen. Men related to the foreman might well be given posts they did not deserve too. This was a situation that persisted throughout the period apparently, as described by a disgruntled 'workshop scribe' in a letter to *The Swindonian* magazine in June 1959: 'Promotion for tradesmen is simply a racket. An inspector falls sick and someone is appointed by the foreman to act in a temporary capacity. When the vacancy occurs this temporary man, in 9 cases out of 10 obtains the post despite a promotion scheme which invites applicants from all interested.'

Gordon saw an advert in the *Evening Advertiser* for timber technology classes in 1948:

It was a three year course at the College, one evening a week. I enrolled and eventually passed my Timber Development Association exam. I learned about the properties of the various woods and their microscopic examination as well as the selling and handling of timber as a business. This enabled me to apply for and fill a vacancy for a timber inspector. Bert Hillman and I covered the Works in the early 1950s; Bert had been a tradesman in the Carpenters' Shop. I lost money because I was no longer getting piecework payments but made up a little with accommodation allowances when I went to a supplier. Frank Morris and Charlie Oliver were doing this job before us in Great Western days; they and ourselves were answerable to Monty Jones [he was 'Chief Inspector of Purchased Materials', a post he took over from Mr Arkell in 1939]. In 1954 I left the Works as the job was no longer based at Swindon; we now covered the whole of the West of England.

Ken Farncombe should have started his apprenticeship on his 16th birthday in March of 1938, but he started six and a half months late. On the carriage side, you did a total of two years turning (operating lathes and boring machine tools), and three years fitting (assembling components and making sure they worked with each other). His pay as a first year apprentice would have been 14s a week, of which 4s was 'war wage'. Ken would have received a pay rise every year until he was getting a total of 28s. It was in the early part of 1938 that the company announced large cutbacks in 'the factory'. Several building programmes finished together and the company did not place further orders; immediately, numbers of men to go were made known. Considering that the country had been steadily coming out of the recession for some time, it was a huge shock in the town. The Swindon workforce, normally very perceptive in these matters, was taken by surprise at this situation and the scale of it. Ken said:

A staged picture showing the repair of wheels and axles of platform trolleys and sack trucks in 15 Shop. Trolleys used where glass was set into the floor to give light to underground areas, such as station subways, were fitted with rubber tyres. (*BRW*)

In 15 Shop, where I started, the men that did survive the discharges went on 'short time', meaning in this case no Saturday morning shift. Apprentices were still being taken on but the men refused to train them. They reasoned that the newcomers were doing the work journeymen should be doing. Until feelings subsided, training was delayed, that's why I started my apprenticeship late. First of all, we were put on simple turning jobs such as making nuts and bolts, then turning parts for the maintenance gang. In September of the following year I worked with the fitters on vacuum brake gear and for the first week of 1940 I was put on a vertical boring machine.

The vacuum brakes which were fitted to all coaches and many wagons provided work for quite a number of fitters. One gang fitted up [assembled] the vacuum cylinders as they came over from being machined: they also repaired defective ones and then tested them all to 26 inches of vacuum. They then went to be fitted to the vehicles. Another gang made the direct admission valves, which admitted the air to the vacuum system on each coach. The foremen at that time were Bill White, machine sections, and Reg Arman, bench fitters. Ashley Walker had been the night foreman in 15 Shop until he went over to 24 Shop to help set up the displaced Shorts aircraft factory in 1940 with assistant Jack Grey. Sam Owen the chief foreman and Bill White were retained beyond retirement while the war was on.

Ken's apprentice training card, which he still has, shows he was turning small brass valves, cocks and fittings for coaches on centre lathes. This was from 8 January 1940 under chargeman Frank Hitchens; he became foreman in 15 Shop in the 1950s.

Afterwards, with the fitters I would be filing these parts to remove sharp edges and, with emery paste and soft soap, make the male and female parts steam tight. Of course these, like every job, had a piecework price and you had to complete so many per day depending on the type. Apprentices always got the badly paying jobs; the men pointed out that their bonus was low anyway so they had less to lose. The maintenance fitters were based in 3 Shop and I would go round helping a gang of them repair saw mills, machine tools and stationary boilers in the C&W workshops. We worked on the boilers Saturday mornings when they were usually shut down, if not a Bank Holiday. This was now wartime and Saturday working was reintroduced. Munitions work

Women worked on the carriage side, in some cases doing the same work as men but separate from them. They started coming into the workshops in larger numbers from April 1917, to replace men away at war. In the Sewing Room women did light trimming machine and hand work using fabrics, canvas, leather and lace. Upholstery, window blinds, axle box pads and netting for luggage racks were among a range of items worked on here. Mr Duck was the trimmers' foreman in the 1930s. Alongside the Sewing or Linen Room were three sections of 'polishers', one of which was all female. Here the art of French polishing and lacquering was practiced to produce high quality finishes on internal carriage woodwork. By the end of the war all three polishing sections of this workshop – No. 10A, seen here – were staffed by women. The displaced men, if they hadn't been 'called up', were presumably moved to 7C Shop or to similar work in the carriage repair shops. Of the 123 females in the Carriage Works in 1947, twenty-four were under 21 years of age. The Central Laundry on the eastern edge of the Carriage Works site, alongside Whitehouse Road, was also staffed by women manual workers. (*BRW*)

from the Ministry of Production started to come into 15 Shop in 1941. I remember turning the stub axles and parts for the wheel assemblies of 25-pounder field guns. Later females came into our shop and that's where I met Dorothy Gleed, my future wife. Trench mortar bomb cases which had been forged then machined elsewhere in the Works, were brought into 15 Shop. Dorothy's job was to spray the cases inside and out; whatever it was dried like brown varnish and presumably stopped rust.

Ken finished his apprenticeship in 1943 and was immediately transferred to the loco side. This was unheard of in peacetime, apart from some senior officials with a locomotive background who took up positions in the Carriage Works. Now, skilled fitters were needed in the locomotive shops. A lot of what was going on in 15 Shop was repetition work and could be done by semi-skilled or 'cat 3' labour. Category 3 men were the semi-skilled and category 4 were skilled men who had served a recognised training; only toolmakers were known as category 5 men. 'I seem to remember they had dilutees from the Cornish china clay industries in the Erecting Shop when I was there,' said Ken. 'Dilutees' was the term used for labour bought in to replace those 'called up' for war service. Italian prisoners of war were also brought in each day to supplement the labour shortage; Reg Willcocks said of them, 'They didn't do much though.'

After the war Ken Farncombe, who had been studying toolmaking at night school, left the railway and went to work at Plesseys, an electrical components firm in Kembrey Street.

> I can't recall exactly when I left but it was during severe weather, possibly December 1945. I quickly learned that without the unions and negotiating committees we had 'inside', the workers were vulnerable to downturns in this company's fortunes. For that reason I returned to the Works in May 1948, now a skilled toolmaker with some experience. After several temporary jobs I became part of 3 Shop toolmaking gang.

The fitters who did the machine tool maintenance for the new carriage workshops were also based here. Most of 3 Shop was laid out for the production of steel and wooden body panelling that would be fitted to carriage body frames next door in 4 Shop. The machines were mainly guillotines, presses and multiple punches, along with an electro-mechanical riveting machine. No. 3 Shop was one of the carriage body shops which were south of the Paddington–Bristol main line.

Ken kept a diary of the moves he made at work in the 1950s. He referred to this and told me that in October 1955 he was made chargeman in the toolmaking gang; in July of 1957 he became a piecework inspector in 15 Shop; three months later he started standing in for various foreman when the need arose. In November of 1958, Ken was made foreman over the 'diesel new build' and the 'bogie' gangs, about twenty-four men in total.

Members of Beryl Odey's family about to leave for Weymouth on 'Trip Day', in around 1930. From left to right: mother Dorothy, young Ronnie Thrush, an adopted cousin who later worked at Eastleigh Railway Works, Aunt Lily, Cousin Olive and Uncle Bill, who was a labourer in the Works. Presumably Bill was younger than Albert, Beryl's father (see the following photo), as only the eldest sons got to learn a trade 'inside'. At 'Trip', when most workers and their families spent their holiday away courtesy of the company's free trains, Albert used his skills at the Midland Bank down in Bridge Street. They hired him to polish and restore their counters and panelling, something the company would not have tolerated had they found out. (Mrs B. Wynn)

The former worked on engines, cabs and gearboxes of carriages and diesel cars in 15 Shop. The latter did the bogie erecting, turning out four completed bogies per week. Ken's father was chargeman in the 'bogie gang'. It was not unusual for fathers and sons to work in the same workshop. In this case, however, Ken was foreman over his own father and this was cause for some publicity in the railway and local press at the time. Fred Farncombe retired shortly afterwards aged 67, having been 'inside' the Works all his working life.

Stan Leach started learning his trade in 17 Shop, the road vehicle workshop, in August of 1935: 'I had been a telegraph boy on 5s a week after leaving school the year before, now I was getting 9s 10d as a first year 'class B' apprentice.' No. 17 Shop was where all the GWR's station handcarts, horse-drawn coal trailers, road carriages, vans and lorries were built, painted and subsequently repaired. It is best remembered nowadays for producing and mounting the bodies, cabs and wheels for motor omnibuses, cartage vehicles and Scammell mechanical horses. Some of the work was lost when the company's passenger omnibus services finished in 1933; some of those vehicles were then converted for haulage. According to the GWR's published statistics, they had 2,010 parcel and goods motor vehicles and 3,700 horse-drawn vehicles for the same purpose in 1935.

'Apprentices were required to attend night school three evenings a week; it was a rush getting home to Purton and back for 7 p.m. We learned about: the principles and practice of woodwork, geometry, engineering drawings and vernier measurement. You could get away with missing the odd night but you had to be careful.' Stan goes on to say:

No. 17 Shop had a blacksmiths' section with three blacksmiths and three smiths' strikers. Jimmy Breakspear was a blacksmith there then, so was Jimmy Griffiths who was a good old time dancer. They produced iron and steel fittings for the wooden bodies and they formed the tyres as well. We were still fitting iron tyres onto the earlier horse drawn vehicles and gun carriages in the 1930s and 1940s. Hot iron was drawn out and curved using a ball hammer and a former; to fuse it together it was reheated and further beaten to make the joint, very clever; later the tyres were welded. They could then be shrunk onto the wooden wheels by heating in a furnace sunk into the floor, as were machined tyres. Cockroaches could be found where there were dark corners and heat from pipes etc. As soon as the fires had died down a bit on the smiths' section, you could see them crawling about in the forges too.

The majority of work undertaken in 17 Shop after 1930 was connected with the company's huge fleet of cartage vehicles. The staff employed on this work came under the Road Motor Department based in Slough. Here, in rather more cramped conditions than at Swindon, was the GWR's main repair depot. Mr Coventry had been Superintendent of Road Transport since it became a separate department in 1922; he had been trained in the Locomotive Dept at Swindon. Stan said:

Mr Coventry kept a close eye on production here and his visits often resulted in men getting laid off, if work was slack. Either way the men became a bit jumpy if it was known the Superintendent was due to be 'about'. One chap was fond of saying, 'Look out he's coming,' when asked where, he would reply: 'On Slough Station.'

Motor lorries were also built for the exclusive hire of firms such as Huntley &
Palmer's biscuits and Reckitt & Coleman's mustard. They were painted in the firm's
own style and livery at Swindon. 'We were required to put maple floors into these
lorries so that heavy containers could be slid in and out,' said Stan. Vehicle painting
and varnishing was done by painters based in 24 Shop. If something was in for repair,
the old paint would have to be burnt off and the surfaces prepared for repainting. No
steel supports were used in any of the bodies before the war; they used hickory, which
was tough and would bend but was expensive. Hickory and ash could also be bent
round in a hoop and covered in canvas. The off cuts were made into 3/8-inch carriage
window blind rods. Elsewhere, wooden hammer shafts and shunting poles were also
made from hickory. Ash was the most common wood for the superstructures; it was
also used for the adjustable horse shafts, along with pitched pine. Horse carts and
trailers were made of elm and some trials were done, covering them with aluminium
sheets, but this was not successful, said Stan: 'The stuff we used reacted with its steel
fastenings, and would corrode, especially in coastal areas.' The drag boxes or brake
blocks were made of cast iron. Before the war the windscreens were plain glass; later,
a layer of cellulose was placed between two pieces of glass so that if it smashed, it
would hold together and be less likely to injure the driver.

Men from the same workshop would speak if they passed one another in the town,
except for the foreman. If he was a churchgoer, he might speak only to men in his
congregation or in his choir. Like Gordon, Stan remembers some men would try to
win favour with the foreman in the days when he could hire and fire people:

> Some of these 'hopefuls', as the men called them, would leave a box of vegetables
> or eggs outside their door with a note wishing them well. This was more common
> when orders were down and men were being discharged. I remember the chief
> foreman coming round with discharge notices before the war. The men knew a lot
> would be going on the 'carriage side' but until the boss stopped and handed out the
> envelope, no one knew who. It seemed to be mostly the last in that were selected: us
> apprentices knew we were alright. Everyone was surprised to hear that Jack Hext got
> an envelope; they said he went as white as a sheet. He was a left wing union man on
> the Works committee, and generally kept in with the right people. When he opened
> it, all it said was 'evolution not revolution': the foreman's idea of a joke.
>
> A lot of carriage men wore their white aprons home of a dinner time; being as only
> tradesmen wore them, I think they wanted to show off. Before the war some of the
> older men wore bowler hats to and from work.

It is said that this was forbidden unless the wearer was a foreman but Stan disagrees. I
wonder whether the supervisors were wary of a confrontation with some of the older
hands if challenged. In 1939 the Civil Defence Organisation set up several emergency
feeding centres around the town in case of mass homelessness due to the expected air
raids. Stan and his father could not get home at dinnertime as they lived at Purton, so
they would walk up to one of these 'British Restaurants', either the one in Maxwell
Street or the one in Savernake Street, where they could get a hot meal. Because of the
anticipated run down of carriage work during 'the present emergency', Stan was called

French polisher Albert Odey and his family are seen here in about 1938 at their home in North Street, Old Town. People at the time said that the air was clearer and healthier in the old (pre-railway) town, away from the factory chimneys. Few wages grades lived up there in those days, but upon being married in 1924, Albert moved into his new wife Dorothy's family home, which she shared with her parents. Their future daughter Beryl, pictured here in the foreground, continued to live in this, the house that her grandfather had built, until she died in 2010.

Albert Daniel Odey was apprenticed to French polishing in about 1912, and stayed 'inside' all his working life. He was never put on short time or dismissed, something the company were quick to do before the war in 1939, whenever orders were down. Men and women both worked as 'polishers' in separate sections in the Carriage Works from the 1870s. They French polished and/or lacquered hardwoods such as mahogany, oak and walnut used for interior woodwork of carriages and furniture. This was a slow process that required several applications of cellulose lacquer, shellac and spirit and needed skill and experience to achieve the right finish. Male French polishers worked in part of 7 Shop or, before 1945, 10A Shop on the south side of the main line. Others were in the carriage repair and repainting shop, where they worked on carriages in for overhaul.

The Odeys were a typical Swindon family in that the men of each generation had been in the Works and formed a lineage back to its earliest days. 'Grandfather Benjamin had been a French polisher's assistant and his brother Edmund had been a blacksmith and had met the King in 1924. [When King George V visited the factory, all the longest serving working or retired men were presented to His Majesty] I found out too that great-grandfather John Odey who was born in 1826 was also in the GWR, as a labourer,' said Beryl.

Beryl Odey was expected to go on to learn her father's trade 'inside' but resisted it: 'I developed a loathing of the distinctive pear drop smell that was always present when dad was around. I didn't want the stained hands of a polisher either: it looked like bad nicotine stains.'

up fairly early on, in 1940, for the army. At this time, apprentices were among the first to be enlisted because of their young age and because, in theory, their work could be done by others brought in. Stan was in his final year of training and doing the work of a skilled man while getting a lot less pay, of course. While he was away, a canteen was opened on the carriage side: 'When I came back women from the canteen were coming round the shops with a refreshments trolley during the breaks.'

Father Fred Leach had been a skilled boilermaker on the loco side but, unusually, had permanently moved to 13 Shop. When his son Stan arrived in 1935, Fred was a wagon frame foreman. The chief wagon frame builders' foreman was Charlie Garrett, also from Purton; they both attended the same chapel. Mr Garrett was later succeeded by Percy Gleed. Fred was in charge of the gangs making the motor landing craft (later re-designated landing craft, mechanical) complete, in 13 Shop during the war. This workshop usually made steel wagon underframes using jigs, on modern production lines. These facilities were expanded to build the 40 feet by 13 feet 6 inches hulls and fit the oil driven engines, propellers and fittings to produce the finished product. Because of their size and the large order, the MLC became one of the best-known wartime jobs undertaken in the Works.

Stan's elder brother, also Fred, was learning fitting and turning in 15 Shop and Uncle Tom Leach was in the stores. They all worked within an area of the C&W Works that, Stan said, was known as 'the canal side'. There were five or six outside toilet blocks around the Works site and in the 1930s they were very basic:

> The long, narrow toilet building behind 15 Shop was made of wood and louvre panels on a brick base. You sat on a low wall which had a wooden top with a line of holes in it, no doubt designed with the intention of stopping you getting comfortable and loitering; there were scant partitions and doors and no wash basins. A chap named Evans was the attendant; he had been injured in the First World War and retained to work in this post. You gave the attendant your check number as you went in; he would record every visit and whether you took more than ten minutes, after which you lost a quarter of an hour. It was said that if Evans caught you smoking in there, he would lock

A whitemetal toolcheck, which was exchanged for tools and equipment going from one shop to another on loan. It would be hung up in the workshop tool stores of origin, to show where the item(s) were. (*Author's collection*)

you in so you did lose time. Later, just after the war, new toilets were built by 24 Shop next to the carriage disinfecting plant, what the men called the 'bug house' or hutch. They were much better; gone too was the unpopular lavatory attendant arrangement.

No doubt these improvements came about when the new Works committees were formed in the early 1940s. Perhaps too the management realised such primitive conditions could not continue with females coming into the workshops.

The disinfecting plant consisted of a steel chamber into which ran a railway track 85 feet long. This would take the latest 70-foot coach or two smaller vehicles, such as flour and grain vans infested with weevils. The carriage doors and windows were opened so that when the chamber was closed and airtight, all the air could be sucked out. The chamber was heated up and gas was pumped in to kill any vermin and organisms. Stan said: 'This treatment was carried out by two or three blokes as and when required.'

Being from Purton, Stan and his father travelled in by the workmen's train. Alf Tutt travelled in with them; he lived near Stan and worked in N Shop.

> I think it cost me about 3s 11d a quarter at that time; I'd been using the train since I was a telegraph boy. In the morning the locomotive brought the train into the platform and went down to the brickworks siding to 'run round' and return to Swindon bunker first. Coming in from Purton, our train was rarely ever late but the Chiseldon people weren't always so lucky. Their train had to cross the main line at Rushey Platt and could be held up. A chap named Roy Green was the regular driver on our train for years; 'old greenie' was also a union man down the Running Shed. Virtually every traveller was a regular and they tended to have the same seat in the same carriage every journey. This was human nature but was bound to cause the odd dispute and some younger men began to challenge this arrangement in the 1950s. Because the train filled up quickly, the loser might then have to stand, much to the amusement of the rest of us. The coaches were stabled near the station, ready to take us home in the evening. After the war, a Bristol bus was waiting to take people on from Purton station if they needed it. Previously, dozens of bicycles were left at the station.

When Stan returned to 17 Shop in 1946, the chief road wagon foreman was Mr Nicholls and the other foreman was Arthur Wiltshire. With so little of his apprenticeship left to do, they took him back on as a skilled man. The first thing Mr Wiltshire said to Stan was, 'You weren't the best apprentice you know,' and Stan replied, 'No, and you weren't the best foreman.' Apprentice Stan Bond was put with him at first: he had an older brother, George, who was a carriage painter in 24 Shop. Probably because of his cheek, the foreman put Stan and his mate to work making howitzer wheels, 102 of them to be made complete. Cast iron 'artillery hubs' were used with the wheels, and had been since before the Great War; they had been developed for gun carriages and were very reliable. 'The army continued to have us make these wheels after the war. You had to make sure 'the flower' or end grain of the wood faced inwards on spokes and rims.'

After that, Stan worked on batches of mechanical horses with Thornycroft chassis with another apprentice, Ray Townsend:

Views of the inside of the Road Vehicle Body Shop aren't easy to find: these two were local press photographs, probably taken in the 1920s. This was a large workshop with no rail access where lorry and van bodies were built for the GWR Commercial Department.

Our gang were to build up the cabs, the flat bodies with high sides and hoopsticks and mount on Scammell 3 ton trailers. If we worked hard we could do one vehicle a day and earned £1 6s a week piecework bonus; this was my first experience of piecework. Charlie Hatcher came over to fit the dashes (dashboards) into all the cabs. The rest of the time he was employed making water closet tanks for coaches in 15 Shop.

Edgar Gardner was a carriage bodymaker who spent his final working years in 17 (Road Wagon) Shop. He had been a very popular and benevolent character and upon his retirement the *Swindon Railway News* described Mr Gardner as an untiring sick visitor who was prominent in setting up a wartime comforts fund for shop mates away on active service. When hostilities ceased, two of their colleagues remained in hospital, so the fund was kept going for them and he continued to seek contributions. The write up continues:

In the administration of the fund, Mr Gardner was ably assisted by Mr Roberts of the Central Wages Office. In addition to the financial assistance provided, Edgar regularly visited the two men at Roundway (Devizes) and later, at their homes. This great effort by Edgar and his mates was not without reward, for one of the two patients recovered and is now working in the shop.

This staged picture shows a horse-drawn vehicle on the left that the company used for 'express parcels services' well into the 1930s. It was probably taken before 1930, as the omnibus in the foreground is of a type that they sold off in the late 1920s. Vehicle chassis were supplied by the specialist builders such as Guy, Thorneycroft and Morris. Swindon would fit the bodies, cabs and trailers and those that they replaced during overhaul were repaired and repainted and would then go into the pool for future use or for dispatch to various outstations. Sometimes the company would buy fleets of complete vehicles from outside firms. In wartime, ambulance bodies were fitted to some vehicles. Trailers for the factory's Internal Transport Department were also made and repaired here; their solid rubber tyres were pressed on in G Shop, on the 'locomotive side'. Engine maintenance requiring machine work was carried out on the company's road vehicles at Slough; otherwise, it was done in the vehicle's home depot. (*Author's collection*)

By 1960, the repair of road vehicles on behalf of the Road Motor Engineer had been transferred from 17 Shop to Bristol.

No. 18 Shop was the Stamping and Drop Forging Shop, just across from where Stan worked. Not only did they do work for the C&W side, they did some work for the Signal Works, the Loco Works and points and crossing work for the permanent way. Stan remembers that:

If the wind was in the wrong direction we could catch the choking air from 18 Shop. The men there went in half an hour early to light the many furnaces including at least twenty that used creosote pitch oil fuel. Not surprisingly, there would soon be black smoke everywhere. If the wind was blowing from the south-west, women from Beatrice Street to Ferndale Road would be out complaining about not being able to hang out the washing.

Bill Peacy was secretary of the National Union of Vehicle Builders during my time in 17 Shop. He was a good bloke and although he was a coach finisher, all his time was spent on union business. The NUVB offices were just across the road from the Works, at No. 1 Bridge Street. Bill could speak Esperanto and had apparently been involved in the Spanish Civil War. In 1948 he got some of us moved when work was slack. I went, with four others, to coach finishing; another five went to coach building. The carriage finishing repairs were done over in what was known as 19B Shop, which was actually part of 24 Shop. Harold Williams was now my shop steward: he would come round and collect 1s 6d union subscription from us all. Incredible as it may seem when money was so tight, the subs were actually 1s 9d per week, and Harold must have been making the amounts up out of his own pocket.

'Finishers' removed worn and damaged internal fittings and replaced them. These included carriage pictures, luggage supports and nets, sliding and hinged doors, ceilings, handrails in corridor coaches, drop lights, mirrors, lavatory pans and wash basins.

An apprentice and I would complete a coach a day if nothing went wrong. We worked on coaches on 'the bank', the roads leading in and out of the Finishing Shop which were nearest the embankment. On one occasion I was trying to screw down a lavatory pan in a coach which had a special soundproofed and fireproofed floor. Try as I might I could not locate any cross members to screw into, under the floor covering. I decided to leave it and put extra long screws in to hold the toilet roll holder. This cured the problem as far as I was concerned because the piecework inspector, Jack Shailes, saw the screws projecting through into the corridor. He made such a song and dance about that, he missed the loose pan in the lavatory. I could rectify the roll holder in time but not the pan. This was one of the tricks of the trade. In winter with no artificial light, we had to stop work at dusk; sometimes we had a sleep in a coach till the hooter went.

The 19 Shop 'finishers' would refurbish coaches required for the mass exodus in July that was 'Trip'. Doug Webb, formerly of 13 Shop, told me that this was done on the sidings at the back of A Shop on the loco side (This was also where the frames for 'Hall' class locomotive 4911, which suffered a direct hit in 1941, were until at least 1948, said George Petfield). Stan said of the 'Trip' coaches: 'They didn't do much to them, just looked em over and gave them a bit of a clean.' Ken Farncombe remembers hearing of men who, on finding a lavatory in need of work to be done, screwed the door to the frame so that it could not be used. This was pre-war and I should think such 'tricks' were only tried on Works holiday coaches that were soon to be condemned. Most of the Works' holiday trains were made up of old third class non-corridor stock. The overhead luggage racks had to be inspected carefully as this was a favourite place to put a sleeping baby when the compartment was full. Occasionally, finishers and other trades were paid overtime to refurbish burnt-out carriages. Stan said that some of the men suspected fires were started deliberately using cotton waste soaked in turps that the men cleaned their hands with. Ron Cox was a coach finishers' foreman, later chief finishers' foreman; he originated from outside the town, Oswestry, so was known as a 'down homer' said Stan.

Various types of carriage repairs were done in workshop areas collectively known as 19 Shop, as well as any alterations and modifications. This building was known as the 'Klondyke', a name it was given when it was the old Carriage Lifting and Paint Shop. Nobody I have met knows how the nickname, which goes back to at least 1900, came

---

CLOSING OF SHOPS

THE CARRIAGE AND WAGON WORKS AND SAW MILLS WILL BE CLOSED FROM 12-30 PM ON THURSDAY, JULY 13TH UNTIL 8-0 AM MONDAY JULY 24TH.

THE WAGES FOR WEEK ENDING JULY 8TH. WILL BE PAID ON THURSDAY JULY 13TH.

AND FOR WEEK ENDING JULY 15TH. ON JULY 21ST. AND 24TH.

BY ORDER. 1933.

A homemade poster probably produced in the Print Room, where engineering drawings were copied. It is endorsed with the Carriage and Wagon Works Manager: Office No. 4 stamp, which made it official and discouraged the men from pasting their own notices onto boards around the Works.

Before the war, 'the factory' closed down production for one week in July and of course at the time of this instruction, 1933, there was no holiday pay. Because the workforce worked 'a week in hand', they did get paid on their return (Monday 24th). That money would be 'short' because the annual holiday commenced on Thursday afternoon and not at the end of the working week, which was Saturday. This reduced pay had to last until Friday week. Wives of wages grades 'inside' had to make savings in advance or put a few things by to be able to put food on the table over this period. Because of the economic situation, they were the lucky ones: their husbands were employed. (*Author's collection*)

about. Unlike building new coaches, some repair work involved working underneath, in inspection pits between the rails. Because of the serious decline of cattle carried by train, these shops converted large numbers of cattle wagons into fruit vans from the late 1930s onward. The carrying of fruit was a business restricted only by limited facilities. It was a straightforward job to remove the floor battens, fit louvre panels and ventilators and replace doors. Stan worked in 19D Shop from 1953; this area was known to the men as the 'buffer, brake and drawgear' shop. He inspected and repaired the various springs, tie rods and brakegear of gas tank vehicles with Sid Adams. The bogies or running gear, including axleboxes, were dealt with by the carriage lifters in 19C Shop. When returned to traffic, the tanks were filled at the adjacent Gas Works so that at the depots, carriage examiners would use them to recharge the gas tanks of their passenger carriages from them. These vehicles, together with milk tanks, fish vans and others, were classified as carriages as they ran in passenger trains. Stan also spent time with the horse box section. Horse box bodies were nearly all made of oak, with some elm fittings, and these would not give horses splinters. Stan was employed putting in greenheart timber floors with oak battens for the tough wear and tear they would receive. Later, he was converting old passenger stock to outstation mess vans and tunnel maintenance vehicles. The other repair shop was known collectively as 24 Shop and they dealt with body repairs and painting.

The amount of stealing that went on sticks in Stan's mind: 'All I ever took home was my carriage key; these were general issue when I went to carriage finishers in 1948.' It was said that you could always tell a Swindon railwayman's house because the woodwork was engine green and the guttering black. This myth was born out of an acknowledgement that Works paint was regularly taken home. It was known as Tate & Lyle paint after the type of tins brought in to transport it, and varnish, out. Some men worked on the principle that if they were bold enough they were unlikely to get stopped. Stan said someone walked out past the gate holding open a newspaper at the racing page, which was not unusual except that he had a large piece of glass between the pages. Another followed one of the managers out one evening, pushing a wheelbarrow; the watchmen on the gate assumed he was with the VIP and did nothing. In one part of 19 Shop reclaimed screws and bolts were sorted by disabled men. Stan knew one of these men had been caught stealing underwear from washing lines: 'The Police searched his home and found a sideboard full of packets of carriage screws. One of his workmates heard about it and was said to have hurriedly buried something under a new concrete path in his garden.'

George Butt started his apprenticeship in wagon building in 1958. He stayed in 13 Shop all his five years, except for 6 weeks learning the theory and practise of welding at the College. Like most other trades 'inside', wagon building was a secondary trade along with wagon riveting:

> My first job was lighting the forges to heat the rivets. Apprentices who started with me were John Glass, Les Plumb, Richard Jolliak and David Miles; Ray Jordan was the Wagon Frame Builders' foreman and his brother Doug was shop steward. Bert Williams was a painter, he worked outside coating the finished frames with red oxide before they went over to 21 [wagon body] Shop. Another fella, Wally King, went round tapping rivets to see they were sound, if they had to come out he hit them with a cold chisel as they had hardened when heated and couldn't be drilled out.

Every operation performed on component parts had a piecework price payable in full if the gang got through a certain amount of work per fortnight. A 13 and 21A Shops' piecework register for 1958 shows how much in old pennies, or shillings if more work was involved, had been negotiated to either mark out, punch, shear, guillotine, bend, straighten, level, drill, joggle, rivet, grind, cut by profile machine, carry, dress down or fit up each part or set of parts if more than one per wagon. The register also shows that unskilled labour not involved in production work was, by 1958, also receiving piecework bonus rather than a fixed day rate. Labourers' work in the wagon workshops included drawing from stores or warehouses smaller items and transporting them to the shop, removing swarf from machine tools and topping up the coolant, sweeping and removing refuse from incoming wagons, keeping shop gangways clear and clean, issuing items from shop stores, cleaning and attending to hand washing troughs and switching on and off all the electric shop lighting, for which they got 4s 6d a week.

These are the men of the Horsebox Shop, part of 19 Shop, in 1951. Those identified are from left to right, back row: Bob Harris, Ron Ferris, Jack Telling, two unknown (probably apprentices), Ken Archer. Middle row: Arthur Selby, Arthur Iles, Stan King, Jack Richards, Cyril (?), Percy Turner, Reg Court, Cyril Newman, Reg Henley, Cyril Mills, Godfrey Price, Frank Peace, Ted Davies, Sid Adams (?). Front row: Arthur Manning, Ivor Ody, Arthur Shaw (or King), Bert Moseley, Harold Parker (the foreman), Perc Henley. (*Ray Townsend collection*)

This was 'Webb's Entrance' in Station Road in the 1940s or early 50s. The name came from a large building material merchants on the other side of the road. These men leaving the Works have now to negotiate a gap in a procession of cyclists also leaving, but from the tunnel entrance further down the road. The entrance on the left led down to a subway with stairways up to the carriage shops either side of the main lines. The cast iron notice says: 'All applications for employment in these Works must be made in the employment exchange.'

A local census dated 1951 shows that 12,671 Swindon men worked on the railway somewhere; that was more than half the working men in the town. Of course, this did not include the many coming in from outside the borough or female workers. (*Swindon Central Library - local studies collection*)

Tailpiece

Further development of road haulage and motor coach travel, as well as an increase in private motoring after the war, did not affect the railway industry noticeably until the 1960s. In fact, the volume of rail traffic carried by the nationalised railways actually went up compared with the immediate pre-war period. Despite this, the new administration started to lose money and wage demands increased considerably. This forced the British Transport Commission to seek to increase charges and fares, thus making railways ever more uncompetitive. The output at Swindon Works continued to capacity because of the backlog of maintenance caused by the war and, later, undertaking contracts for the modernisation plan. The workforce in the late 1950s was only slightly lower than in the heyday a few years earlier and this was partly due to less labour-intensive workshop methods.

To young men in particular, the railway industry was looking tired and old-fashioned compared with the new car and electrical component firms arriving in the town. They were offering higher wages and cleaner working environments. This, together with a feeling 'inside' that work was being deliberately diverted elsewhere, led inevitably to rumours, and by the mid-1950s it was noticeable that morale had started to go down. The men had long since realised their prospects would be better elsewhere. Many left and could not be replaced by men of the same calibre, if at all. Eight smaller Locomotive Works had closed by the end of the decade but this still wasn't enough under the modernisation and rationalisation plan and Swindon was one of those under threat. The contracts were available but some of those in power thought the facilities here were unsuitable for investment. All Stan Leach's father said was, 'It's dead son,' and this summed up the feeling at that time. 'Workshop scribe', writing in *The Swindonian* in 1959, gives another reason for the deterioration: 'In private enterprise times, one foreman and one inspector sufficed for more men than four foremen and two inspectors do today.' The older hands were quite happy to see out their time 'inside' but many of the younger men moved on. Despite the new impressive diesels and all the Western Region publicity and optimism that accompanied them, these men guessed, correctly as it turned out, that there was little future in this Railway Works in the decade to come.

Bibliography

The Story of the Home Guard in the North-East Wilts Sector. Swindon Borough Press: 1944.

Swindon Works and its place in British Railways History. The Railway Executive: 1950.

British Machine Tool Engineering: April to June 1950.

GWR Two Cylinder Piston Valve Locomotives. E. J. Nutty: 1947.

Swindon Railway Village Museum. Museum Division of Thamesdown Borough Council.

The Locomotives of the Great Western Railway: Part Eight. The Railway Correspondence and Travel Society: 1953.

Road Vehicles of the Great Western Railway. Philip J. Kelley. Oxford Publishing Co: 1980.

Locomotives Illustrated No.140 & No.152: Swindon's New Century: Parts 3 & 5. RAS Publishing: 2001.

Caerphilly Castle. W. G. Chapman. G.W.R: 1924.

Fletcher's Directory of Swindon: 1930 and 1959.

Great Western Progress: 1835–1935. Great Western Railway: 1936.

Swindon Steam: 1921 to 1951. K. J. Cook. Ian Allan: 1974.

Working at Swindon Works: 1930–1960. P. Timms. History Press: 2007.

The Railway Works and Church in New Swindon. Frederick Fuller. Red Brick Publishing: 1987.

The Education Committee Handbook: Various editions from the 1930s and 1940s.

The Western's Hydraulics. J. K. Lewis. Atlantic: 1997.

The Great Western Echo: Various editions from the 1970s.

Internal Publications

The Great Western Railway Staff Magazine: Various editions.

New Lamps for Old: The BRWR System of Travelling Stores Vans. Stores Department: 1950s.

Fuel Efficiency on the Footplate. CME Department of the GWR: 1945.

GWR Swindon Engineering Society Transactions: Various papers.

The Swindon Railway News: 1960-63.

Advanced copy of a paper read at the Institution of Mechanical Engineers in November
1959: *The Swindon Built Diesel Hydraulic Locomotive,* by G. E. Scholes.
Diesel Rail Cars. The CM&EE's Department, Swindon: 1956.
Memorandum of Procedure (with subsequent updates). The GWR Secretary's office,
Paddington: 1932.
An investigation report by the Associated Industrial Consultants Ltd: March 1956.
The Annual Report of the Chief Mechanical and Electrical Engineer: 1956.

Newspapers

The *Evening Advertiser*
The *Swindon Messenger*